IMAGES
of America

AROUND BOONVILLE

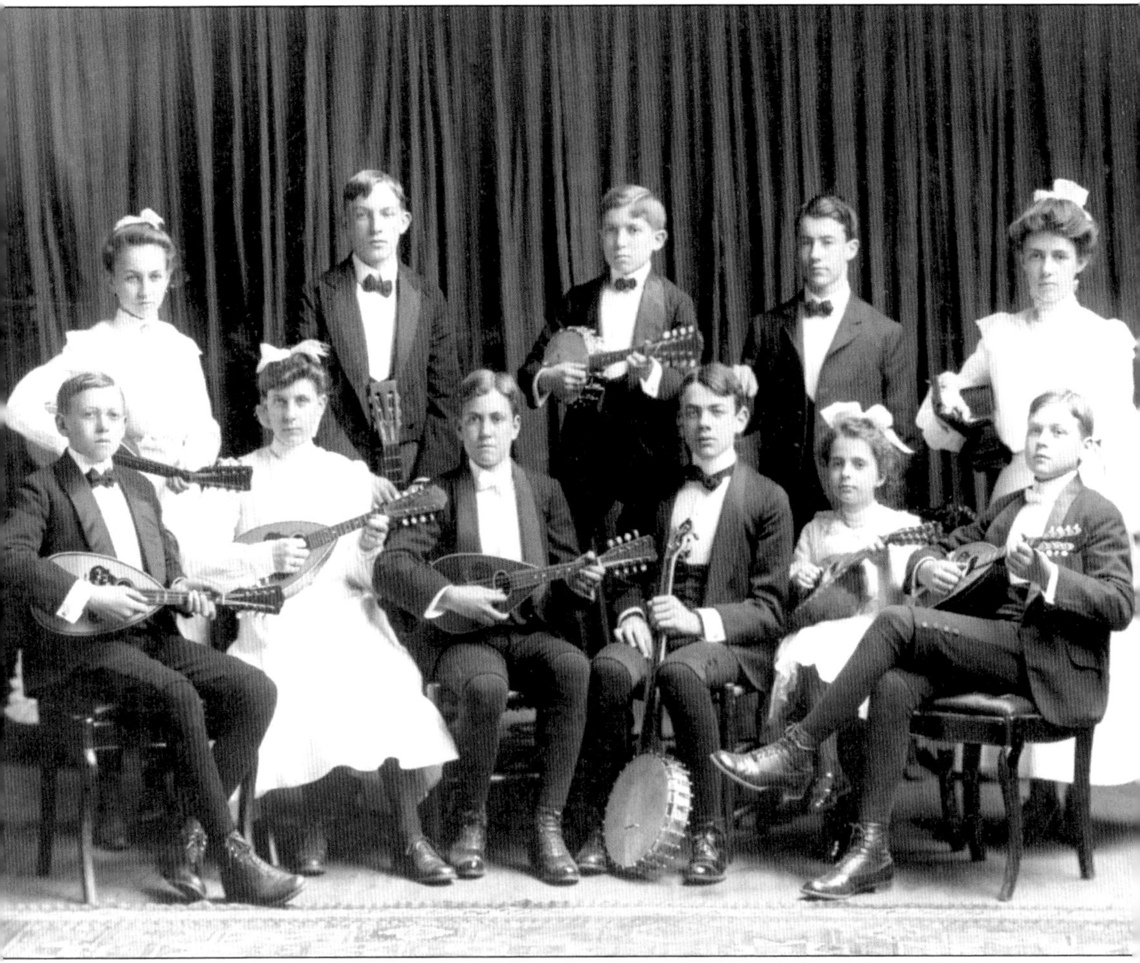

A mandolin craze swept America in the 1890s. This photograph from about 1902 features the Euterpe Banjo and Mandolin Club, composed of Boonville High School students. (Courtesy of Ed Fynmore.)

On the cover: In the 1890s, J. H. Nellis (standing next to gramophone) ran a bakery and restaurant at the corner of Church and Main Streets. The establishment featured a separate ladies' parlor and promised to appease diners' appetites for oysters. (Courtesy of Ed Fynmore.)

IMAGES
of America

AROUND BOONVILLE

Harney J. Corwin

ARCADIA
PUBLISHING

ISBN 978-0-7385-6502-6

Published by Arcadia Publishing
Charleston, South Carolina

Printed in the United States of America

Library of Congress Catalog Card Number: 2008942591

For all general information contact Arcadia Publishing at:
Telephone 843-853-2070
Fax 843-853-0044
E-mail sales@arcadiapublishing.com
For customer service and orders:
Toll-Free 1-888-313-2665

Visit us on the Internet at www.arcadiapublishing.com

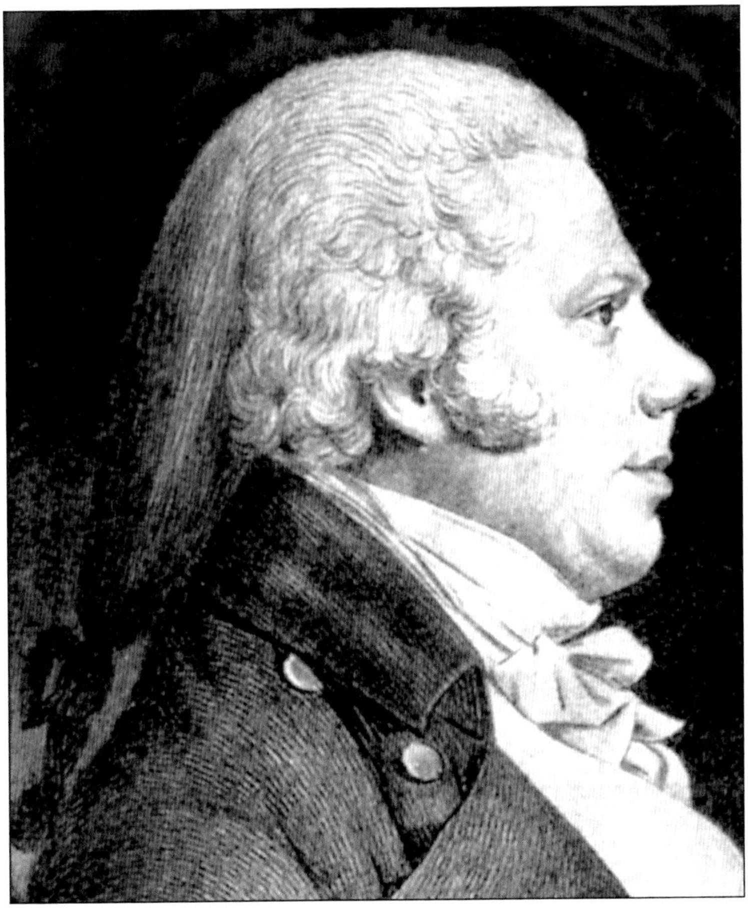

In 1791, John Lincklaen and Gerrit Boon beheld their first sugar maple near Bethlehem, Pennsylvania. "We stopped for a moment to admire this, the object of our search," Lincklaen remarks in his journal. "Mr. Boon, at that instant, seemed to descry beneath its bark the treasures of Peru, while I, for my part, would have wished to carve on it the name of my sweetheart." The engraving depicts Gerrit Boon. (Author's collection.)

Contents

Acknowledgments		6
Introduction		7
1.	Village Green and Public Square	9
2.	Upper Main Street	29
3.	Canal Street and Lower Main Street	45
4.	Erwin Park	57
5.	Around Town	65
6.	Churches and Schools	81
7.	Farming, Logging, and Mining	93
8.	Country Roads	105
9.	Great Outdoors	117

Acknowledgments

I wish to thank the following, without whom the book would not have been possible: Virginia Best Clarendon, Henry Daskiewich family, George R. Davis, Dale Ferris, Vincent T. Fitch, Joe Gaetano, Peter Hayes, Ed Fynmore, Irma K. Marcy, Chris and John Markham, Larry Myers, Jim Pitcher, Marty Podskoch, Jerry Putnam, Linda and Richard Sanford, and Charlotte Capron Willoughby.

I also extend my gratitude to the following organizations: Adirondack Central School, Boonville History Club, Boonville Municipal Commission, Boonville Volunteer Fire Department, Dodge-Pratt-Northam Center, Erwin Library, Oneida Historical Society, Port Leyden Library, Rome Historical Society, St. Joseph's Church, Utica *Observer-Dispatch*, and Woodgate Free Library.

INTRODUCTION

By the end of 1855, the newly incorporated village of Boonville had evolved into a thriving farming community. Nestled in the Black River valley between Tug Hill to the west and the Adirondacks to the east, Boonville was the largest population center between Utica and Watertown. Graceful elms towered over handsome, if generally modest, frame houses, and ornamental wooden fences divided landscaped yards from plank sidewalks. At the center of the village was a large business district with about 40 shops as well as a full complement of skilled mechanics and trained professionals. Prosperous dairy farms and cheese factories surrounded the village. The recently opened Black River Canal connected the village to the outside world as did the even newer Black River and Utica Railroad. There was very little about the village to suggest that its founding was an afterthought—the result of a failed dream.

Boonville sprang up in the midst of what was to have been the largest sugar plantation in the New World. In 1791, a Dutch banking consortium known as the Club of Three dispatched Gerrit Boon to America. This syndicate (which would soon become the Holland Land Company) charged Boon with the task of identifying large tracts of land for speculation. In particular, the Club of Three wanted to acquire a maple forest that would sustain a vast native sugar industry. The investors hoped such an enterprise would prove lucrative and lure Yankee settlers into the wilderness. With a background in sugar refining, Boon eagerly embraced the idea of a great northern sugar bush. In search of suitable land for a plantation, Boon and his companion, John Lincklaen, traveled 2,600 miles throughout the Northeast. As these two agents traveled the backwoods from Vermont to western Pennsylvania, they discovered that frontier communities were likely to succeed only if land speculators were willing to extend capital assistance and material support to settlers. Such generosity, they realized, was a matter of self-interest. By inducing settlers to improve the land, investors would enhance the value of their own holdings.

The agents' travels ended abruptly in 1792, when Theophile Cazenove, the syndicate's general agent in Philadelphia, purchased three nearly contiguous tracts in northern New York for the sugar enterprise. The largest of these was Adgate's Western Tract, some 45,000 acres along Black River—within which the present-day township of Boonville is largely situated. To the south was the 25,000-acre Servis Tract located west of West Canada Creek and a 6,000-acre parcel of land belonging to Baron von Steuben. Boon thought these three tracts would answer his needs splendidly, and in 1793, he established his headquarters at Oldenbarneveld, near the center of the Servis Tract. Boon's associate Lincklaen went on to found the village of Cazenovia.

Boon hired men to clear 17 acres near Oldenbarneveld of all trees except sugar maples. In a memoir, Boon declared that he planned to develop another 10,000 acres should his experiment succeed. By his reckoning, a maple plantation this size would yield one and a half million pounds of sugar annually. Since workers were both scarce and expensive, Boon decided to forego the use of sap buckets and set up a gravity-feed system instead. Through an intricate network of tubes, sap was allowed to drain from the trees and flow toward a central collection point. The spring weather was ideal, and all went well at first. Sunny days and freezing nights produced an abundance of sap. However, exposed to the elements, the wooden tubes soon warped and cracked, causing massive leakage. These tubes were hand-tooled in Albany and were costly to produce. Desperate to rescue his project, Boon had slats milled and nailed together to form triangular conduits, but the seams leaked badly, and little sap was collected. Accountants in the Netherlands later estimated that the sugar project cost 38,000 guilders and that only 800 guilders worth of maple sugar was produced. Some writers have alleged that Boon labored under the illusion that maple sap flowed year round, but given Boon's extensive inquiries into sugar production, this charge has little merit.

Boon wished to try his experiment again in 1794. He had the support of Cazenove, but the Dutch investors, desiring to cut their losses, ordered Boon to sell off the land. The Adgate Patent in the north was divided into 150-acre lots, with a site reserved for a village along Mill Creek. Boon named the settlement Kortenaer after Adm. Egbert Bartholomeuszoon Kortenaer (1604–1665), hero of the Second Anglo-Dutch War. The location had its advantages, including ample waterpower, abundant building materials, and reasonably fertile soil. But the settlement was isolated, with only crude trails linking it with Fort Schuyler (Utica) and Fort Stanwix (Rome) to the south. When Boon reached the area in 1792, Black River did not appear on any map. Eighteenth-century maps describe the region as "impassable," a "dismal wilderness." It was so forbidding that even the Iroquois visited only to hunt.

Adopting a paternalistic stance, Boon commissioned the erection of a sawmill and gristmill on Mill Creek as well as a general store and tavern on the public square. In addition, he advanced money to skilled workers, including carpenters, masons, tanners, blacksmiths, lime-burners, quarrymen, hatters, shoemakers, and a physician, and he built houses for many of them. Boon encouraged settlement outside the village by hiring men to clear the land and build homes for farmers. At first, settlers from New England poured in, and land sales were brisk. By the end of 1794, nearly one-fourth of the Adgate Tract had been sold at $1.50 an acre, with the better land going for $2 an acre. But land sales soon stalled so that between 1795 and 1813, only 1,600 acres were sold. Word had circulated that the growing season was short—four months at most—and that farming was difficult. Fortunately, the region's climate placed Boonville in what was then called the "dairy zone," a temperate latitude thought ideal for raising milch cows. Milk, rather than maple sap, would be the economic mainstay of the community. After placing his settlement on a firm footing, Boon was recalled to the Netherlands in 1798 to answer for his failed sugar project, now widely known as the Kortenaer Fiasco, and Adam Mappa of Oldenbarneveld was left to collect land payments. Although land sales languished, the rudiments of an organized community were in place. Today the sugar maple remains the dominant hardwood. In autumn, leaf peepers visit the area to admire the colorful foliage, and in the spring, local farmers still produce maple syrup—just not on the scale that Boon had dreamt of.

One

Village Green and Public Square

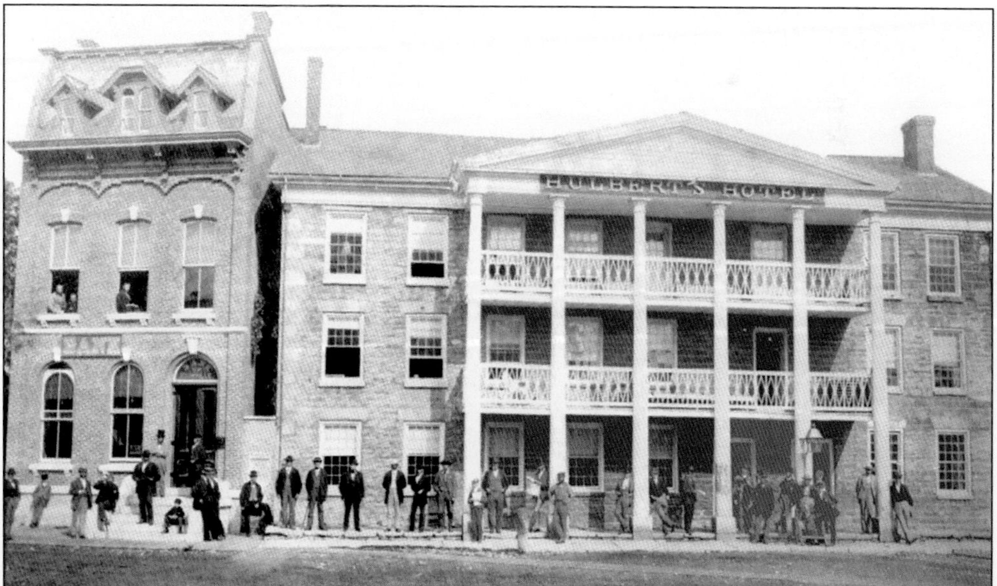

Built of local limestone by Ephraim Owen, the Hulbert House (right) has been a Boonville landmark since 1819. Richard Hulbert bought the building in 1839, adding the third floor and portico during the 1850s. The names of such luminaries as Ulysses S. Grant, Phil Sheridan, Horace Greeley, and Buffalo Bill appear on its ledgers. This photograph dates from the late 1860s. (Courtesy of Ed Fynmore.)

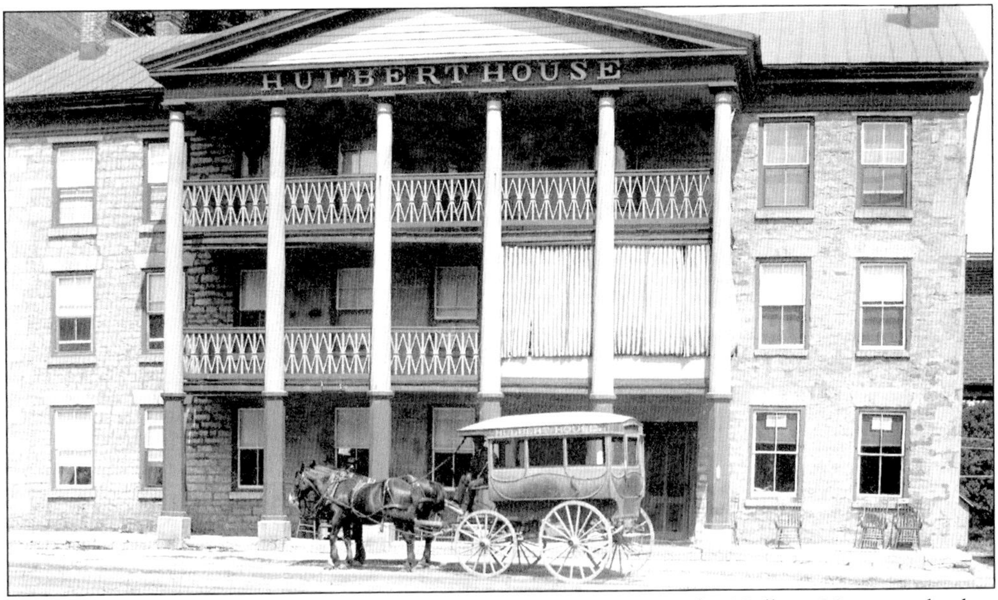

Horse-drawn taxis conveyed passengers from the train station to the Hulbert House and other locations. Between 1855 and 1867, Boonville was the northern terminus of the Black River and Utica Railroad. Travelers who wished to continue their journey north could take Ela Merriam's stage along old New York State Route 12 (now 12D) to Lowville. Other smaller lines conveyed passengers to Hawkinsville, Lyons Falls, Constableville, and Moose River Settlement. (Courtesy of Ed Fynmore.)

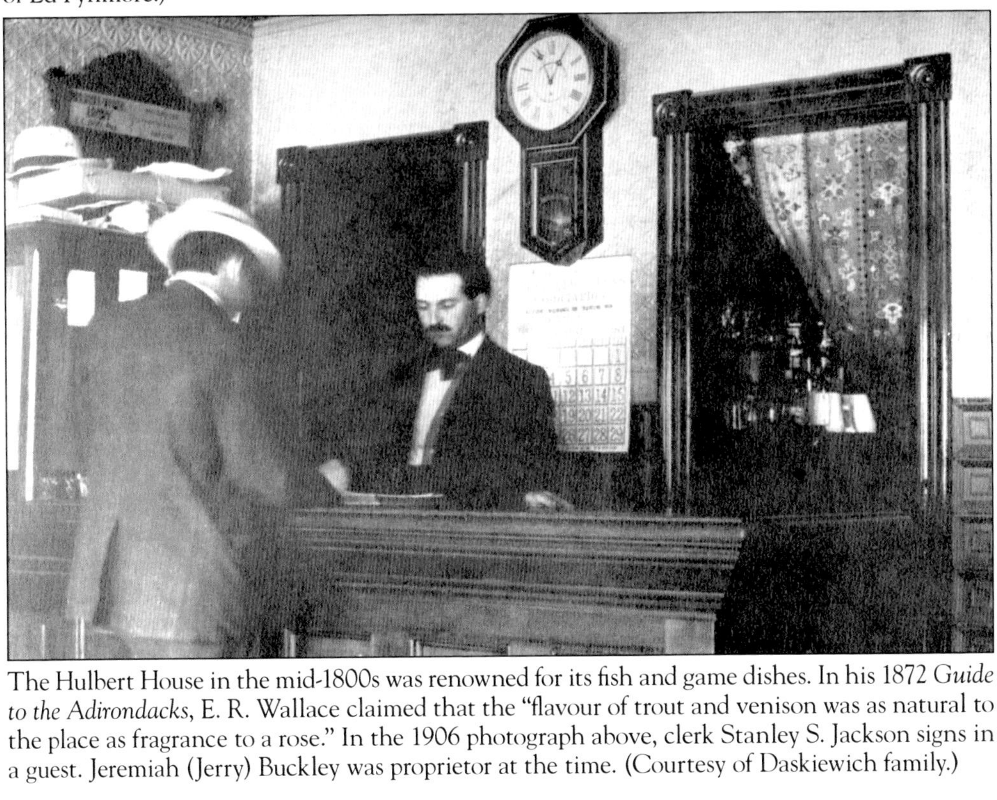

The Hulbert House in the mid-1800s was renowned for its fish and game dishes. In his 1872 *Guide to the Adirondacks*, E. R. Wallace claimed that the "flavour of trout and venison was as natural to the place as fragrance to a rose." In the 1906 photograph above, clerk Stanley S. Jackson signs in a guest. Jeremiah (Jerry) Buckley was proprietor at the time. (Courtesy of Daskiewich family.)

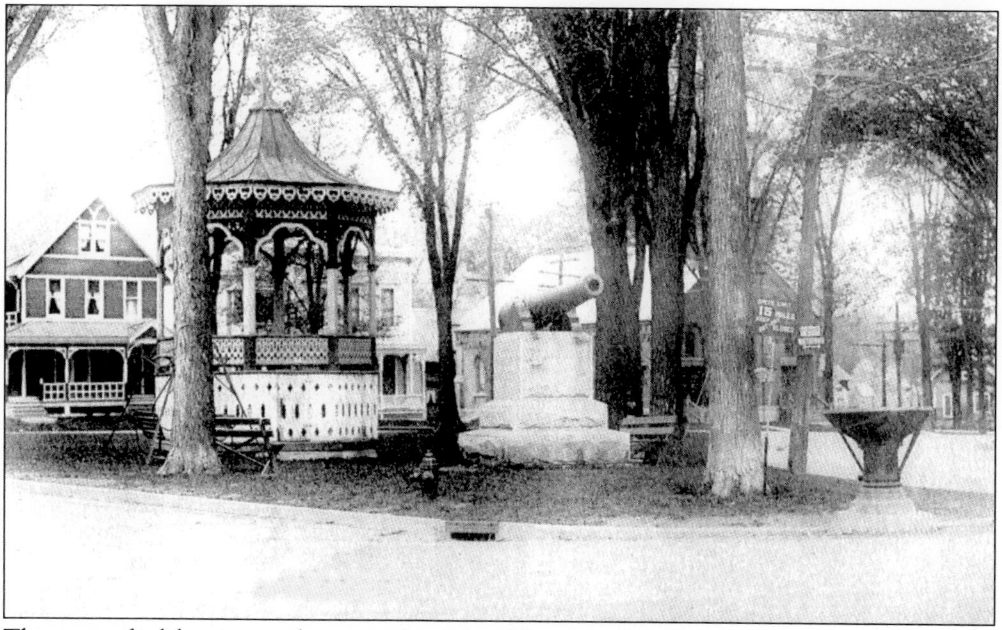

The scene of celebrations and memorial services alike, the village park is at the heart of Boonville. The park is bounded by three streets: Schuyler (left), Main (right), and Post (distance). Guide boat builder Riley Parsons and David H. Miller erected the bandstand in 1882. The park acquired a cast-iron horse trough in 1898 and a Civil War monument in 1901. The six-and-a-half-inch smoothbore cannon dates from the Mexican War. (Courtesy of Ed Fynmore.)

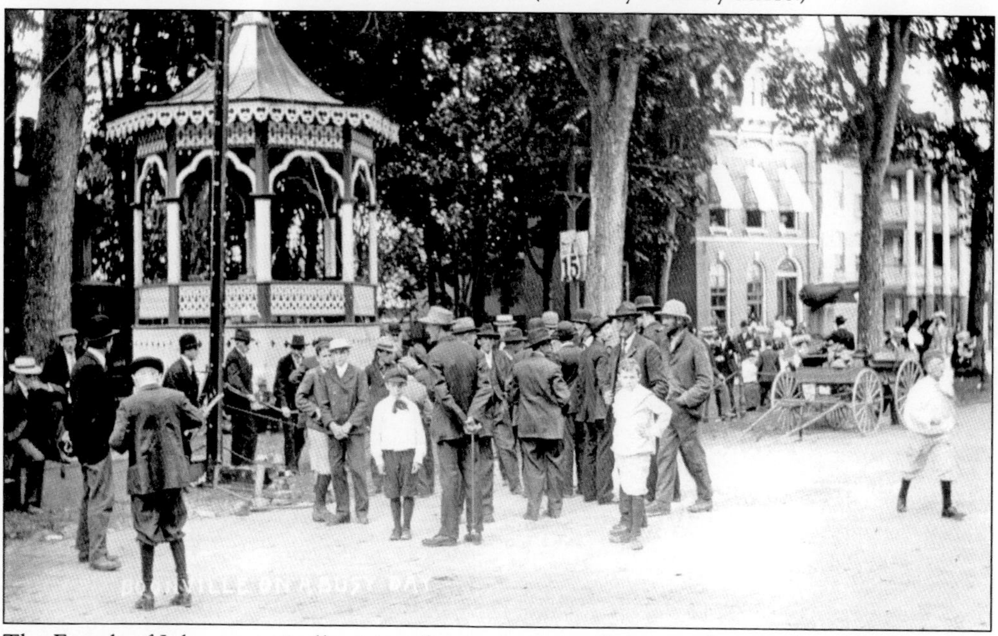

The Fourth of July was typically a time for patriotism and conviviality. In this 1909 Henry M. Beach photograph, a crowd has gathered in the village park where a test-of-strength machine sits in front of the bandstand. The day's festivities included an afternoon parade and band concert, greased-pole climbing, and Russian knife throwers. The day concluded with fireworks and a firemen's ball at the Comstock Opera House. (Courtesy of Ed Fynmore.)

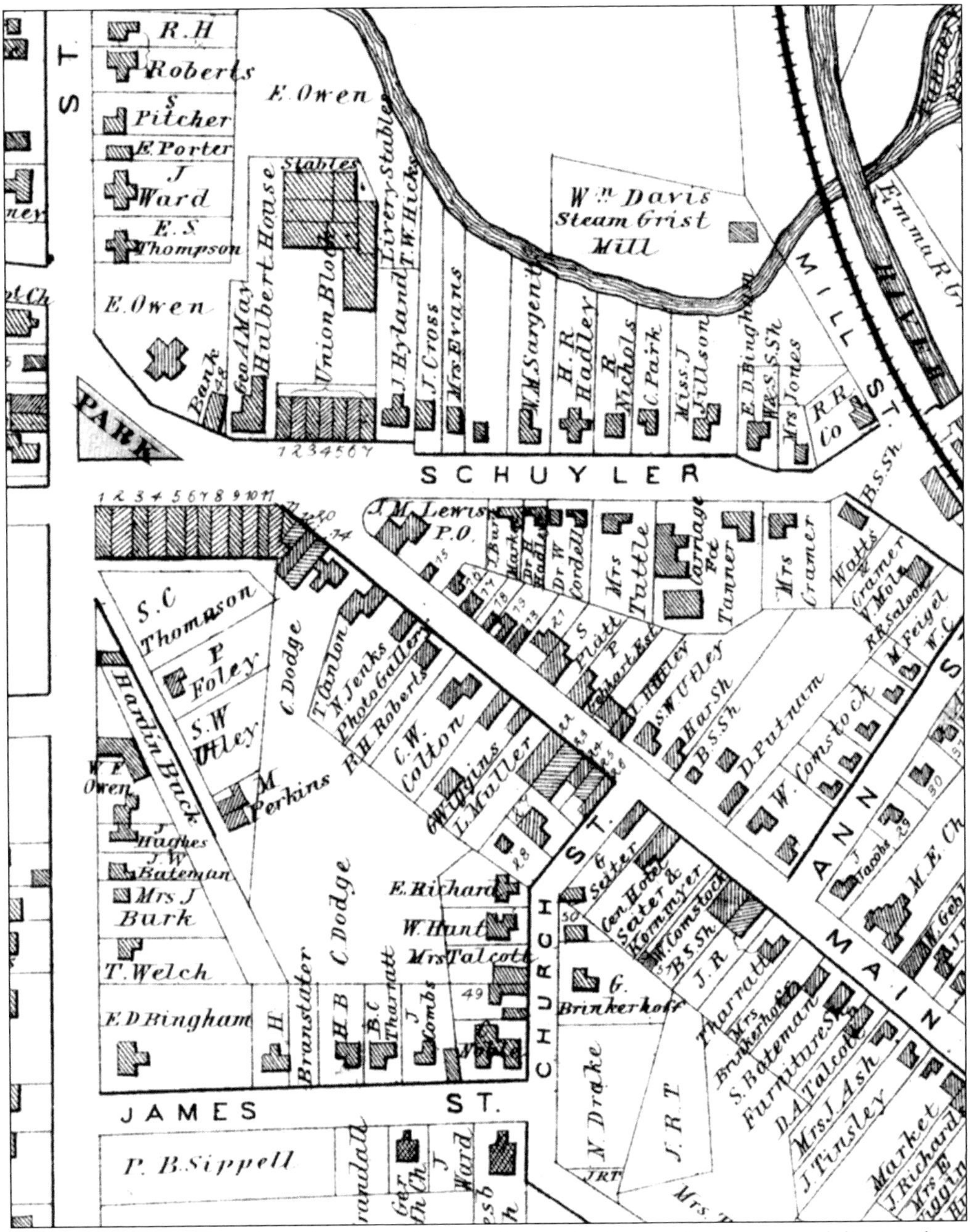

As this D. G. Beers map from the *Atlas of Oneida County* indicates, the commercial district along Main and Schuyler Streets by 1874 was lined with closely spaced buildings. Many of the larger three-story buildings, commonly referred to as blocks, were subdivided and housed a number of tenants. The village at this time had 20 named streets and a population of more than 1,500. (Author's collection.)

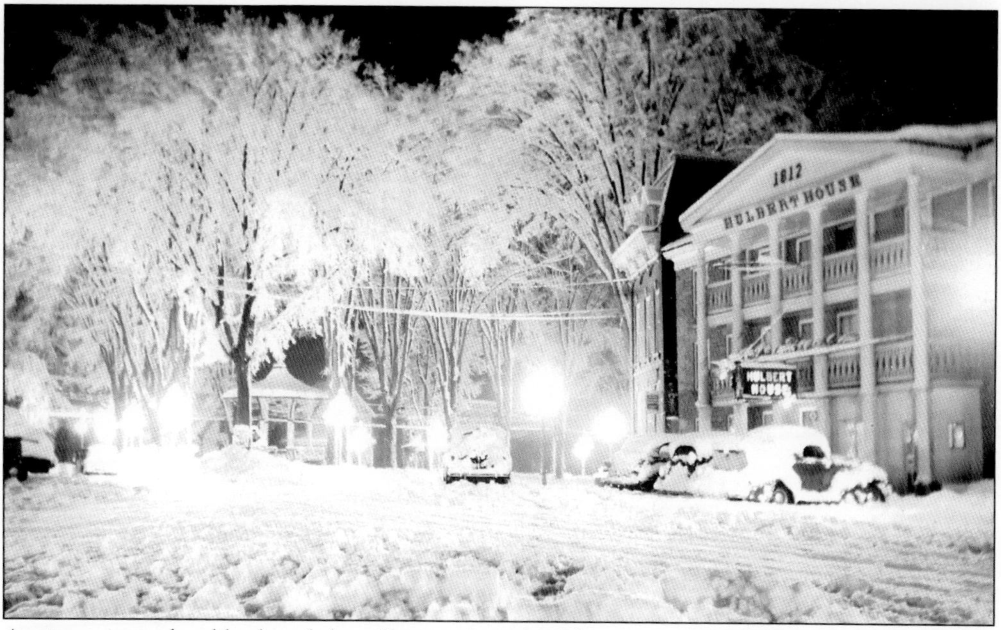

A winter storm has blanketed the village park and public square. Boonville averages 210 inches of snow annually, much of which results from lake effect, the collision of warm, moist air from Lake Ontario with the colder air of the Tug Hill Plateau, reputedly making the region the snowiest east of the Rockies. This photograph by Jim Fynmore dates from 1943. (Courtesy of Ed Fynmore.)

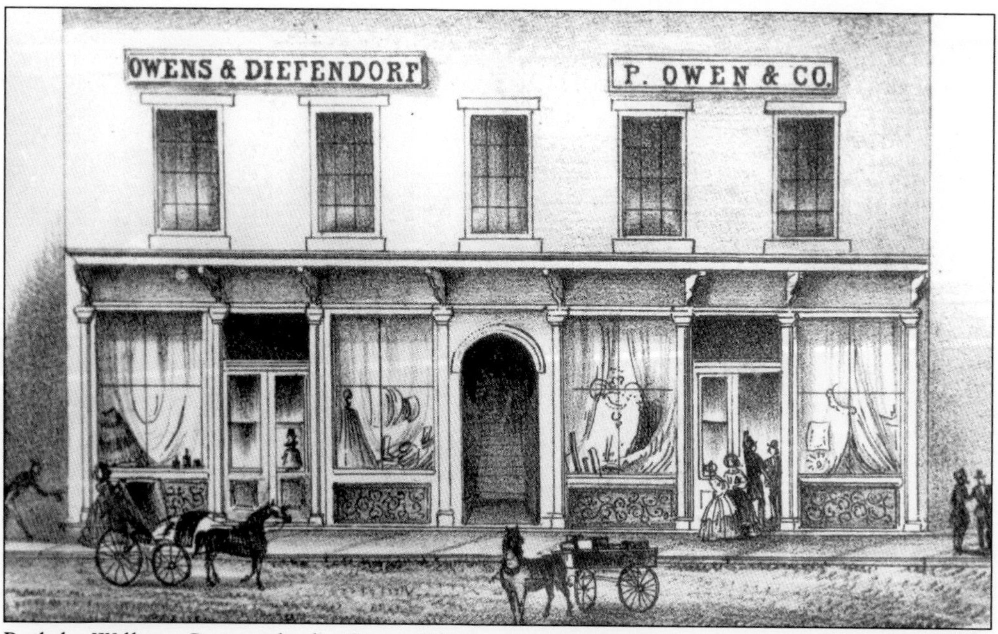

Built by William Comstock, the Owens Block sits on Schuyler Street opposite the village park. In 1857, this block housed two of the seven dry goods stores operating in Boonville: William F. Owens and James H. Diefendorf's (left) and Philip and John Owen's (right). The Owen brothers maintained this store from 1854 to 1868. They began manufacturing clothing on a massive scale at Utica's Globe Woolen Mills in 1870. (Courtesy of Ed Fynmore.)

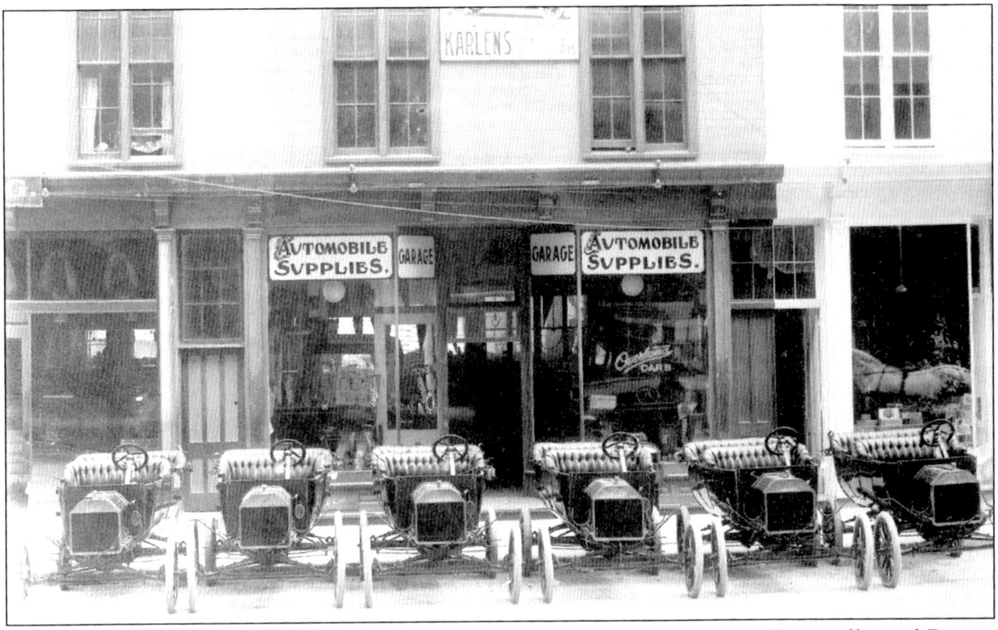

In the early 1900s, villagers talked of establishing a trolley line between Boonville and Rome, but interest in the project waned as automobiles became more common. Samuel Karlen, an electrician and representative for Overland Motor Company, was the first car dealer in Boonville. His shop and garage, pictured here, were in the Owens Block. In this 1913 photograph, newly arrived roadsters await the attachment of fenders. (Courtesy of Ed Fynmore.)

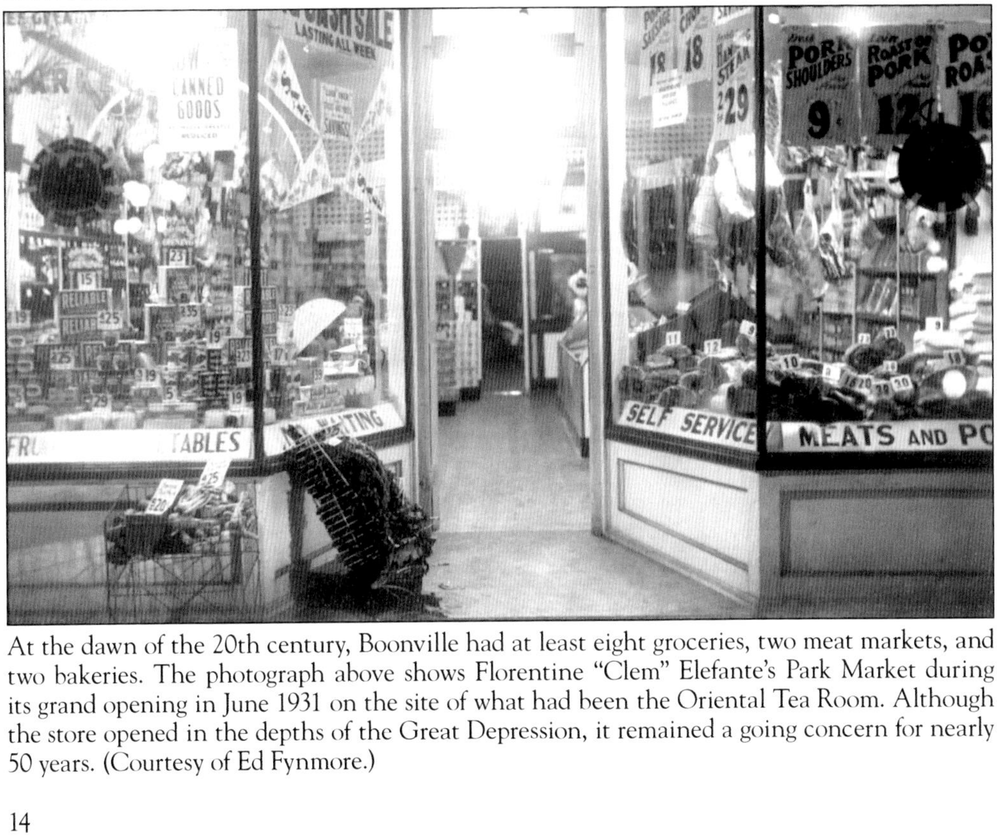

At the dawn of the 20th century, Boonville had at least eight groceries, two meat markets, and two bakeries. The photograph above shows Florentine "Clem" Elefante's Park Market during its grand opening in June 1931 on the site of what had been the Oriental Tea Room. Although the store opened in the depths of the Great Depression, it remained a going concern for nearly 50 years. (Courtesy of Ed Fynmore.)

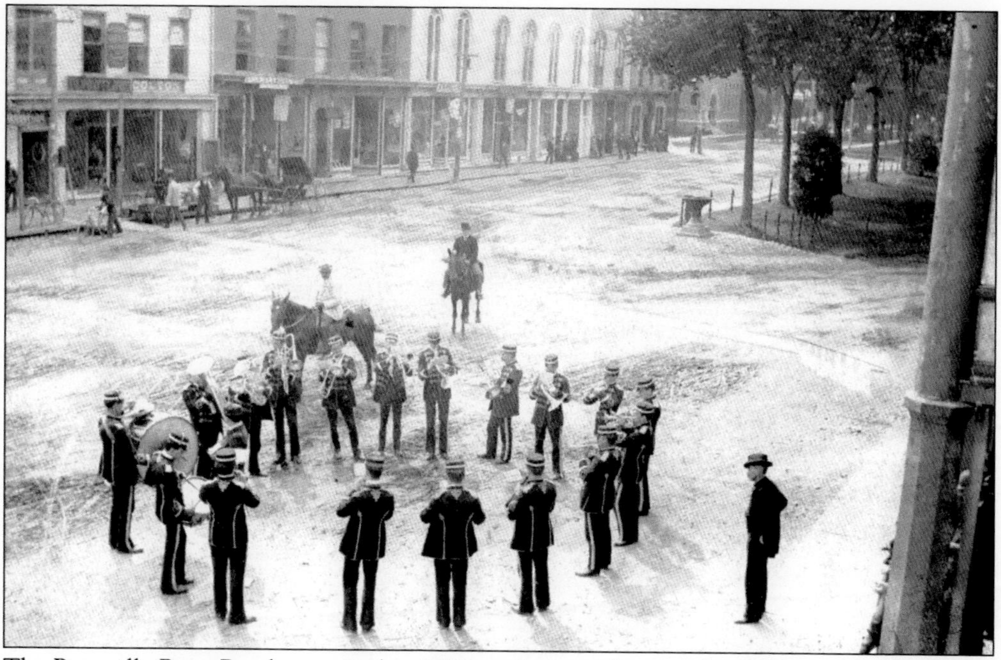

The Boonville Brass Band, organized in 1876, performs in front of the Hulbert House. Buildings lining the south side of Schuyler Street date from the 1830s to the 1870s. These mid-century commercial structures are typically topped with cornices and ornamental brackets, and the windows often feature carved lintels. This photograph was taken around 1900. (Courtesy of Larry Myers.)

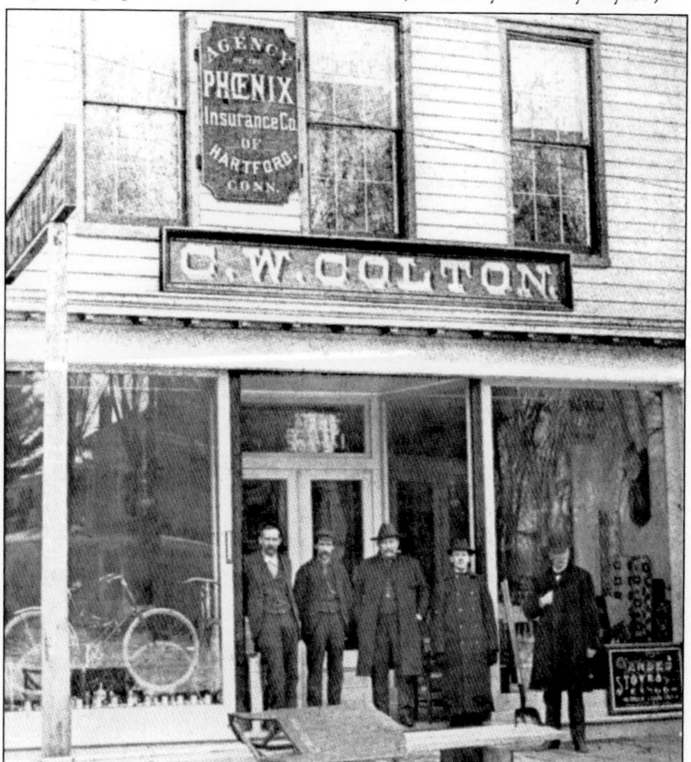

C. W. Colton's hardware store was in the Bamber Block, built in the 1830s near the corner of Schuyler and Main Streets. Standing from left to right are Francis Shedd and Irving Patmore (store employees), Clarence Sperry (attorney), Edwin Traxel (harness maker), and Chauncey W. Colton (proprietor). The William D. Sippel Insurance Agency and Walter Ballou's law office were upstairs. The photograph dates from about 1895. (Courtesy of Ed Fynmore.)

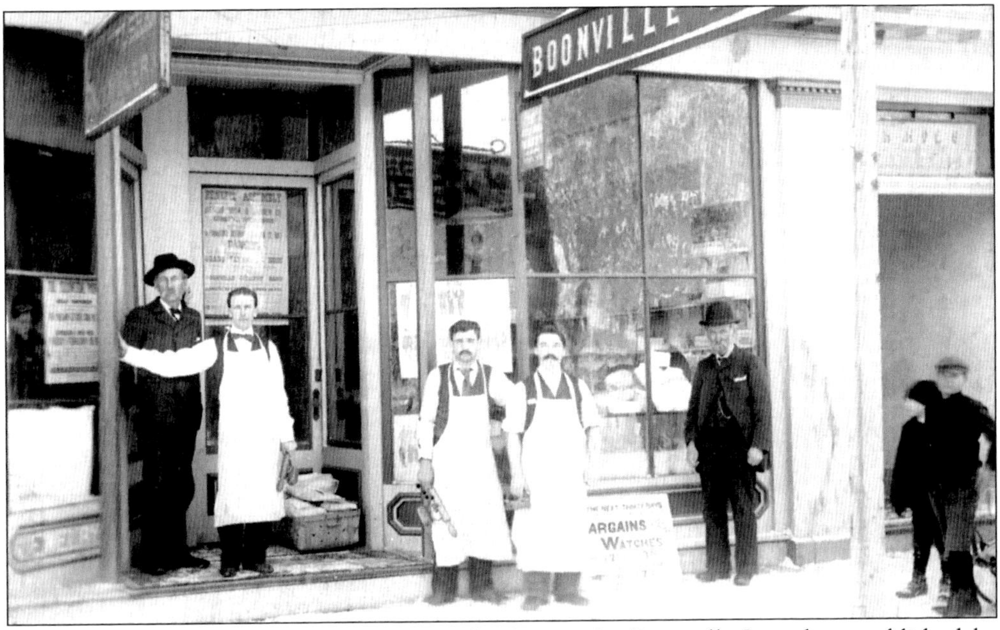

Sharing the Bamber Block with C. W. Colton's was the Boonville Laundry, established by Ai Austin in 1884 and managed by Sidney W. Hines. In 1897, Welsh émigré Evan Oldfield bought the Boonville Laundry but, wishing to devote more time to his music store, sold the business to John A. Sears in 1911. Nelson B. Felshaw's jewelry store is on the left. (Courtesy of Vincent T. Fitch.)

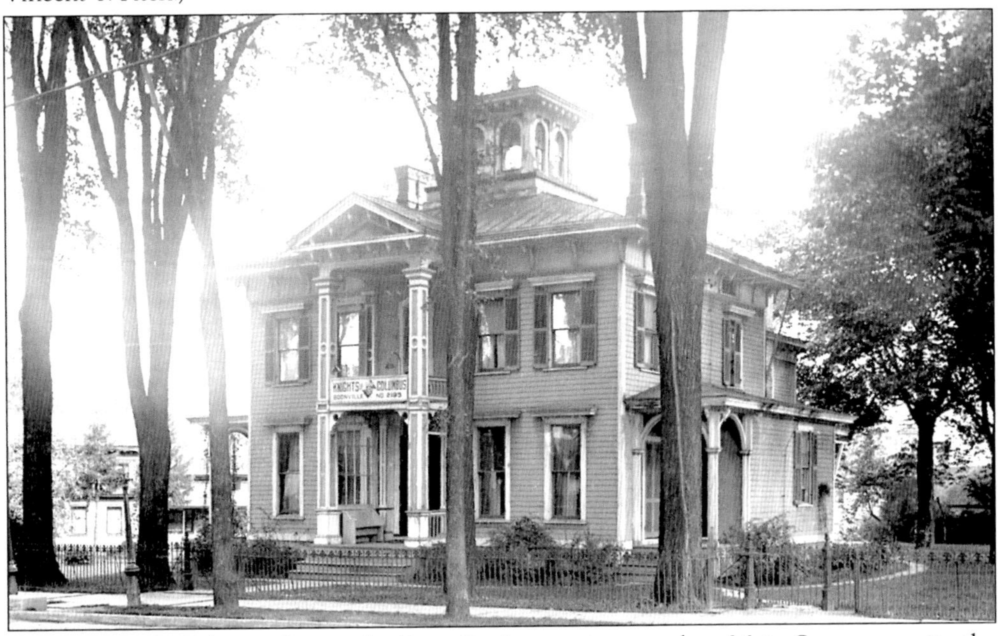

Built in 1831 by Ephraim Owen, the Peter Erwin mansion stood on Main Street opposite the village park. In 1920, Fr. Dennis C. Flynn and Aubrey Seiter founded the Knights of Columbus, with the Erwin mansion serving as that organization's home until 1927. The Knights of Columbus had 47 charter members, with Adolph Seiter serving as the first grand knight. (Courtesy of Vincent T. Fitch.)

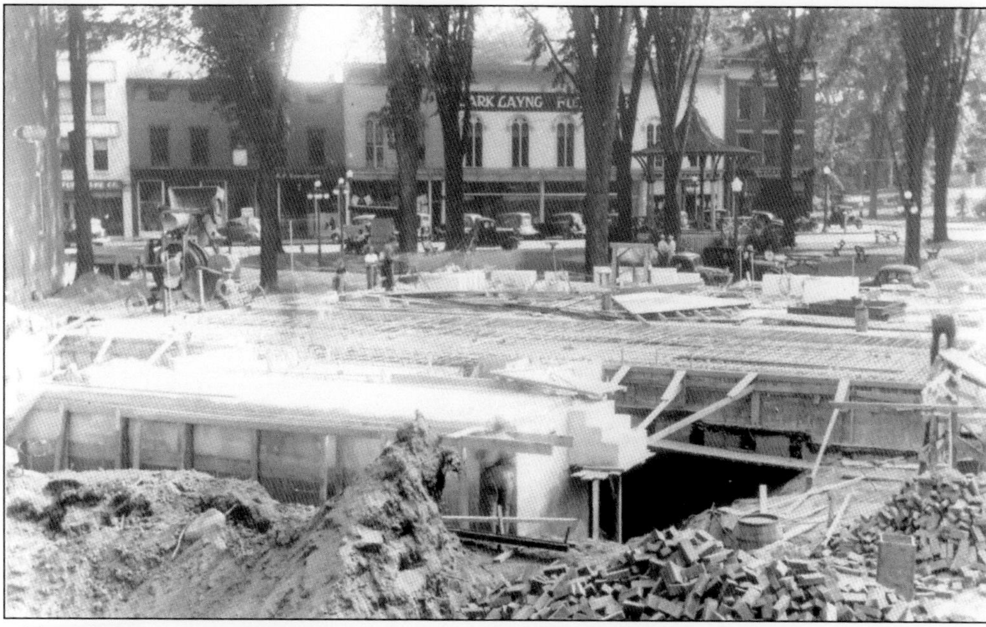

Although Boonville backed Herbert Hoover in the 1932 presidential election, the village benefited greatly from Franklin Delano Roosevelt's New Deal. In 1933, Boonville received a grant from the Works Progress Administration to build a modern sewer system. That same year, the federal government selected the Erwin property as the site for a new post office. This photograph from the summer of 1937 shows the post office under construction. (Courtesy of Ed Fynmore.)

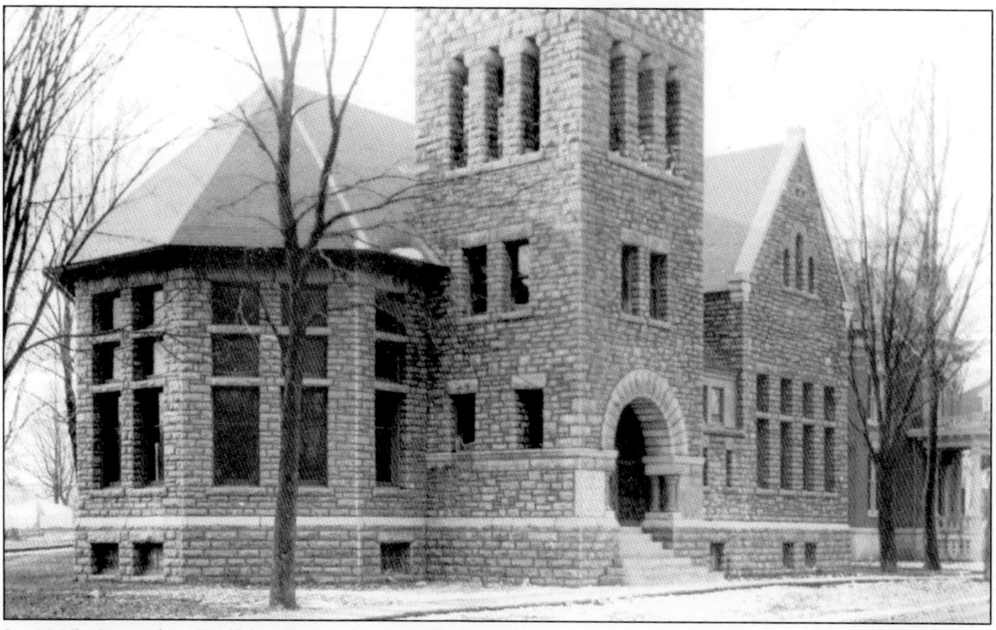

In 1885, Cornelius Bulkley Erwin bequeathed money to construct and maintain a public library. Designed by C. L. Vivian of Ithaca and completed at a cost of $13,000, the Erwin Library and Institute sits on the southwest corner of Schuyler and Post Streets. The land was donated by Louisa, Mary, and Sophia Post. The library opened its doors in September 1891, with attorney Leander W. Fiske serving as the first librarian. (Courtesy of Ed Fynmore.)

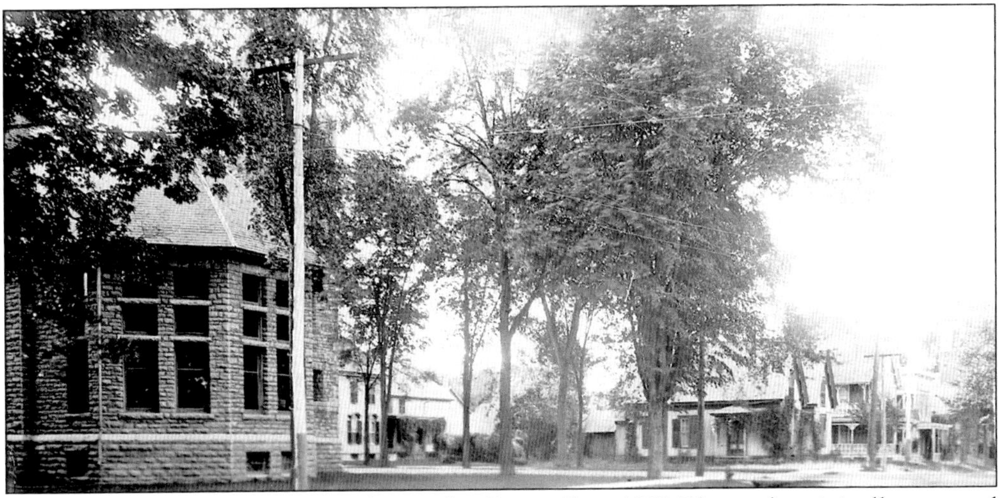

The Black River and Utica Railroad arrived in Boonville in 1855. The tracks originally traversed Post Street (right) at an angle, crossing Schuyler Street in front of what would be the Erwin Library and Institute (left) and terminating at a roundhouse near present-day Erwin Street. Initially, two trains ran daily in each direction. The trip to Utica took two hours and cost $1.25. (Courtesy of Larry Myers.)

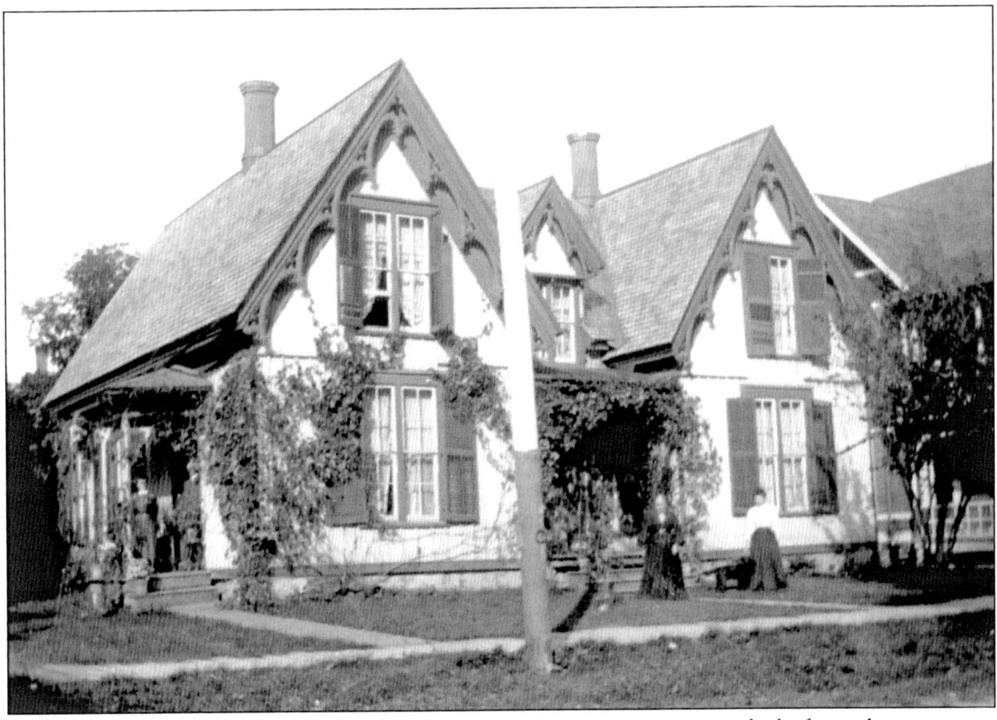

Talcott's Tavern, opposite the village park, was a convenient watering hole for rail passengers. Built by business partners Jesse Talcott and Wetmore Hall, the structure exemplifies the Gothic style popular in the 1850s. By the early 1900s, the tavern became the residence of Eugene Nellis. Part of the building was a cigar shop in which one could purchase Boonville handmade cigars, manufactured by Thomas B. Mitchell for some 40 years. (Courtesy of Ed Fynmore.)

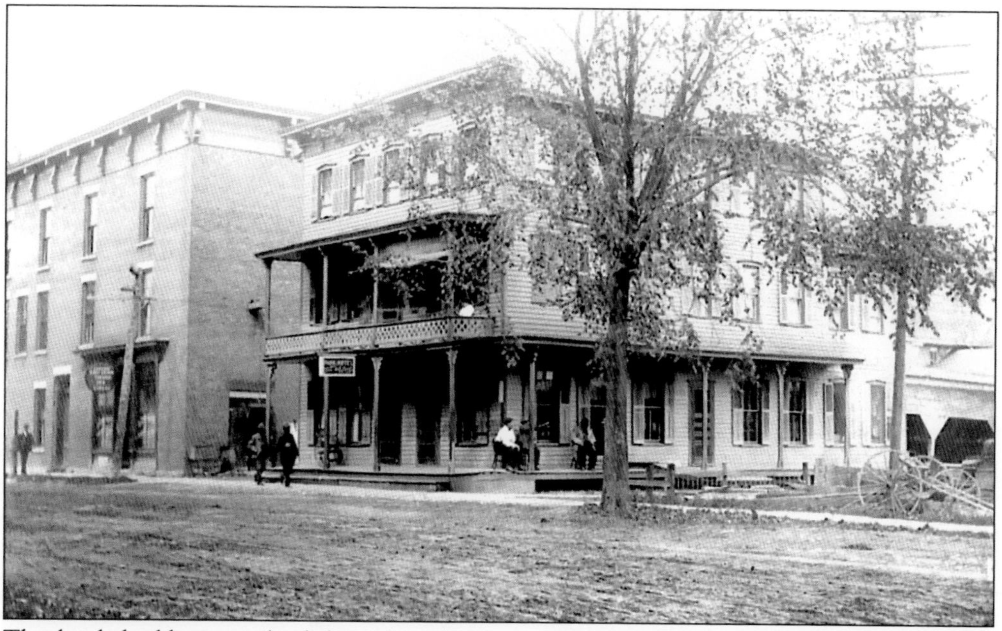

The brick building on the left is the Thompson Block, home to Schuyler C. Thompson's National Bank from 1872 to 1905. The main entrance to the bank was on Schuyler Street. Behind the bank, on Post Street, is the Park Hotel built by George Marcy in 1885. The Union church, erected around 1827, had once straddled the sites on which the bank and hotel were built. Shared by Methodists, Presbyterians, and Universalists, the church was moved to make way for the railroad. (Courtesy of Ed Fynmore.)

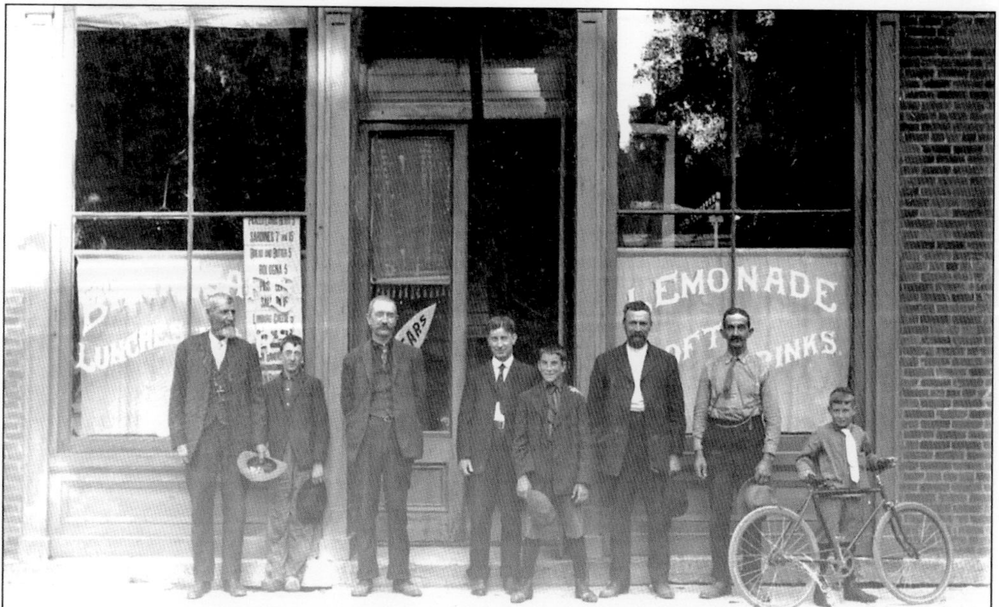

At the dawn of the 20th century, F. Y. Sanborn was managing the Boonville Union Store in the Thompson Block. By 1906, the Bank Café (above), established by Ed Burris, was a going concern in the building's rear section. The Great Atlantic and Pacific Tea Company, Boonville's first national chain grocery, moved into the Thompson Block in 1916. (Courtesy of Vincent T. Fitch.)

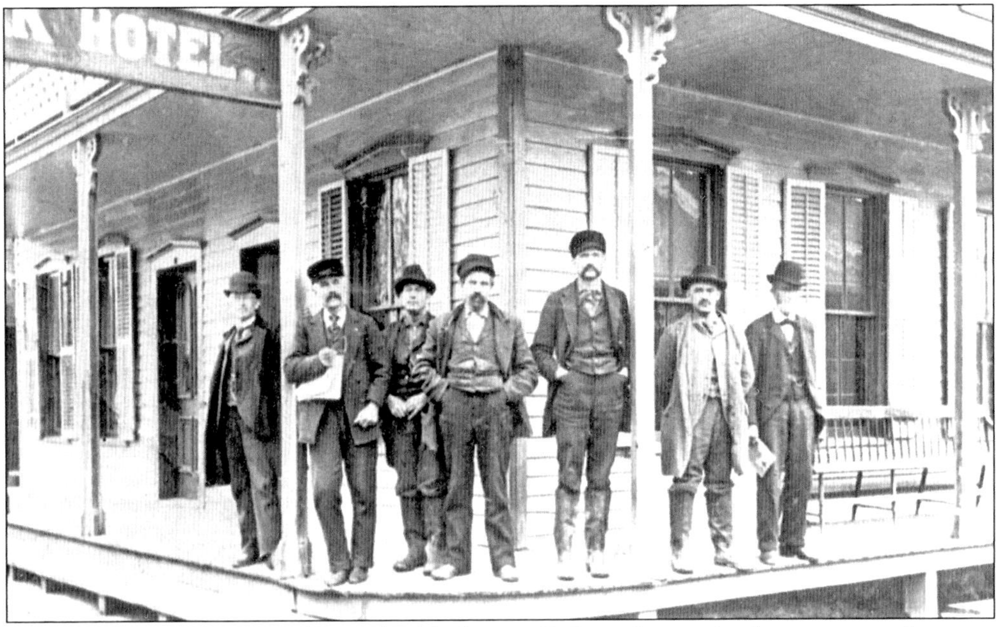

Park Hotel (above) was one of several public houses. Risking the wrath of temperance advocates, Charles Kilkenny and George B. Kitts built the three-story Boonville Brewery in 1889. Located on the feeder canal opposite the state shop, the brewery manufactured K&K Cream Ale for a year before burning down. The brewery was rebuilt but burned down once again in 1891. (Courtesy of Ed Fynmore.)

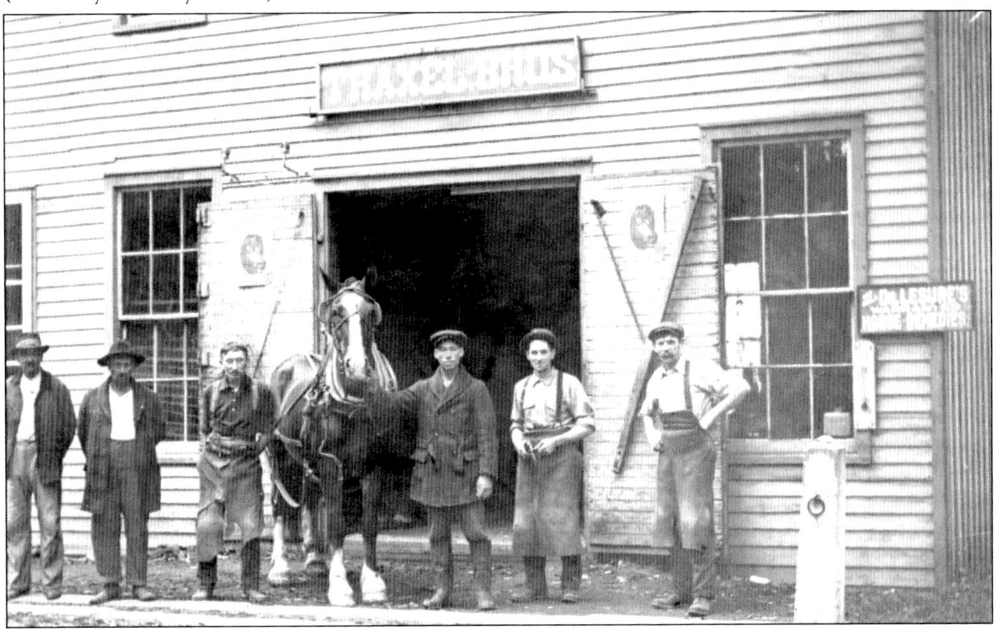

After the railroad tracks on Post Street were torn up in 1872, Henry Hicks established a livery and sales office at the corner of Railroad Avenue. In the late 1890s, Henry Traxel and his sons George and Fred ran a livery and blacksmith shop at the location. Painters Routen Jones and W. J. Tuttle had their offices here. In 1929, Fred Ziegler bought the building, replacing it with a gasoline station. (Author's collection.)

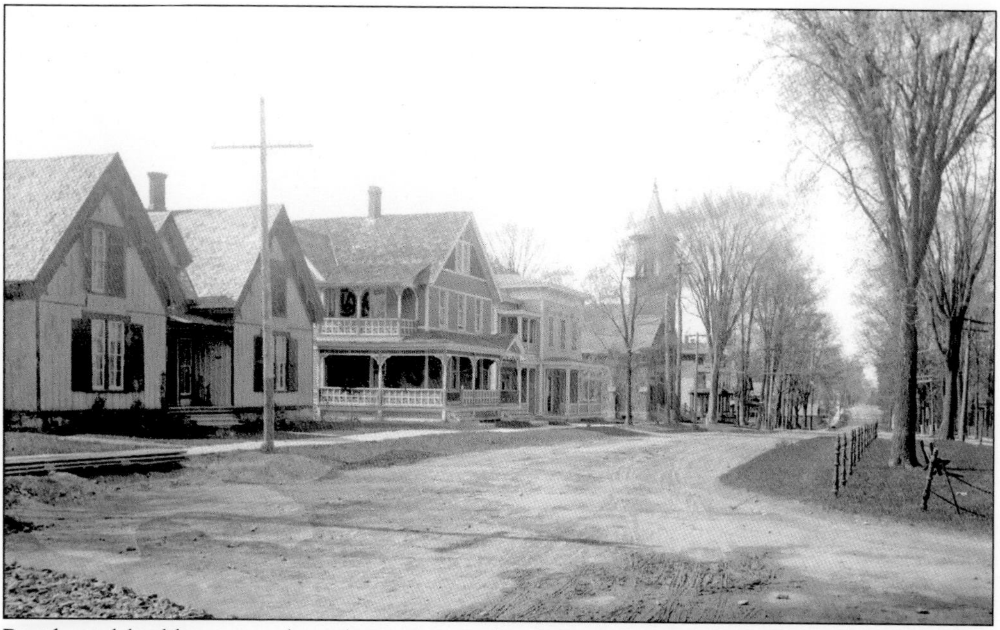

Residential buildings now line the western side of Post Street opposite the village park. The Cottage Inn once stood on the site occupied by the second building from the left but burned down about 1847 and was replaced by the Buck Block. In 1855, E. P. Owens purchased the Union church and moved it to the site occupied by the third building from the left. (Courtesy of Larry Myers.)

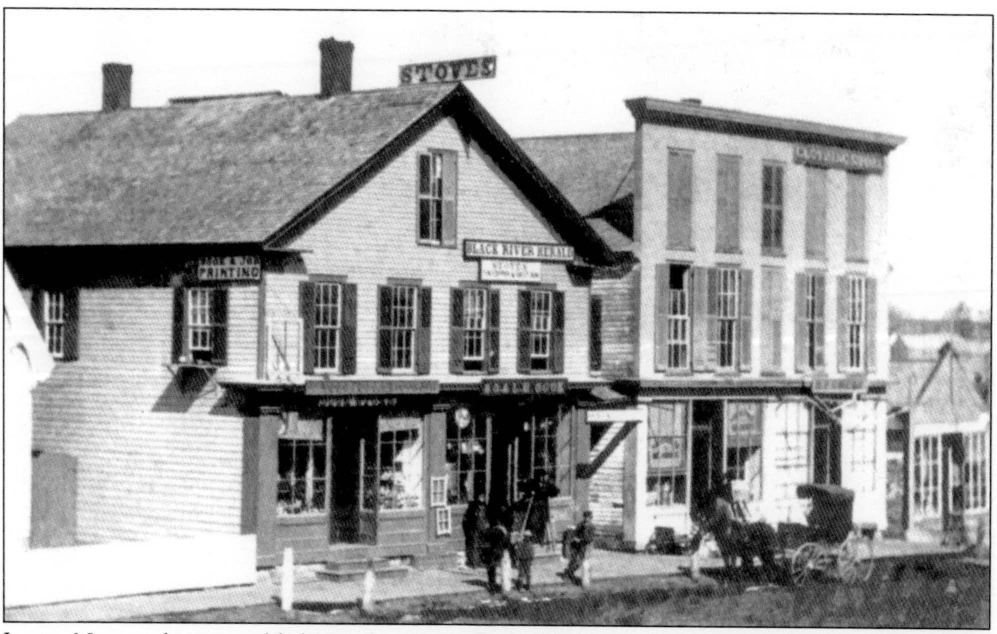

James Norton began publishing the *Boonville Ledger*, a weekly newspaper, in 1852. Three years later, L. C. Childs acquired the paper and, changing its name to the *Black River Herald*, published it upstairs in the Buck Block (left) behind the photography shop of Norton Jenks. Struck by lightning, the Buck Block and the Owens Block to its right burned down in 1887. The photograph dates from about 1860. (Courtesy of Ed Fynmore.)

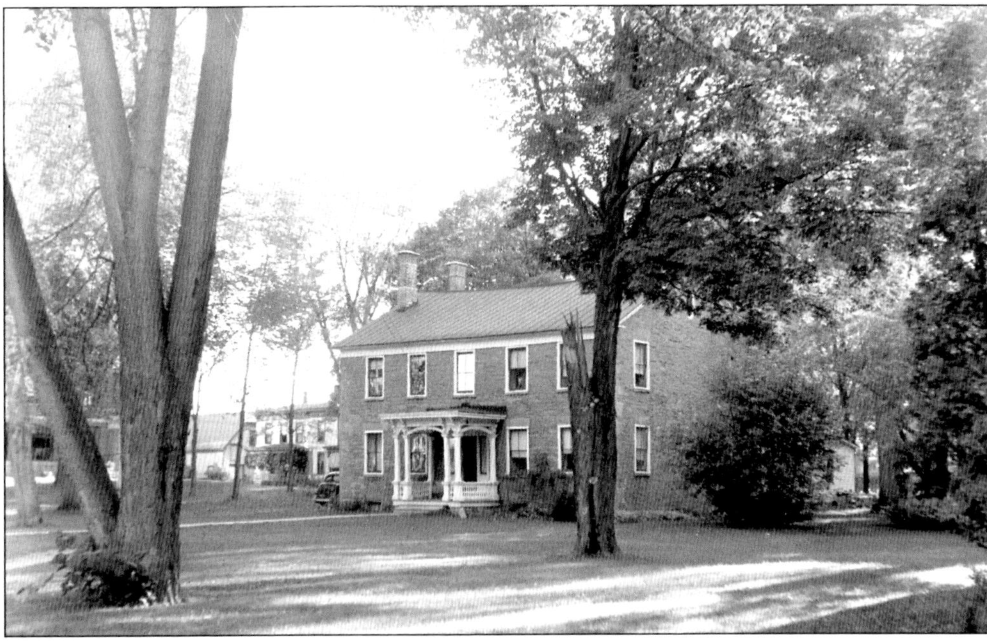

This limestone building at the corner of Post and Schuyler Streets was erected prior to 1817 when John G. Post acquired the property. The local chapter of the Independent Order of Odd Fellows (1887) used the house as a lodge from 1904 to 1947. Also active in the 1880s were the Free and Accepted Masons, Rescue Temple of Honor, and Independent Order of Good Templars. (Courtesy of Erwin Library.)

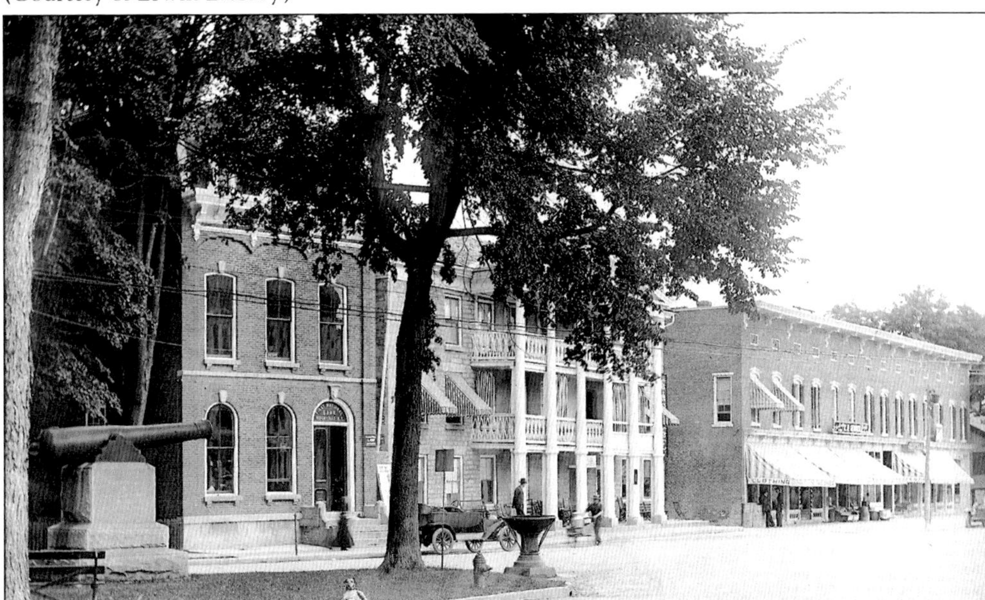

The brick building on the left originally housed the Bank of Boonville (1866). To the right of the Hulbert House is the Union Block (1862–1868), the second floor of which has been home at various times to the Boonville Glove Factory, Elmer Sawyer's chair shop, the Adirondack Bicycle Club, Women's Christian Temperance Union, and the GAR. In 1884, the Boonville Roller Skate Rink Company opened in the basement of the Union Block. (Courtesy of Larry Myers.)

The Bank of Boonville was rechartered in 1876 as the First National Bank. Posing on the bank steps are, from left to right, Claude Hobart, Eugene C. Dodge (president), Charles Jenks, and James P. Pitcher. In 1927, the bank moved into a new building across the street. In 1929, Black River Telephone Company (established in 1900) moved into the building. At the time, John J. Domser managed the company, as he had since its inception. (Courtesy of Ed Fynmore.)

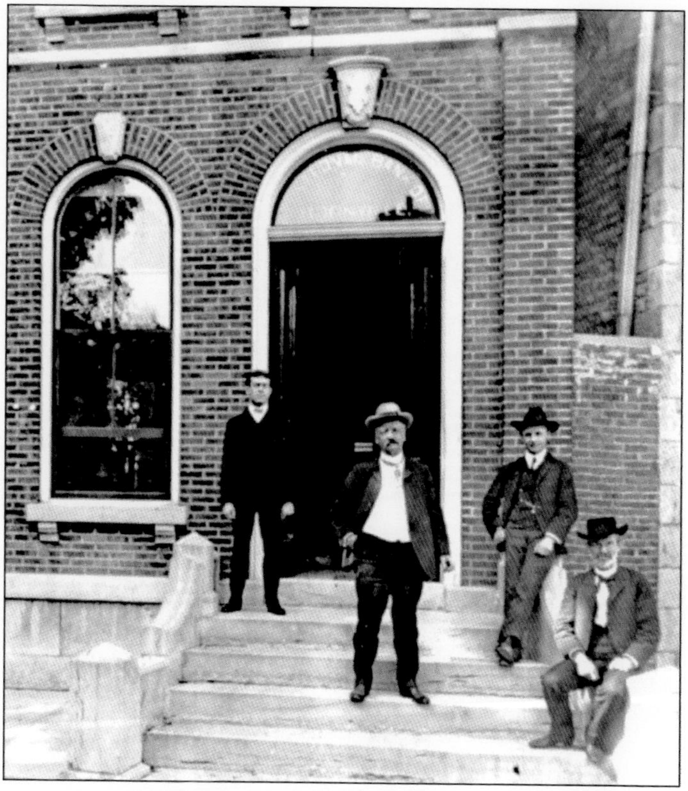

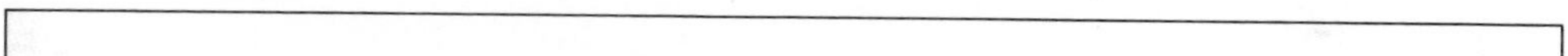

This 1911 excerpt from Henry M. Beach's panorama of the public square shows Fred Marcy's clothing store at the left end of the Union Block. In an earlier era, clothier Byron P. Graves maintained a shop there, regularly outfitting sportsmen for their journey into the Adirondack wilderness. A hunter himself, Graves enjoyed stalking panthers and donated a stuffed mountain lion to the Erwin Library. (Courtesy of Ed Fynmore.)

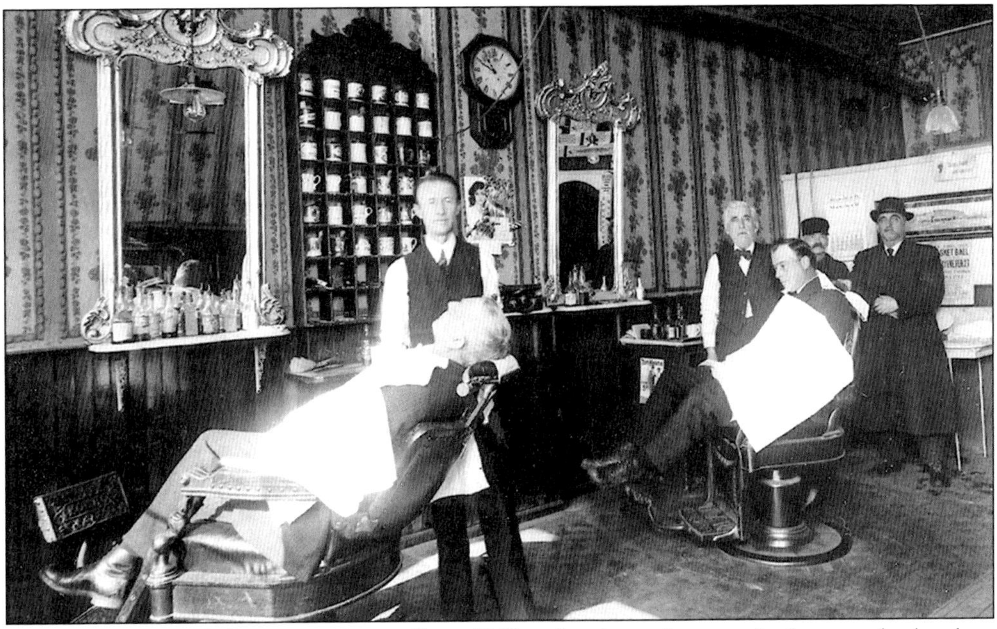

Utica native Fred Pfeifle came to Boonville in 1865 and within a few years had set up a barbershop in the Union Block. Over a career of more than 40 years, Pfeifle claimed to have shaved a long list of notables, including Chester A. Arthur, Artemus Ward, Gen. Franz Sigel, P. T. Barnum, Edwin Booth, Mark Twain, and Tom Thumb. He also shampooed the hair of Mary Todd Lincoln. (Courtesy of Ed Fynmore.)

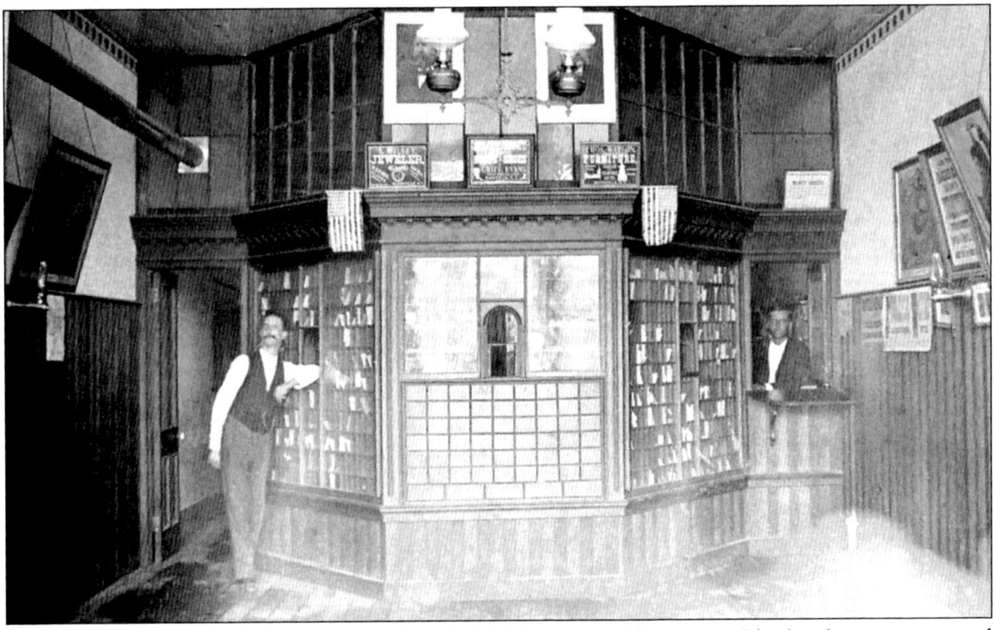

Around 1868, the post office moved from the Barlett Block to the Union Block, where it remained until 1938 when the current post office opened. Pictured here are Louis Manchester and Henry McClusky, who was postmaster from 1878 to 1882. Although rural free delivery began in 1902, home delivery did not commence until 1915. The first letter carrier was Jesse E. Lewis, who covered the whole village twice a day. (Courtesy of Erwin Library.)

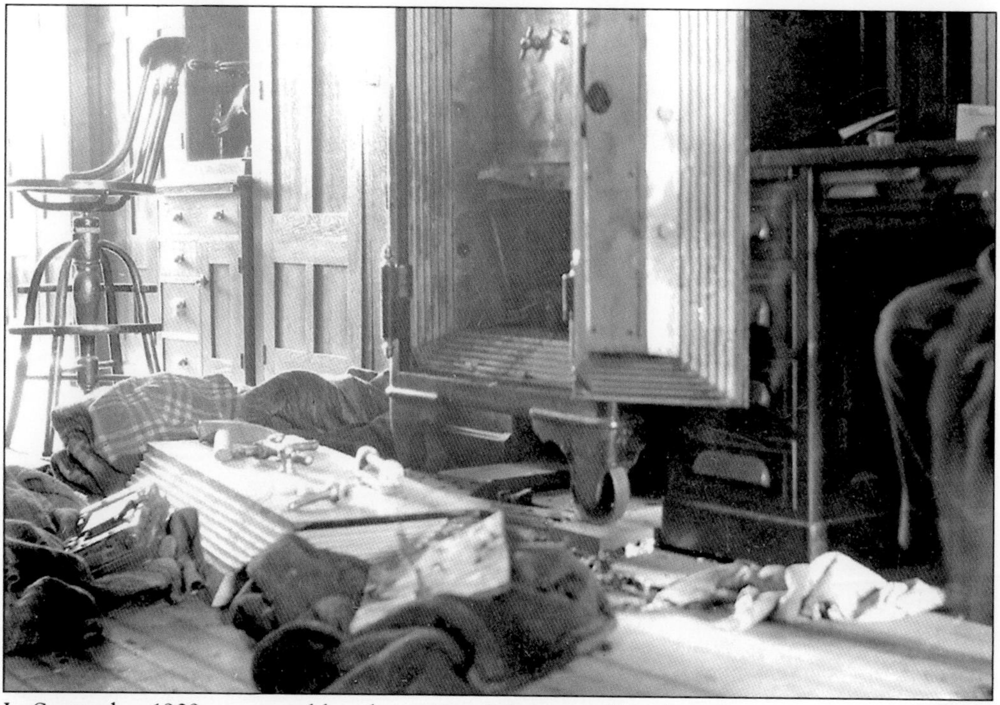

In September 1909, nocturnal burglars entered the post office through a rear window and blew the safe open with nitroglycerine. The thieves made off with about $500 in stamps. The post office was robbed again in August 1911 when burglars dynamited the new safe and absconded with nearly $3,000 in stamps and cash. Frederick M. Wooley was postmaster on both occasions. (Courtesy of Vincent T. Fitch.)

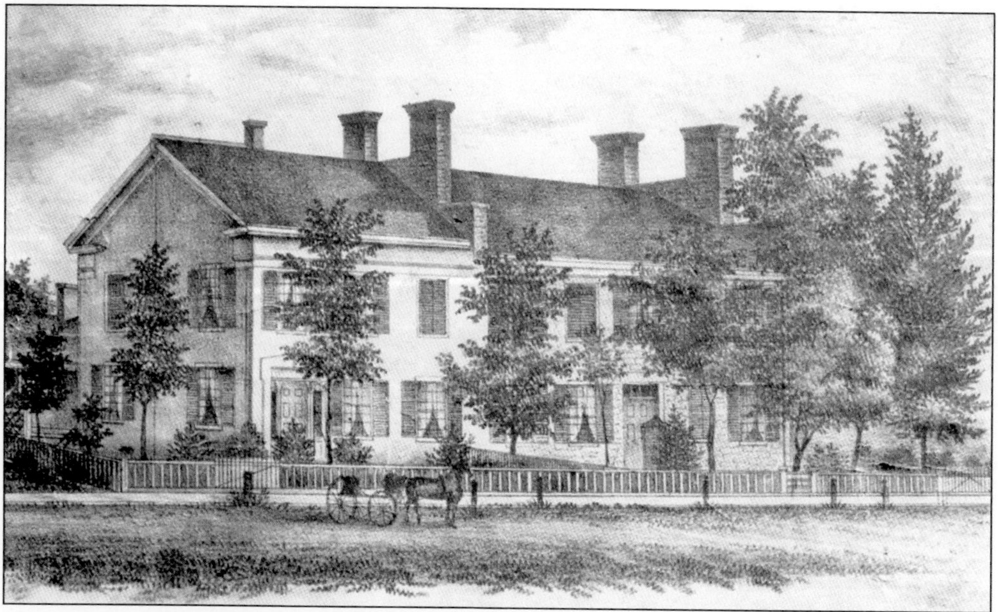

This vignette from Benjamin Clark's 1857 map of Boonville depicts the James Hyland–John Cross home, a two-family structure dating from the 1830s and located on Schuyler Street just east of the Union Block. (Author's collection.)

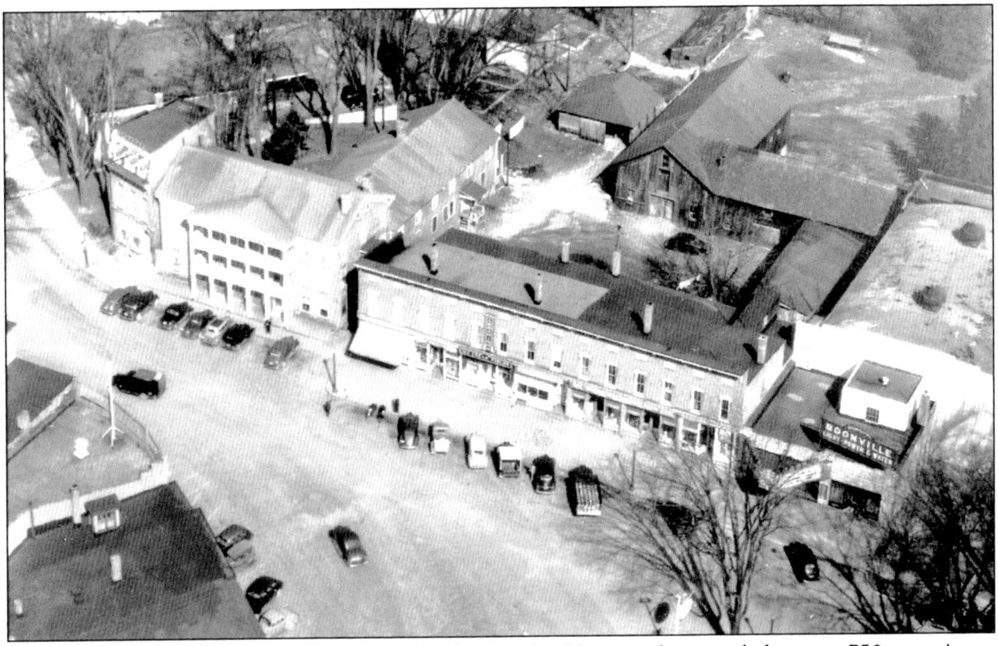

In 1937, Joseph Sternberg razed the Hyland-Cross building and erected the new 750-seat Avon Theater on the site. Two years later, Sternberg renamed the theater Franjo after himself and his wife, Frances. Film studios screened first-run movies here to gauge audience response before general release. Between 1937 and 1952, the municipal commission maintained an office in the building. (Courtesy of Ed Fynmore.)

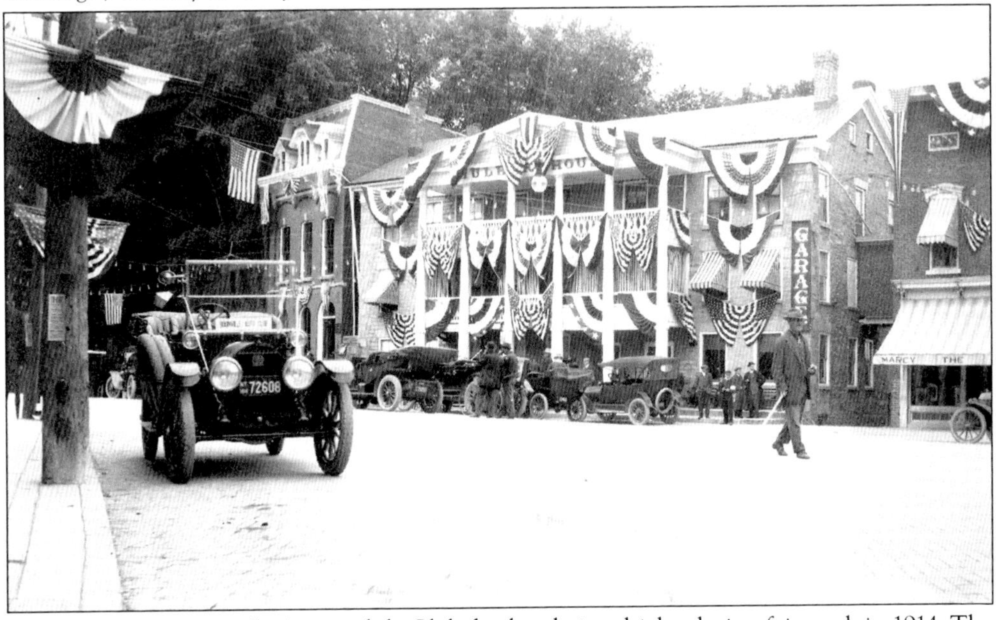

Members of the Boonville Automobile Club display their vehicles during fair week in 1914. The automobile club, organized three years earlier, sponsored group excursions and lobbied for better roads. According to a *Boonville Herald* newspaper estimate, Boonville boasted nearly 50 cars in 1911. Automobile dealer and professional decorator Sam Karlen had the task of hanging bunting in the downtown area. The brick pavement was laid in 1912. (Author's collection.)

Henry D. Ryder's three-story hardware store occupied the site of what had once been a single-story trading post owned by the Holland Land Company and managed by John Storms (reputedly the only person in Boonville to have ever owned a slave). John Post and Peter Schuyler acquired the store and operated it at this location for more than 40 years. (Courtesy of Ed Fynmore.)

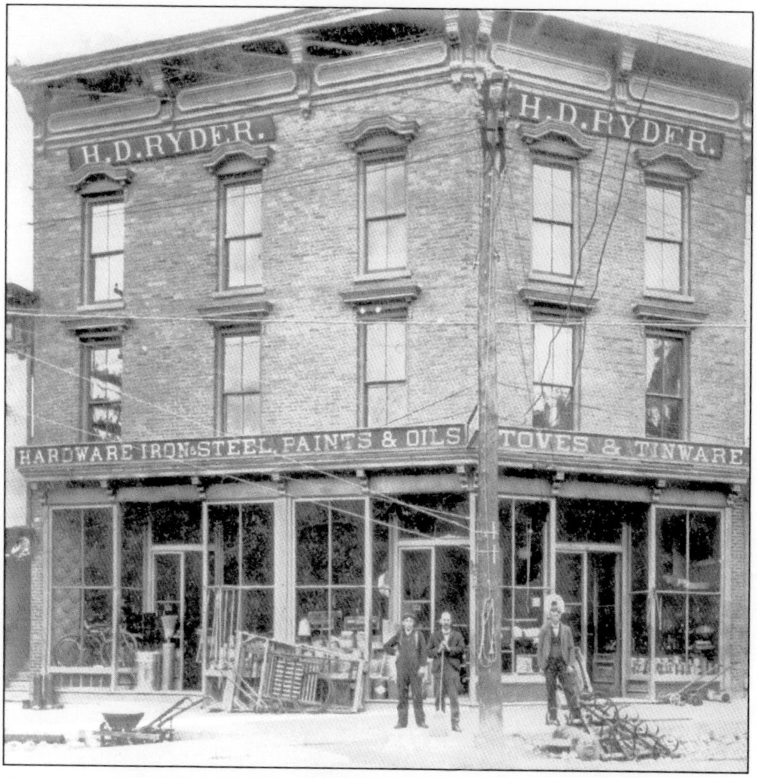

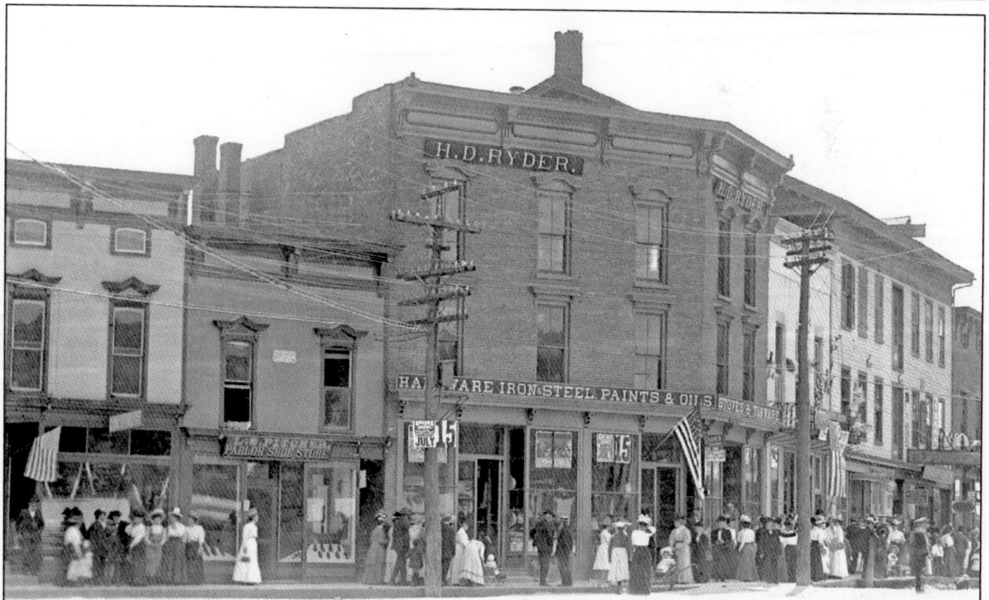

In 1899, Ryder acquired his hardware store (center) from Brinkerhoff C. Tharrett. Situated between Roy Pitcher's shoe store (left) and Shafer and Reber's stationery store (right), Ryder's store flourished at the corner of Main and Schuyler Streets until 1925, when the First National Bank purchased the site and razed the building. The crowd in this 1909 photograph has gathered to watch a parade by the John H. Sparks Circus. (Courtesy of Larry Myers.)

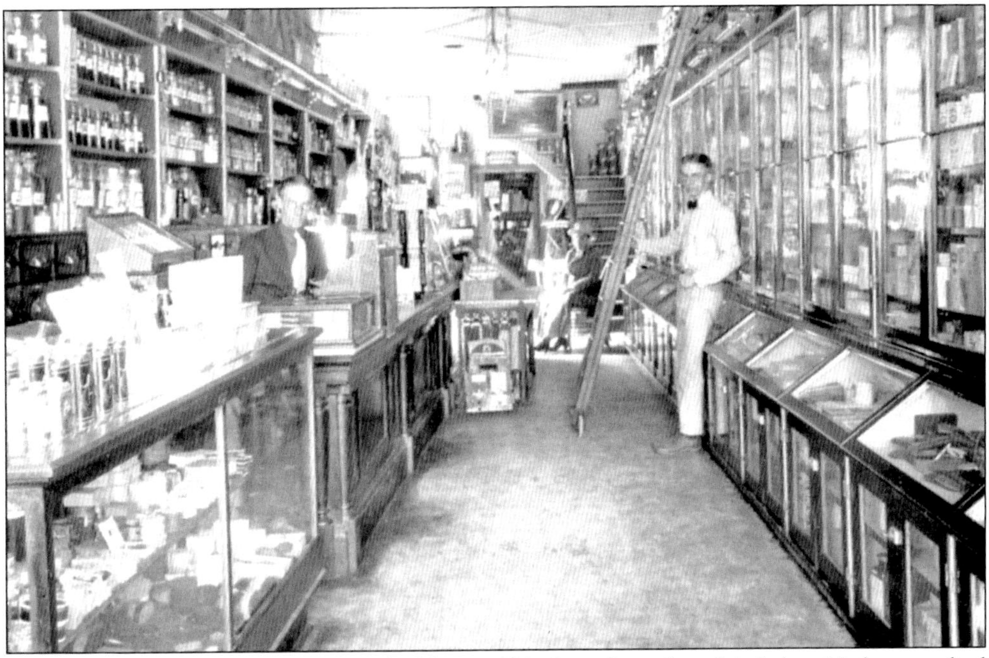

As a child in Nicholville, Silas J. Sanford learned blacksmithing from his father. He later studied optometry in New York City and then attended the Albany School of Pharmacy, graduating in 1906. The following year, he purchased E. B. Austin's drugstore and operated a pharmacy on the site for some 45 years. (Courtesy of Linda and Richard Sanford.)

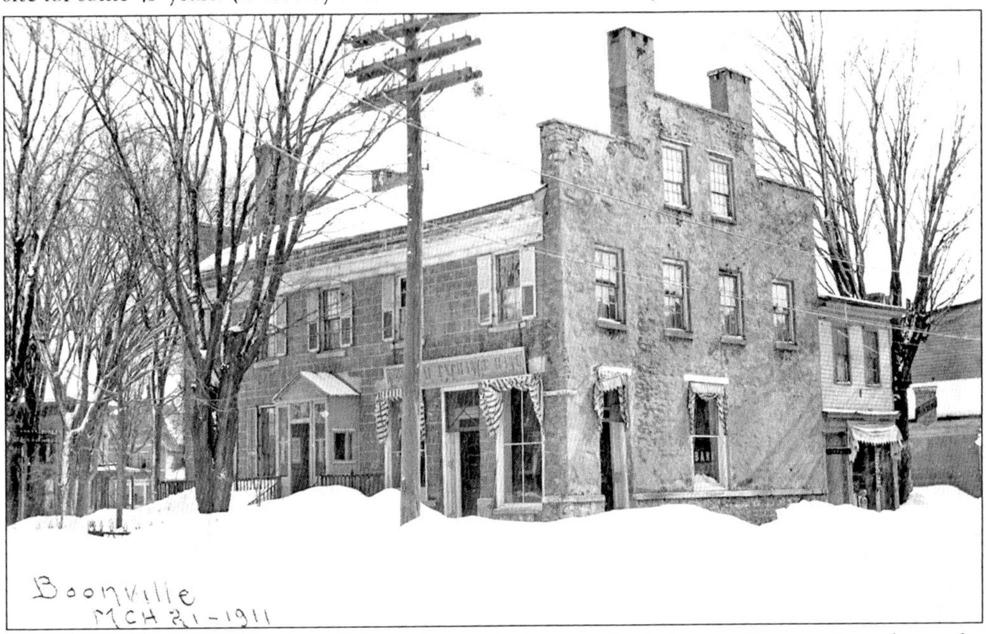

Gerrit Boon's associate Andrew Edmunds was the first settler in Boonville, erecting a home for his family in 1797. The wooden building, located at the eastern corner of Main and Schuyler Streets, also did duty as a tavern and post office. In the 1830s, Dr. Ralph O. Lord erected a limestone building on the site (above). This structure, commonly known as the Barlett Block, briefly housed Ela Merriam's Valley Bank (1852–1854). (Courtesy of Jerry Putnam.)

Two

UPPER MAIN STREET

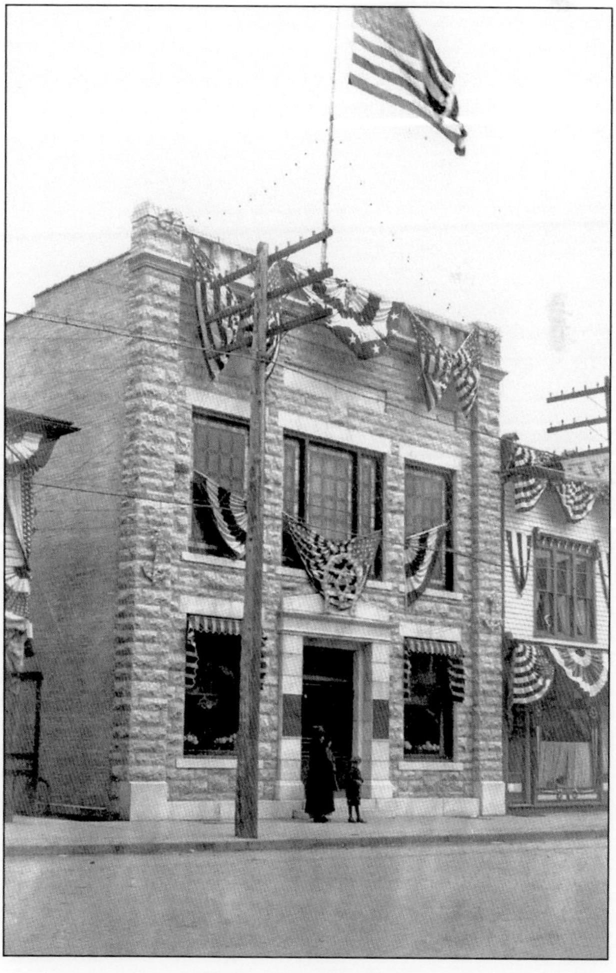

Herbert R. Tubbs and Eugene Hayes organized the National Exchange Bank in 1905 (the year the Thompson Bank ceased operations). In 1913, the bank moved from the Barlett Block into a new limestone structure on Main Street (seen here). At the time, the building on the right housed the office of Dr. Wallace Douglass. The photograph is by George Pollard. (Author's collection.)

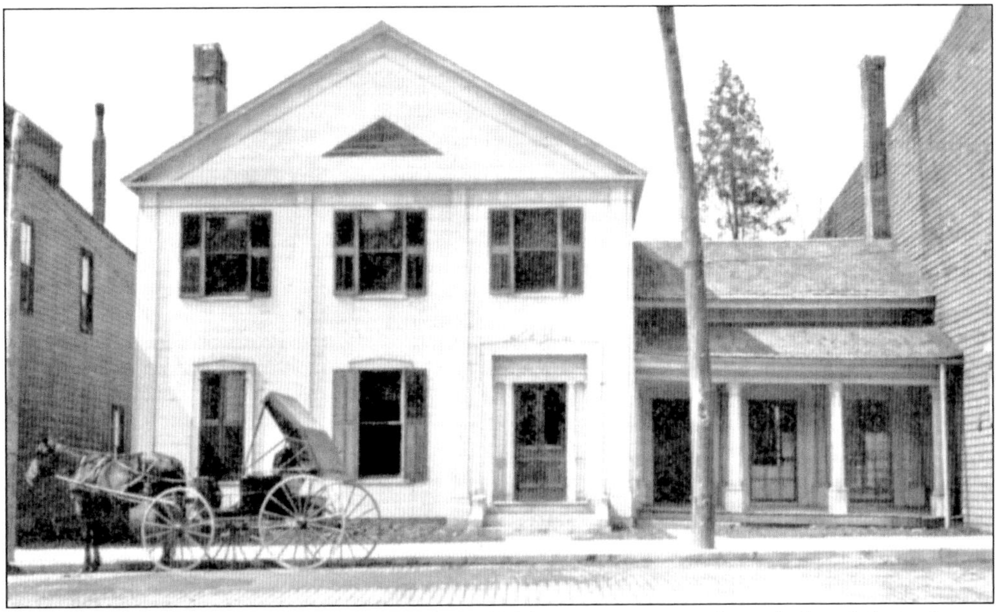

The Free and Accepted Masons organized in 1825 but, wanting members, forfeited their charter in 1835. They reorganized in 1850 and met in the Beale Block. In 1908, the Masons purchased this building from attorney Albert L. Hayes for use as a temple. The structure, once the residence of Philip Schuyler, sat on the south side of Main Street kitty-corner from the Barlett Block. (Courtesy of Larry Myers.)

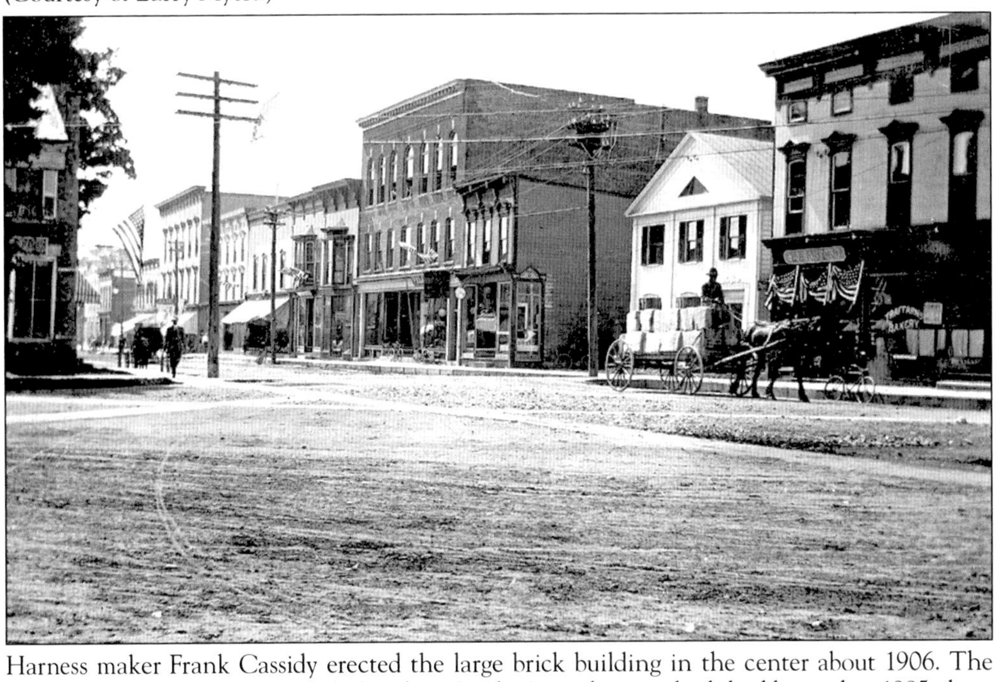

Harness maker Frank Cassidy erected the large brick building in the center about 1906. The structure was built on the site of Theodore Conlon's residence, which had burned in 1885 along with the Clark, Conlon, and Mowers Livery in back. West of the Cassidy Block, from left to right, in 1910 are (first) Charles Lewis' variety store, (second) the Masonic temple, and (third) Silas Sanford's pharmacy (left) and Edward Traffarn's bakery (right). (Courtesy of Ed Fynmore.)

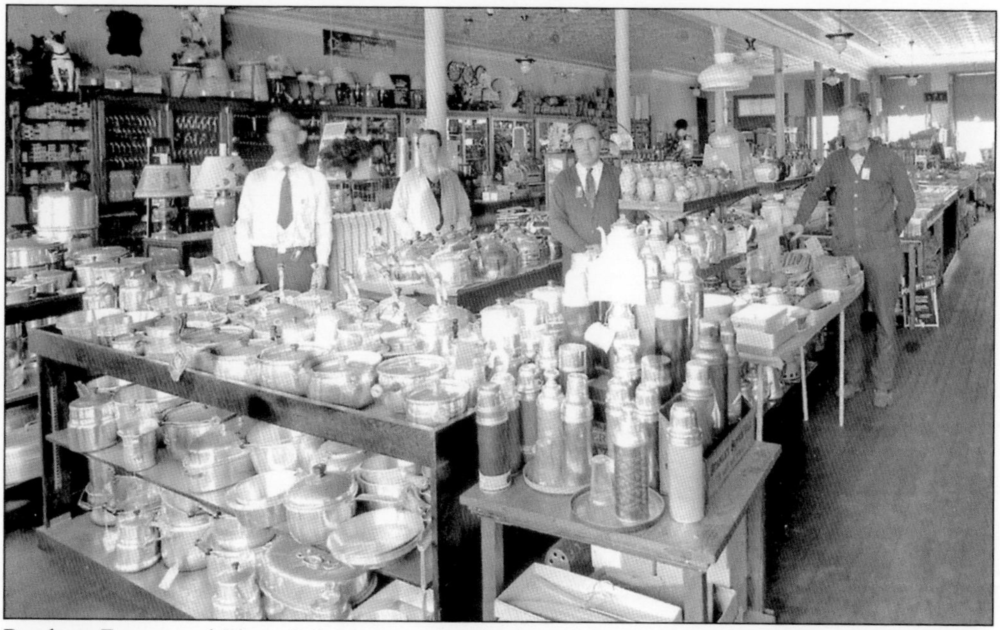

Brothers Ernest and Elwin Palmer ran a hardware store on the first two floors of the Cassidy Block. In 1861, the brothers' father Elbridge Palmer (1834–1911) came to Boonville from New Hampshire. After going into the hardware business with Leon Muller and later with Brinkerhoff Tharrett, Elbridge formed Palmer Brothers in 1895. Pictured from left to right are Elwin Palmer, Loretta McGuire Stoeber, Ernest Palmer, and Sylvester Turner. (Courtesy of Erwin Library.)

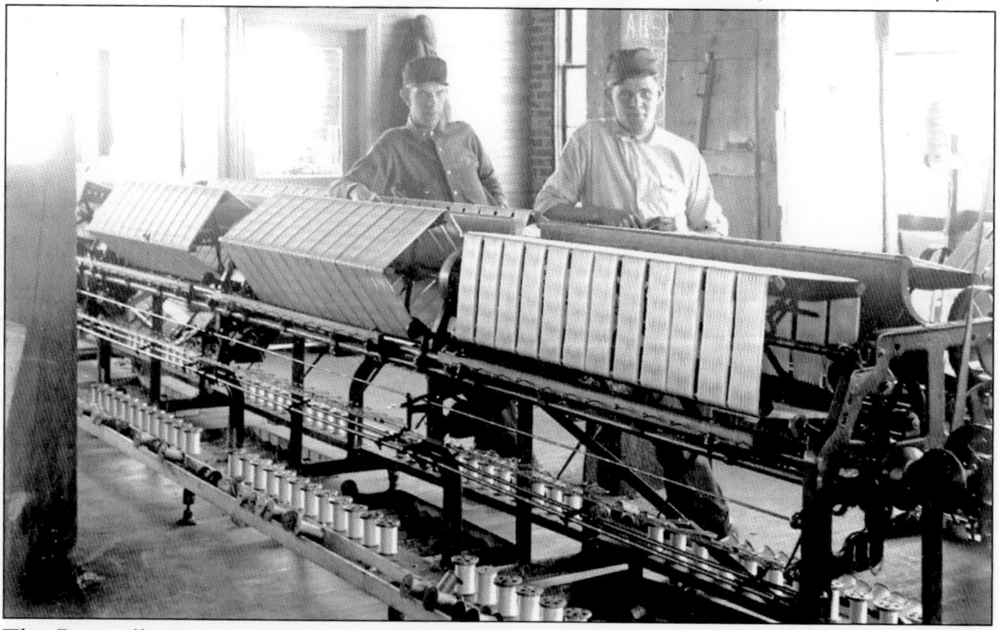

The Boonville Knitting Mill was the first textile mill in the village. Organized by Charles Thompson, Ben Capron, and others in 1902, the mill set up in a new building on the west bank of the canal but lasted only about six months. More successful was Ludwig Littauer's silk-throwing mill (pictured here). From 1907 to 1916, the mill occupied the third floor of the Cassidy Block. (Courtesy of Vincent T. Fitch.)

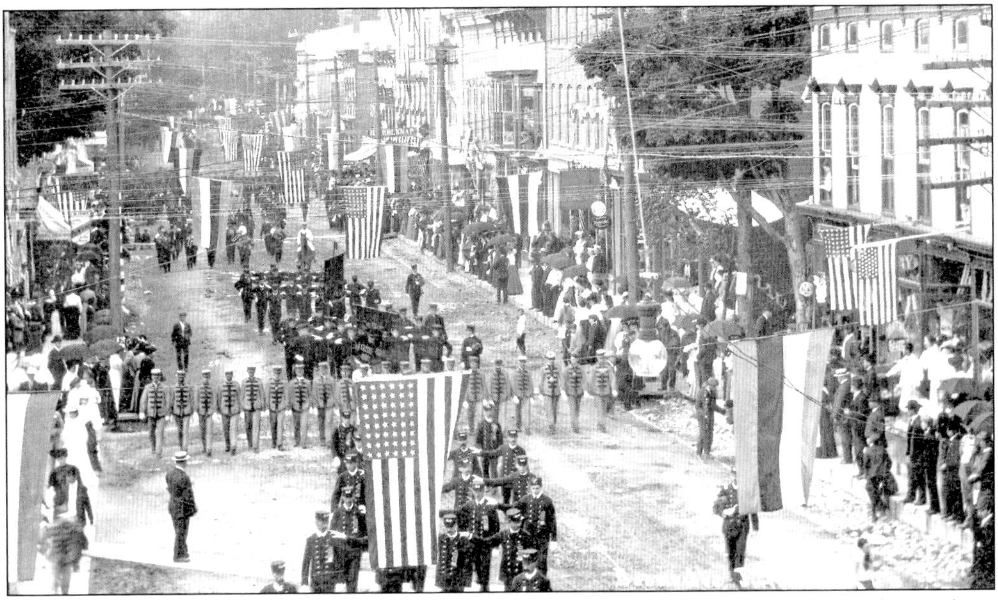

The July 4, 1906, parade advances under a maze of electrical wires. In 1898, August J. Schweinsberg and Charles Thompson formed the Boonville Light and Power Company. With a steam-driven, direct-current generator located on Mill Creek, this privately owned company furnished the village with street lighting for five years. As demand for electricity increased, the village formed a light commission in 1902. (Courtesy of Larry Myers.)

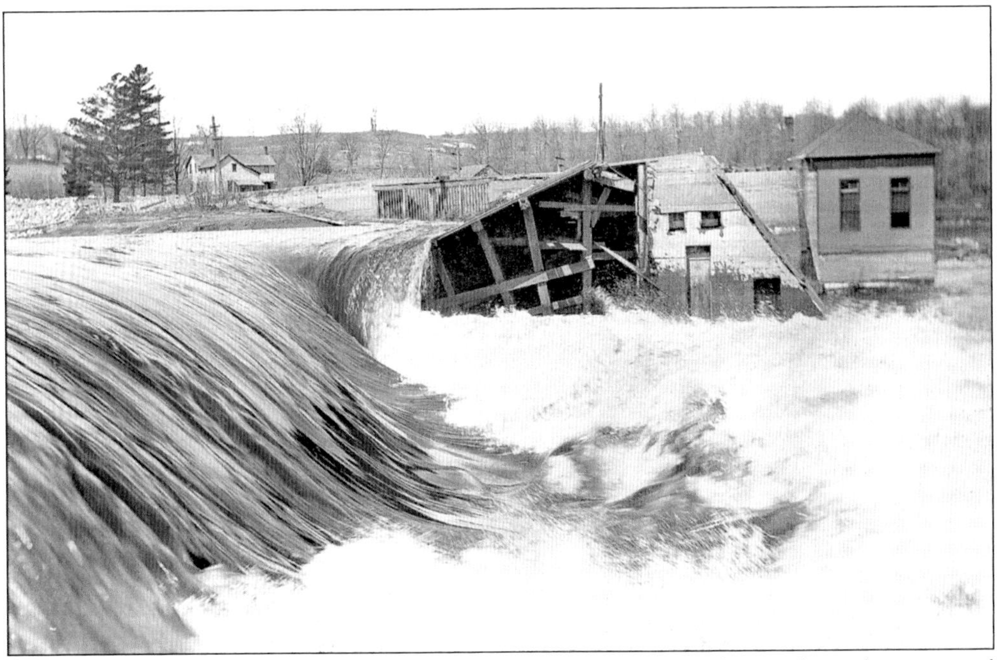

In 1903, the light commission purchased land on Black River near the Denley rail station and ordered a wooden dam built. Finished the same year, the municipally owned power plant boasted two 100-watt generators and one 90-watt generator. On April 17, 1912, the wooden dam washed out, but within a few months, a new concrete dam was in place. (Courtesy of Larry Myers.)

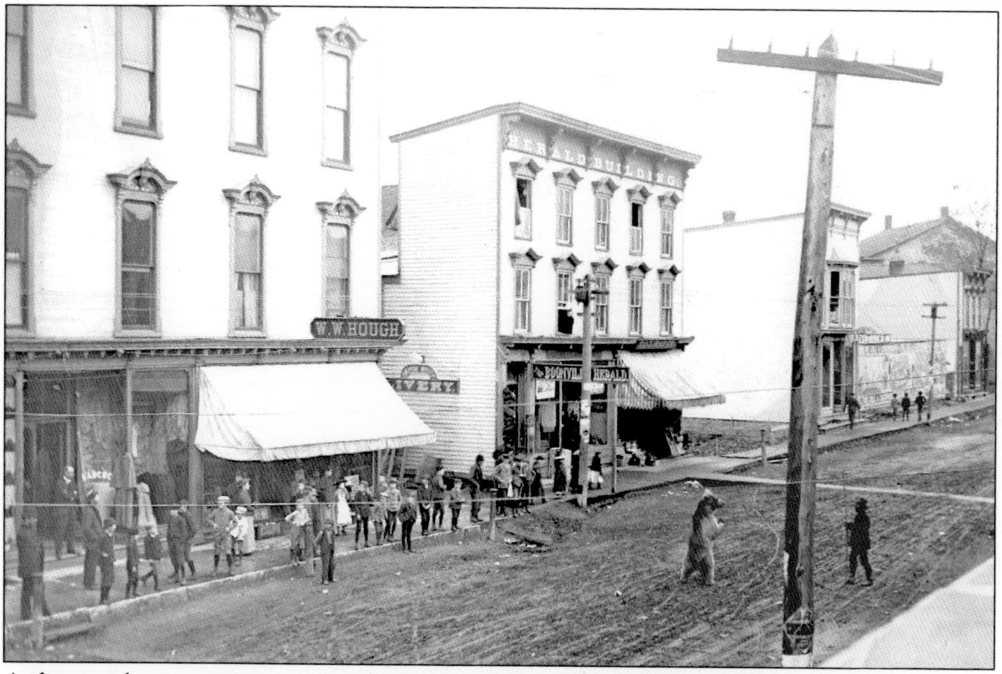

A dancing bear entertains a crowd on Main Street. The building at left is the Empire Block, built in 1886 by merchants Jesse P. Babcock, Alonzo Perrigo, and William W. Hough. In this photograph from about 1902, the block houses Hough's groceries (right) and Babcock's women's apparel (left). Northwest of the Empire Block is the Herald Building, home to the *Herald*, Perry's dry goods, Dr. Gustavus P. English's surgery, and Church's taxidermy. (Courtesy of Ed Fynmore.)

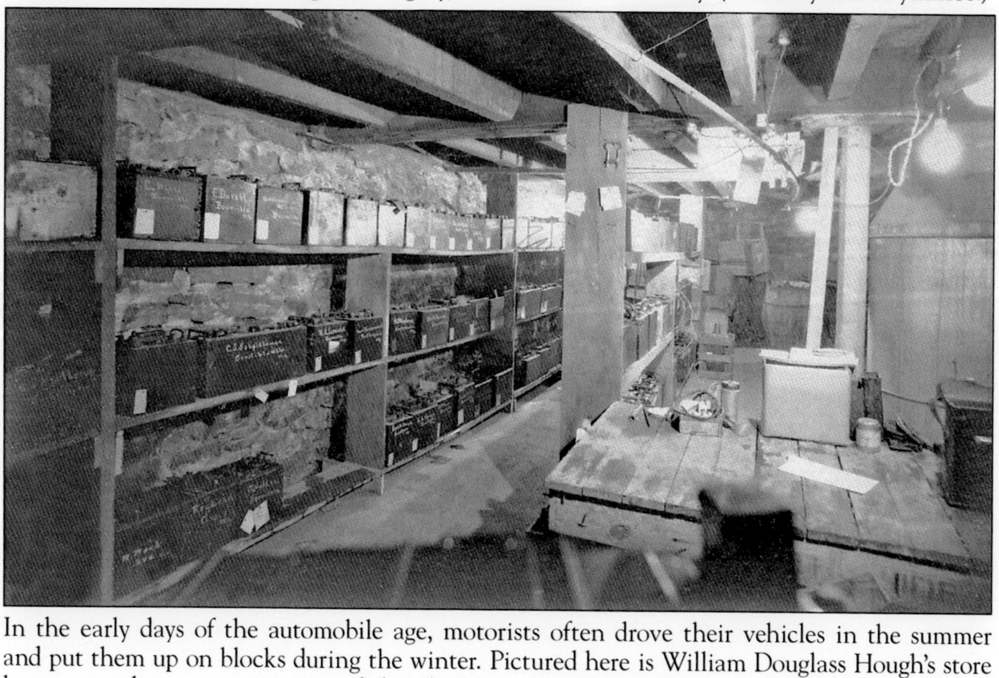

In the early days of the automobile age, motorists often drove their vehicles in the summer and put them up on blocks during the winter. Pictured here is William Douglass Hough's store basement, where car owners stored their batteries during the off-season. Hough also sold Delco generators and electrical appliances. The photograph dates from 1921. (Author's collection.)

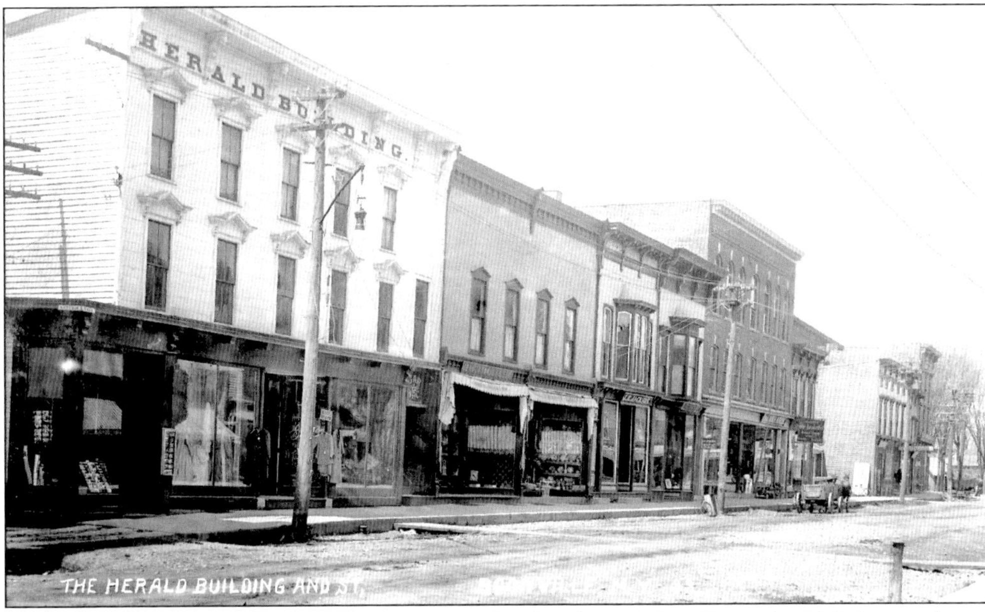

In the 1850s, Harvey Willard ran a proprietary school on lower Main Street. In 1862, he purchased the *Black River Herald*, renaming it the *Boonville Herald* and later moving it from Post Street to a new building on Main Street (site of the former Methodist church). In 1892, J. W. Donnelly founded the rival *Boonville Record*. In contrast to the *Herald*, which championed the Republican Party, the *Record* threw its support to the Democrats. (Courtesy of Larry Myers.)

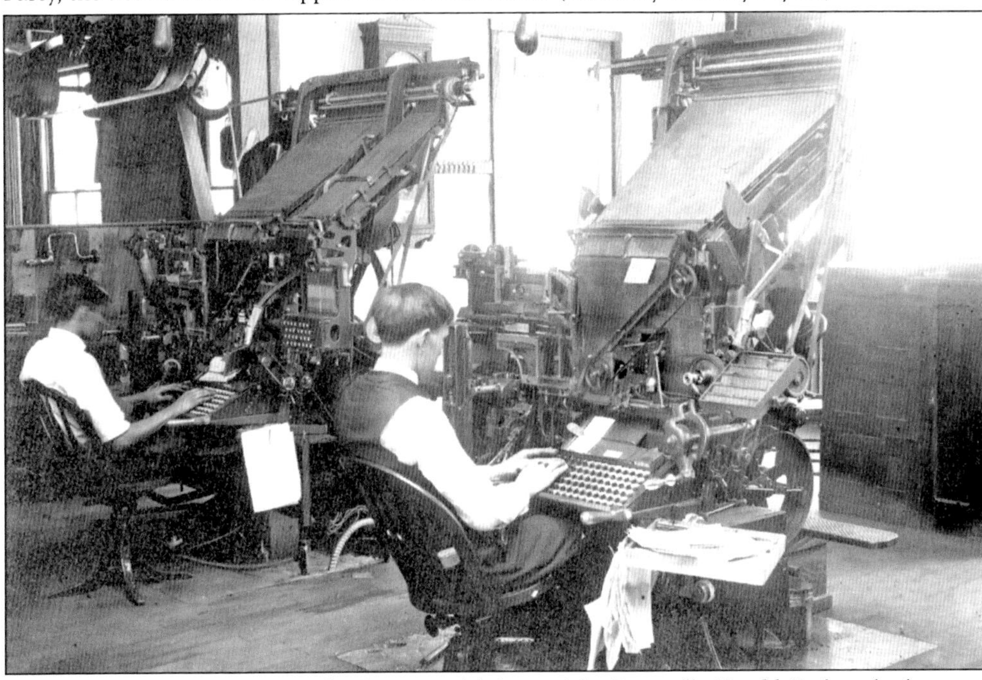

Compositors set type at the Willard Press, publishers of the *Boonville Herald*. Before the linotype machine was introduced by Ottman Mergenthaler in 1894, compositors cast type by hand. Harvey Willard purchased his first linotype about 1896 and acquired a second one in 1914. Willard Press was located behind the Herald Building. (Courtesy of Ed Fynmore.)

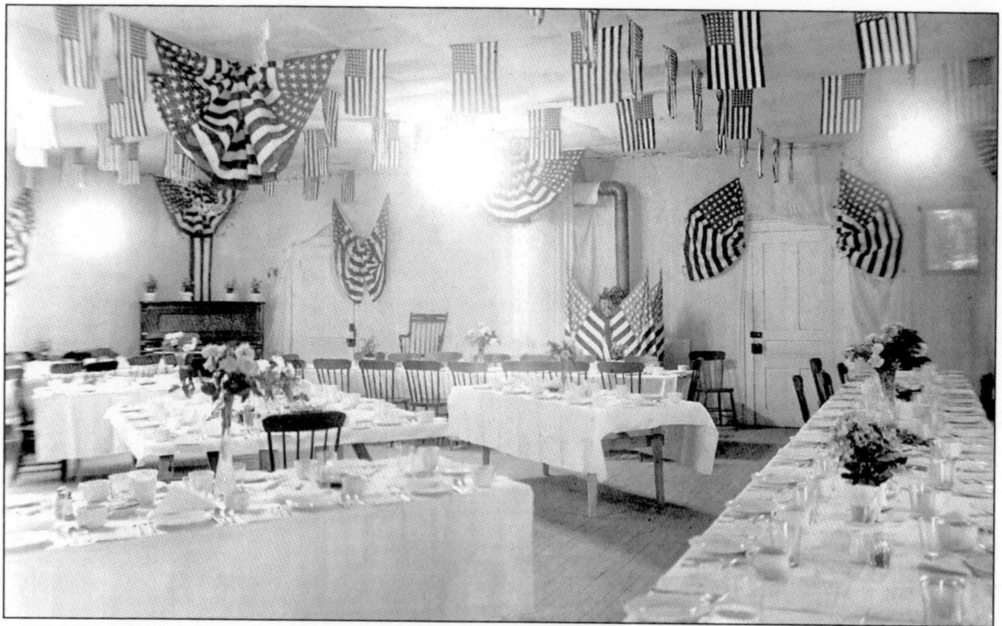

The upper floors of several downtown buildings served as meeting halls. After gathering in a private home for 18 years, the Cornell Study Club began meeting upstairs in the Hayes-Cavanagh Block (above) in 1929. Organized locally by Marion Groh, the club brought farm families together to discuss topics related to agriculture and home economics. Cornell University furnished study pamphlets, and each session typically featured a speaker. (Courtesy of Erwin Library.)

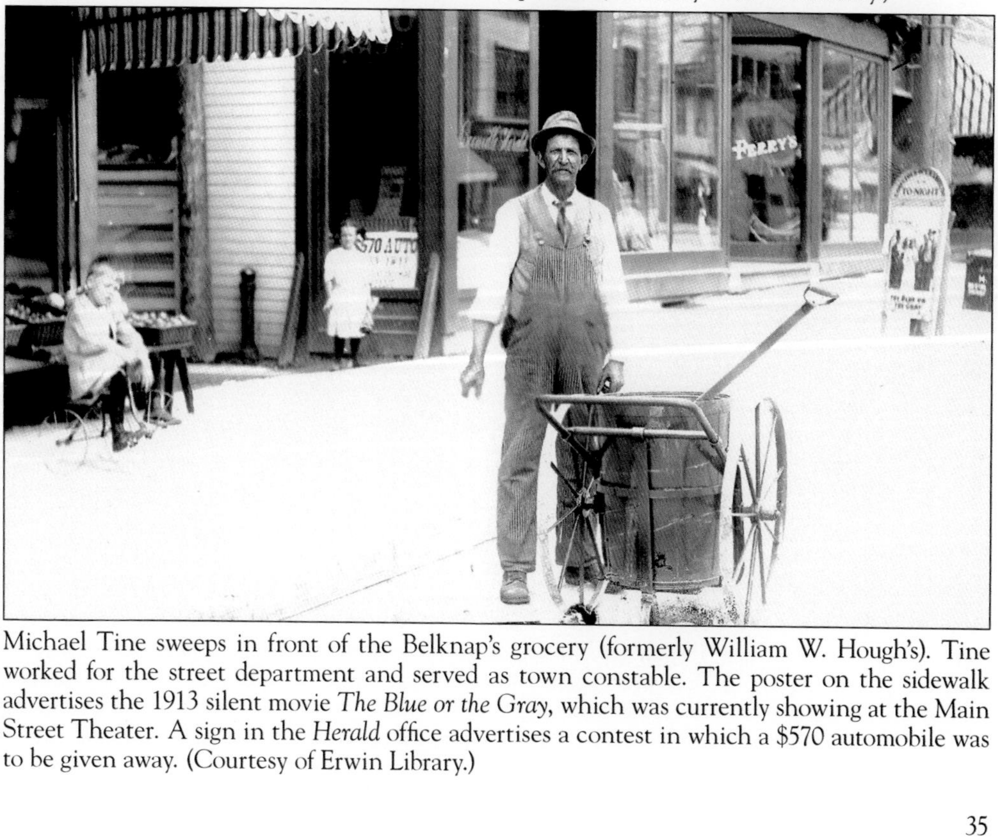

Michael Tine sweeps in front of the Belknap's grocery (formerly William W. Hough's). Tine worked for the street department and served as town constable. The poster on the sidewalk advertises the 1913 silent movie *The Blue or the Gray*, which was currently showing at the Main Street Theater. A sign in the *Herald* office advertises a contest in which a $570 automobile was to be given away. (Courtesy of Erwin Library.)

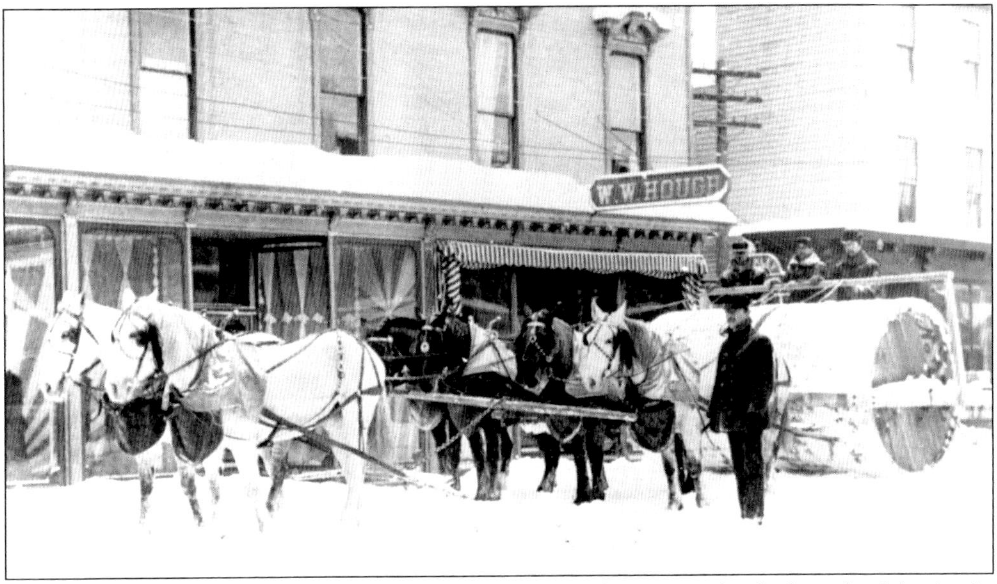

The village used a locally made water-filled roller to pack down snow for the benefit of sleighs. In this 1904 photograph by F. A. Moore, street commissioner Fred Whiter, three drivers, and three teams of horses command the 5,500-pound snow roller stationed in front of the Empire Block. In a 1928 referendum, town residents voted to purchase a $9,500 rotary highway plow. (Courtesy of Erwin Library.)

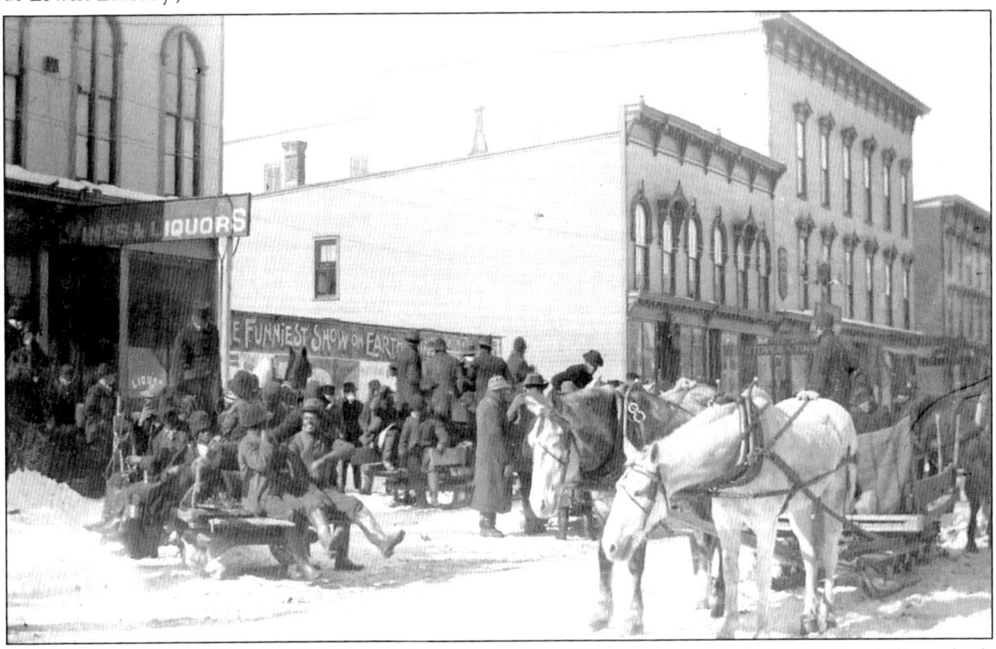

In 1891, contractors imported African Americans from Tennessee to help build the Adirondack and St. Lawrence Railroad. Ill-prepared for the northern winter, many of these workers came to John Cavanagh's shoe store for appropriate footwear. In the photograph, a crowd has gathered outside Joseph Larrivey's liquor store, awaiting a performance at Nicholas Schweinsberg's Opera House. The opera house would later become the Main Street Theater and, still later, the Avon. (Courtesy of Erwin Library.)

In 1893, Julius F. Guillaume (left) opened the Peanut Emporium on Main Street just northwest of Thomas McCormick's harness shop. Sitting are constable John H. Sackett and C. M. Wheeler. Later Frank Traffarn ran a variety store here, sharing the building with several others, including Fred Eppel, who maintained a shoe store affectionately known as "Tammany Hall," a gathering place where friends and cronies discussed politics and local affairs. (Courtesy of Vincent T. Fitch.)

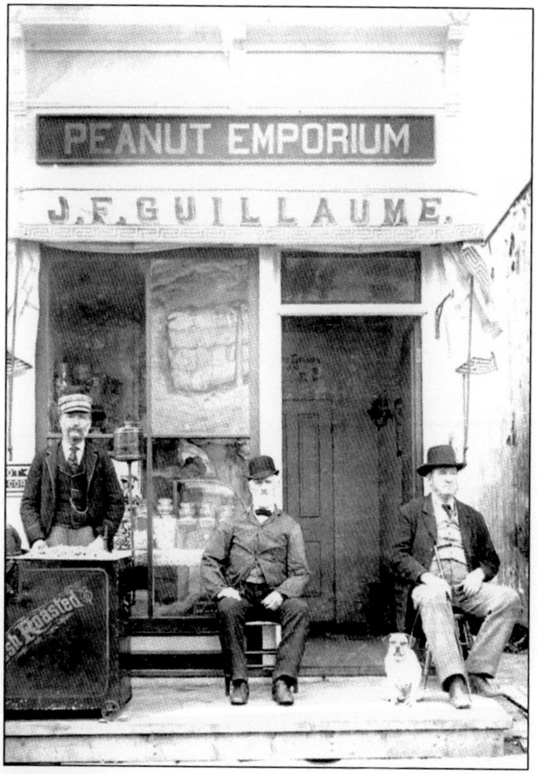

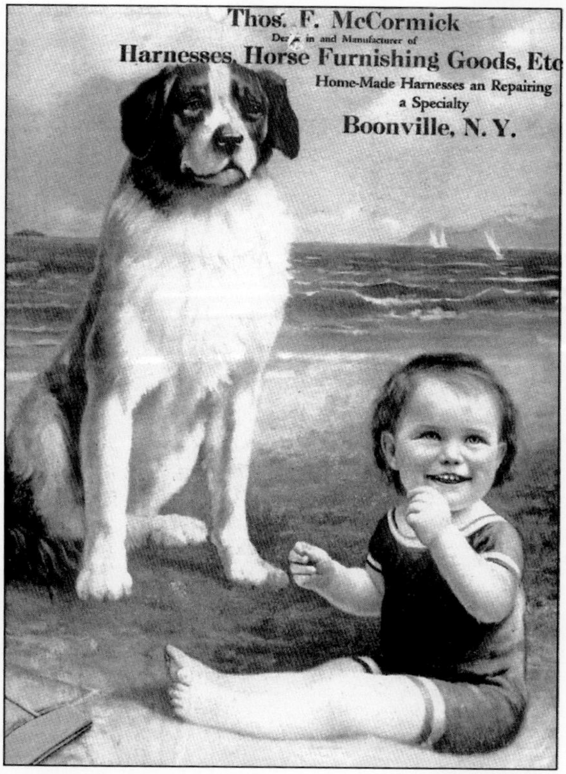

For years, McCormick's harness shop was located between Traffarn's variety store and McCann's Imperial Hotel. Later McCormick moved the shop to the southeast corner of Church and Main Streets. His was the last remaining harness shop in Boonville. According to harness maker Clark Layng, a skilled worker in 1906 could expect to earn $10 for a 59-hour week; by 1917, wages rose to $27 for the same number of hours. (Courtesy of Jerry Putnam.)

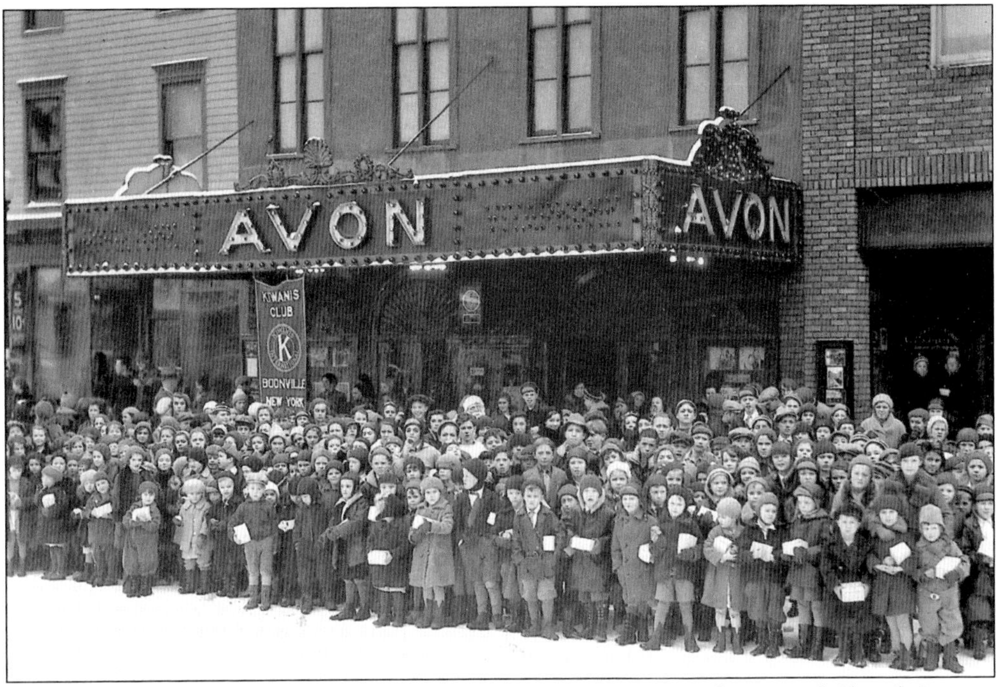

The Avon Theater, owned by Alphonse J. Cyr, was near the corner of Main and Church Streets. In 1926, after a hotly contested election, local citizens voted to allow the showing of Sunday movies. During the holiday season, the Kiwanis Club, organized in 1929, treated children to a program at the Avon. Ryder's new hardware store, opened in 1927, is on the right. (Courtesy of Ed Fynmore.)

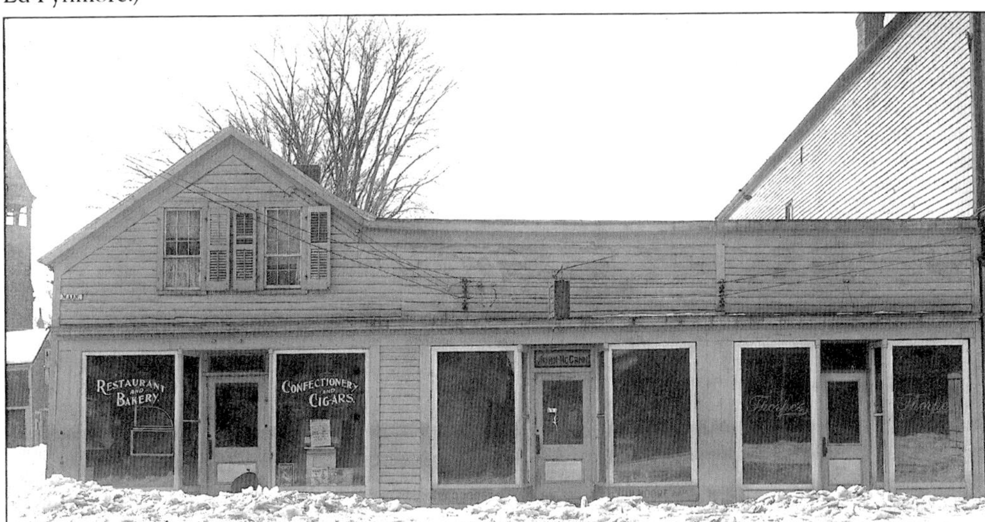

Baker G. H. Schneider maintained a shop on the left side of this building located at the southwest corner of Main and Church Streets. A sign in the window promises an "honest scoop" of ice cream. John McCann's liquor store was in the center, and Frank Thorp's barbershop was on the right. The tower of the old 1856 firehouse is visible in the left background. (Courtesy of Jerry Putnam.)

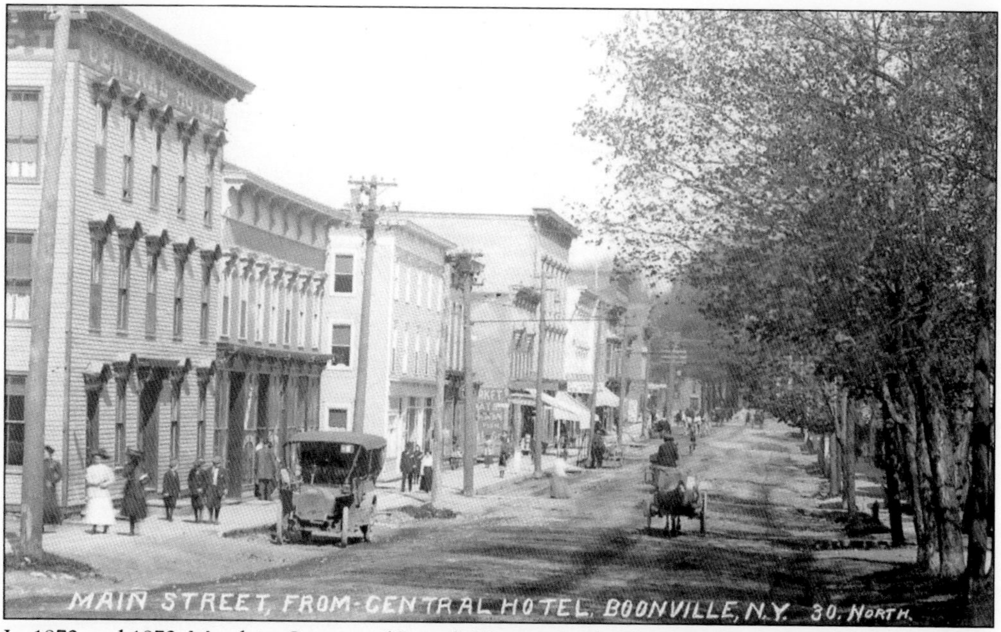

In 1872 and 1873, Matthias Seiter and Joseph Kornmeyer built the Central Hotel (left), owned at different times by Herbert Paddock, Jerry Buckley, Philip McGuire, and E. J. Kirley. About 1900, the McCann Block (third from the left) replaced the one-story building featured in the previous photograph. This structure was home to John McCann's Imperial Hotel and George Kent's pool room. The hotel boasted two bowling alleys in the basement. (Courtesy of Ed Fynmore.)

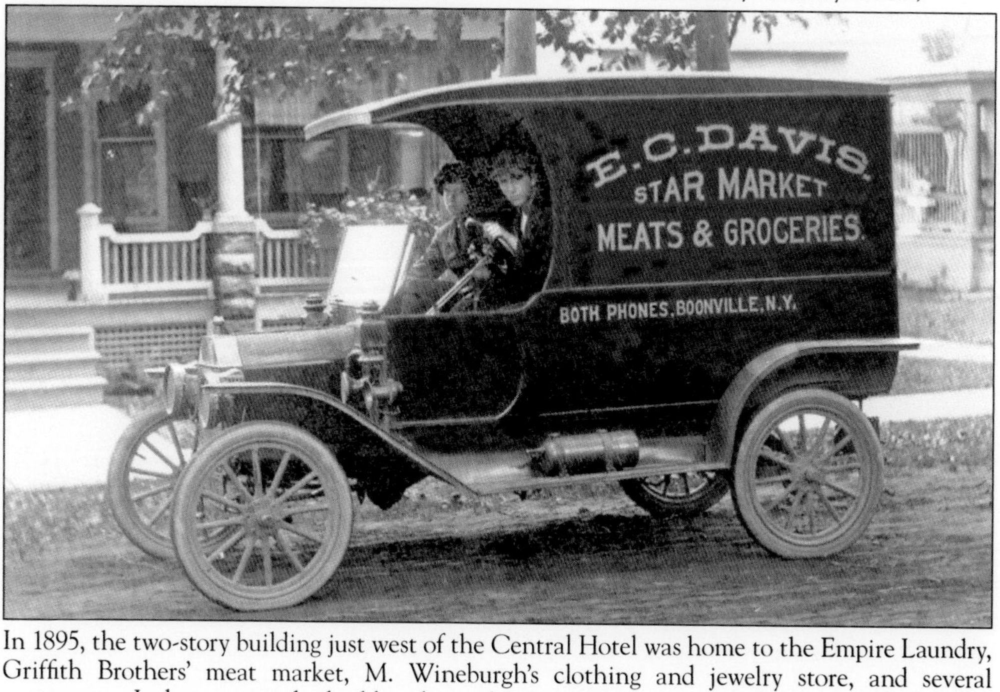

In 1895, the two-story building just west of the Central Hotel was home to the Empire Laundry, Griffith Brothers' meat market, M. Wineburgh's clothing and jewelry store, and several apartments. In later years, the building housed Star Market, owned at different times by Dora Powers, E. C. Davis, Guy Enearl, and Fred Manning. Behind Star Market on Church Street was the Globe Hotel. (Courtesy of Erwin Library.)

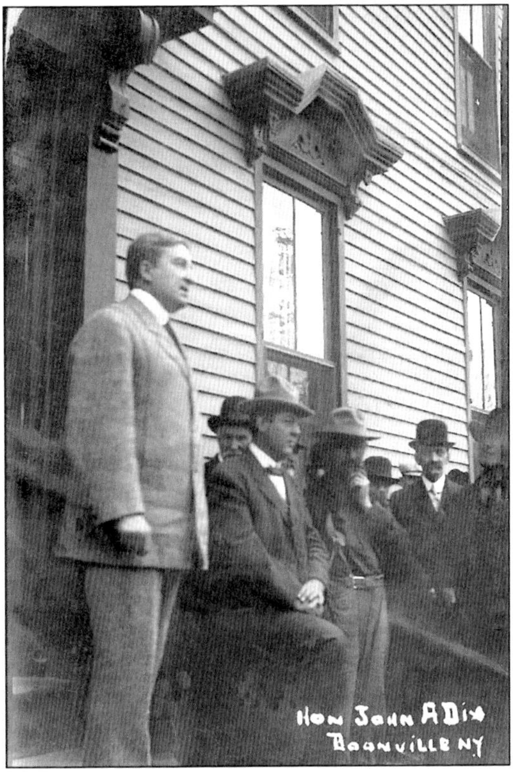

Gov. John Alden Dix (left) speaks to a crowd gathered in front of the Central Hotel. Dix, a Democrat, served as governor from 1911 to 1913. With partner Lemon Thomson, Dix owned the Moose River Lumber Company at McKeever. To the right of Dix is George O. Bridgman, a Civil War veteran and former mayor. From 1904 to 1927, he served as superintendent of the municipal commission. (Courtesy of Larry Myers.)

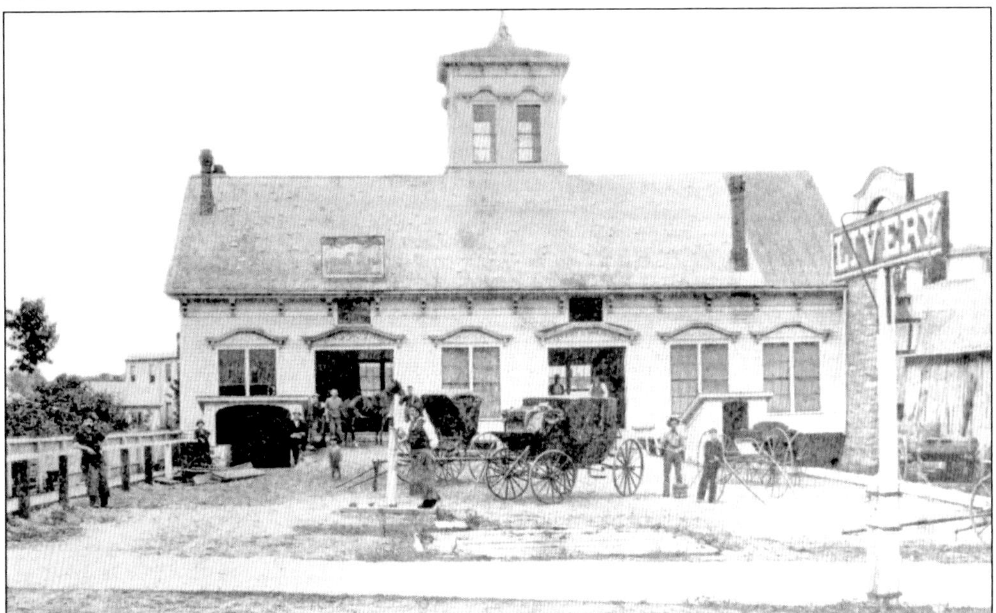

Elijah Comstock built this livery and blacksmith shop east of the Central Hotel. His son William (Billy) Comstock (1822–1907) worked here as a blacksmith and later built many of the houses on Ann Street as well as the Comstock Opera House. Following Billy's death, Herman Earl and Ebert Cronk ran the livery, and William Baker operated the blacksmith shop, one of the last in town. (Courtesy of Ed Fynmore.)

Wooden sidewalks are clearly visible in this 1878 Ackerman Brothers photograph. The building on the left, which housed the shop of machinist Charles L. Jillson, was replaced and occupied by Jacob Vollmar's clothing store in the 1880s. In the building to its right, John Hyland and Griffith Evans made shoes upstairs, and James McClusky sold groceries downstairs. (Courtesy of Ed Fynmore.)

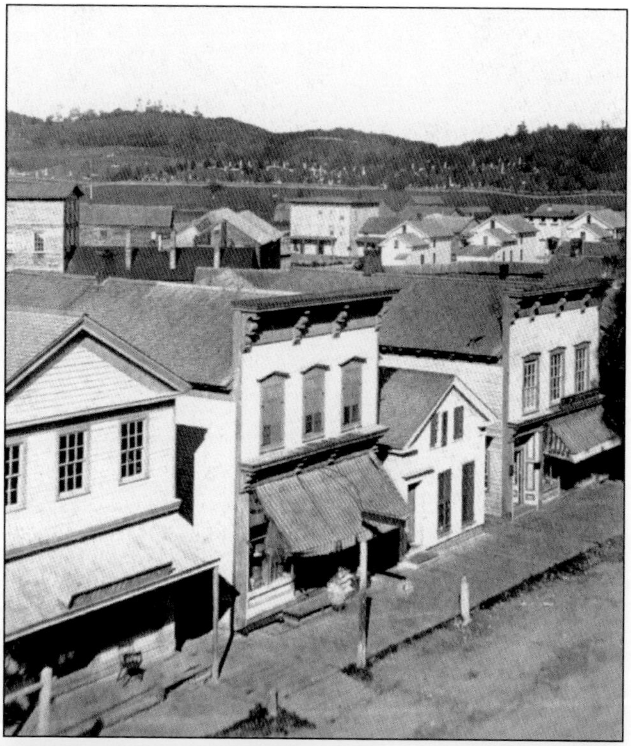

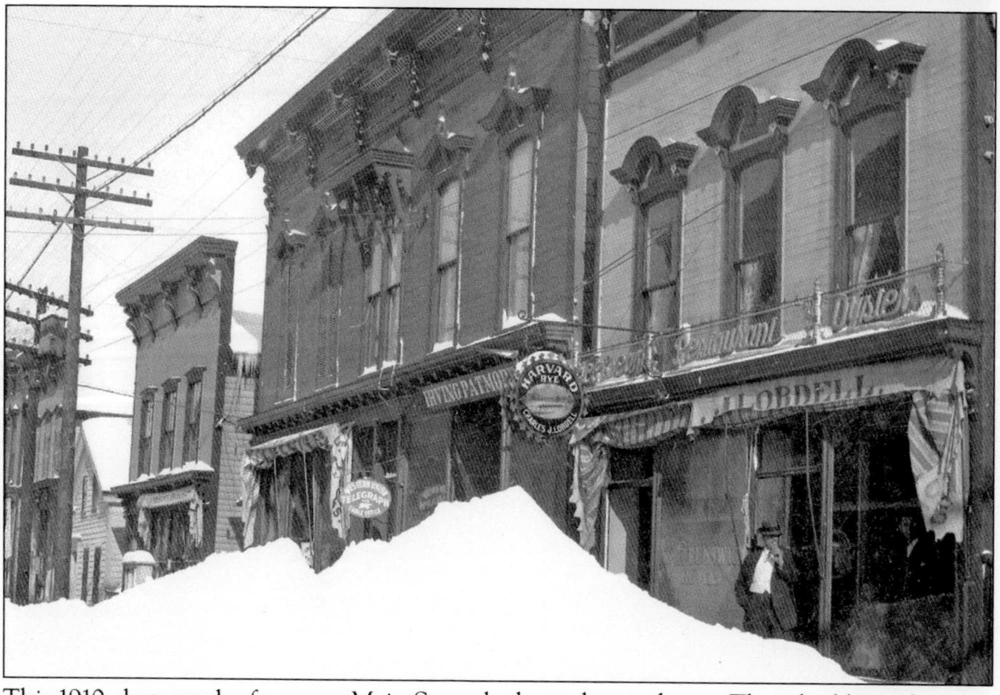

This 1910 photograph of a snowy Main Street looks to the northwest. These buildings, from left to right, house (first) James McClusky's grocery; (second) Ed Mather's barbershop; (third) Charles Prescott's pharmacy; (fourth) Irving Patmore's plumbing, a Western Union office, and the grocery of Herman C. Sears; and (fifth) Charles Lobdell's Brunswick Hotel. (Author's collection.)

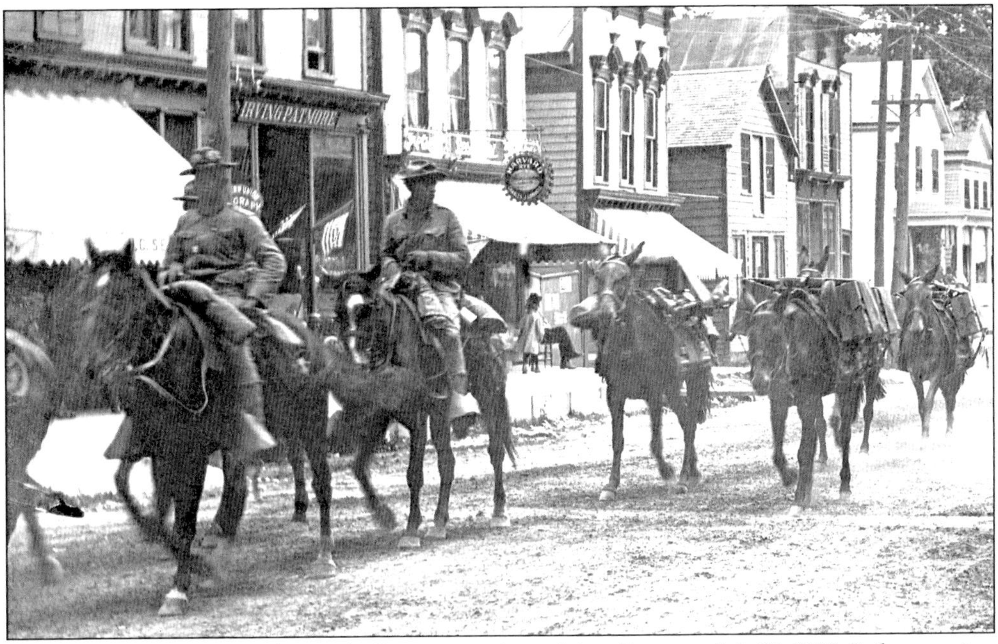

The African American 10th Cavalry Regiment rides up Main Street on July 28, 1910. Before moving on to Pine Plains (Fort Drum), the regiment bivouacked on the Boonville fairgrounds. Housed in the buildings, from left to right, are the grocery of Herman C. Sears and Irving Patmore's plumbing, the Brunswick Hotel, Taft's bakery, Artemus Church's taxidermy, Gilbert Sawyer's printing, John Sears's Boonville Laundry, and Dr. R. C. Hurlbut's veterinary clinic. (Courtesy of Larry Myers.)

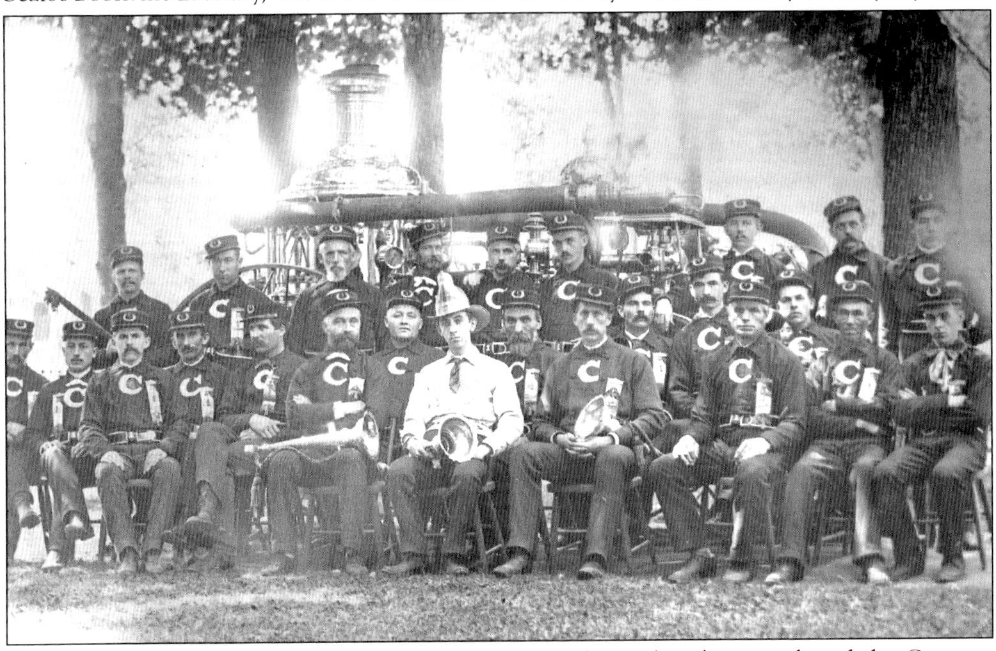

The Cataract Fire Department was organized in 1855 when subscribers purchased the Cataract Engine No. 1 for $1,560. In later years, the fire department was divided into the Acme Hose Company and the Rescue Hook and Ladder Company. This division continued until 1956. The fire chief in this 1888 photograph is carriage maker Edward L. Woolley. (Courtesy of Ed Fynmore.)

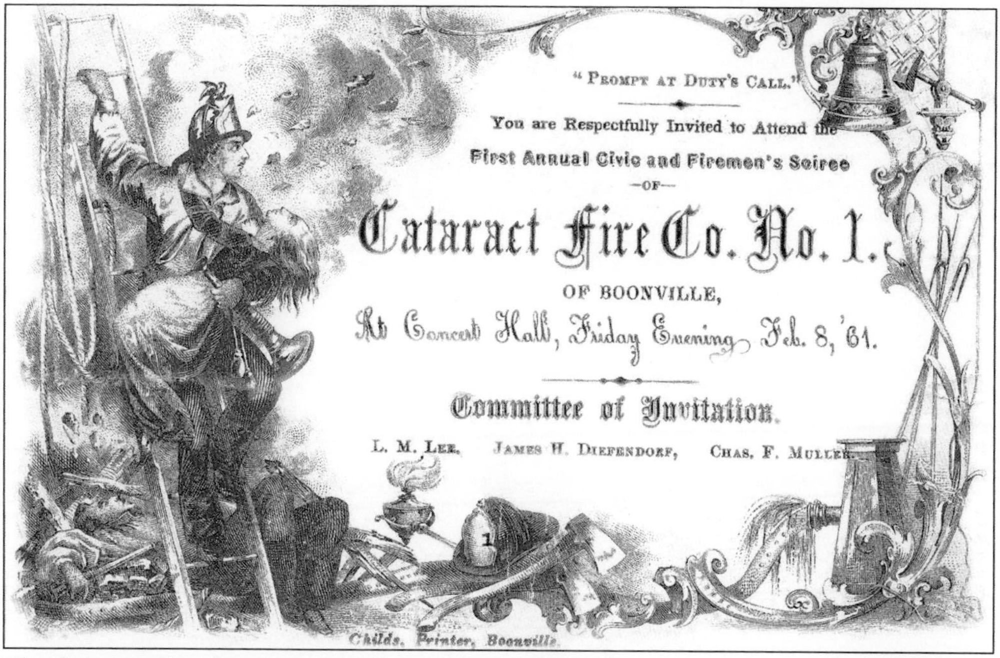

The Cataract Fire Company was dedicated to fighting fires, but it also promoted fellowship and social intercourse. This card, printed by L. C. Childs, announces the first annual Civic and Firemen's Soiree to be held at the concert hall on February 8, 1861. At that time, the fire department had about 65 members. (Courtesy of Jerry Putnam.)

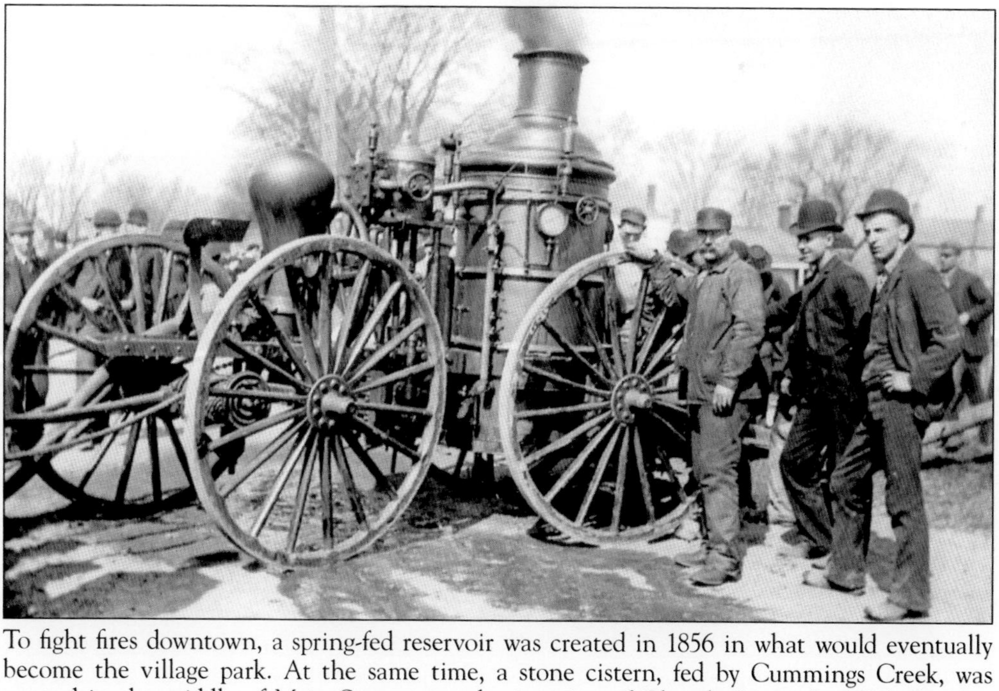

To fight fires downtown, a spring-fed reservoir was created in 1856 in what would eventually become the village park. At the same time, a stone cistern, fed by Cummings Creek, was erected in the middle of Main Street near the junction of Church Street. In 1896, the new water commission ordered a reservoir built on Jackson Hill, and in 1897, water mains and 55 fire hydrants were installed throughout the village. (Courtesy of Ed Fynmore.)

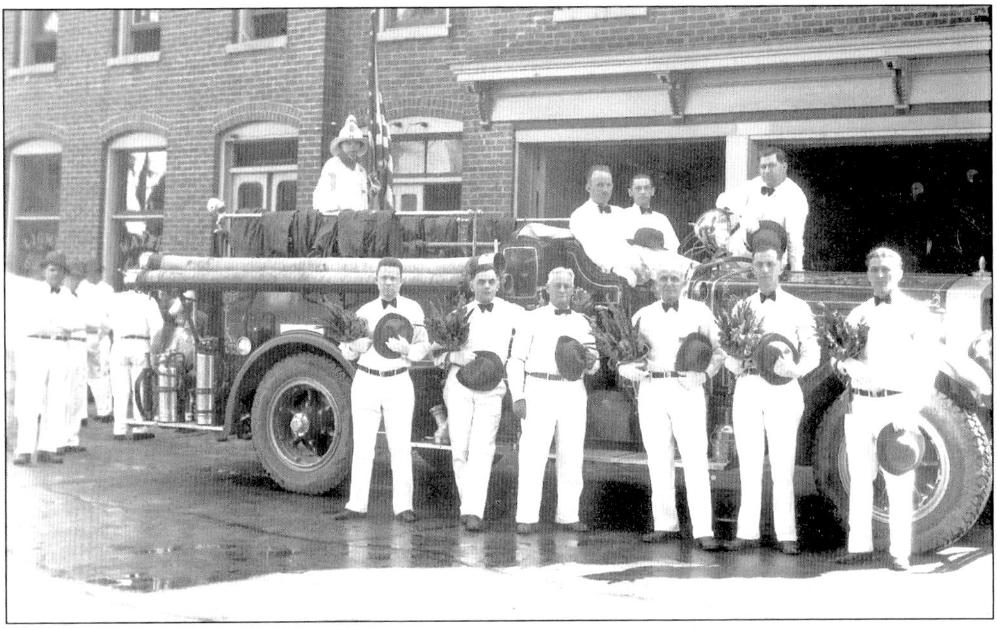

Firemen in white dress uniforms pose with the department's American LaFrance pumper, purchased in 1929 for $12,500. In 1909, citizens voted to erect a municipal building (left) adjoining the fire hall. The municipal commission maintained offices on the first floor of this building until 1937, and the second floor served as a jail until 1938. (Courtesy of Boonville Fire Department.)

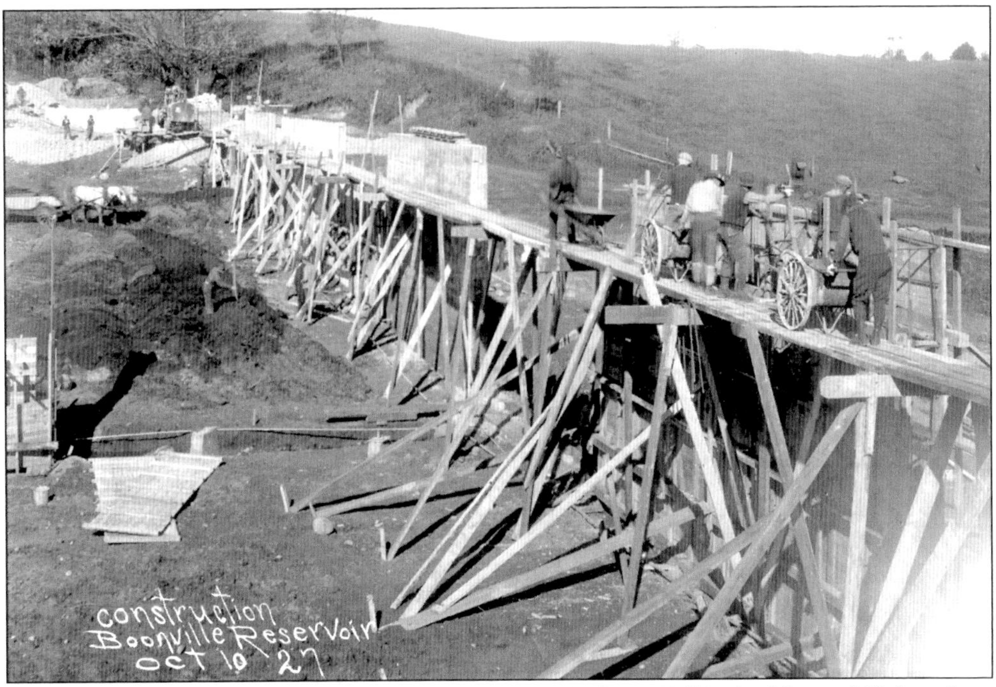

In 1913, the village enlarged the existing reservoir on Jackson Hill by building a 240-foot dam. This reservoir held about two million gallons of water. In 1927, the village contracted with Fort Schuyler Engineering of Utica to build a new, lower reservoir on Jackson Hill, shown here. The photograph is by George H. Pollard. (Courtesy of Boonville Municipal Commission.)

Three

Canal Street and Lower Main Street

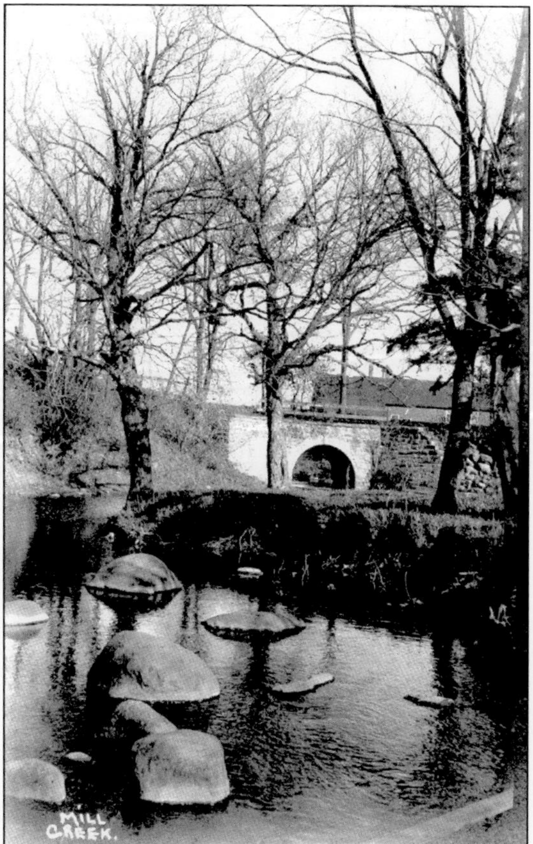

Mill Creek rises in the highlands southwest of Boonville and flows through the village in an easterly direction, draining into Black River some two miles away. To provide power for early mills, the stream was dammed in at least four places. (Courtesy of Vincent T. Fitch.)

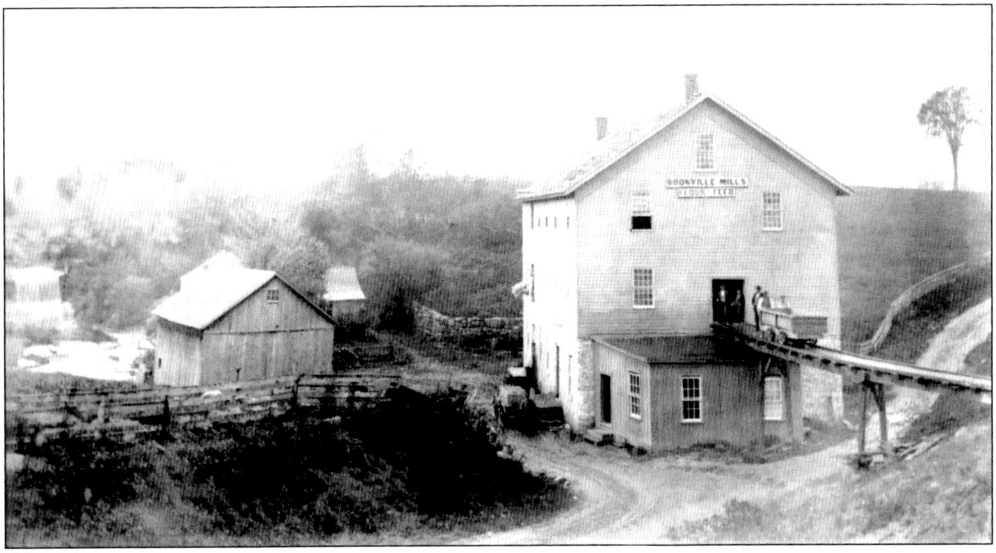

Boonville Mills is one of the oldest going concerns in the village. In 1795, Gerrit Boon and Andrew Edmunds erected a sawmill on Mill Creek to provide building materials for the new settlement. The mill burned down the same year but was rebuilt the next, and a gristmill was added. In 1817, Levin Jillson erected part of the present Boonville Mills just downstream. (Courtesy of Ed Fynmore.)

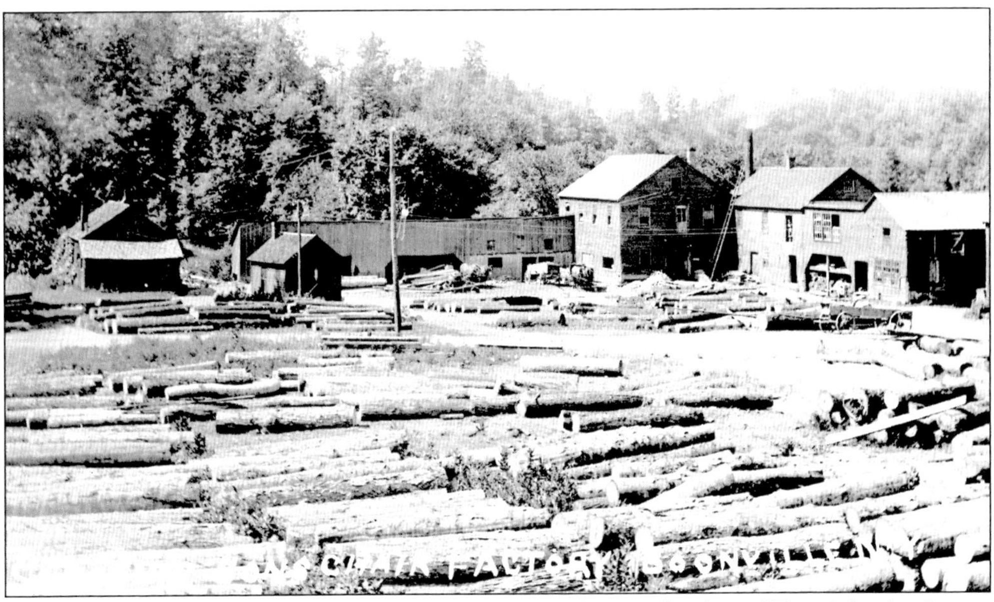

In 1817, Ephraim Owen erected a sawmill on Mill Creek near the foot of East Schuyler Street. After operating it for more than 30 years, Whiting Tuttle sold the mill to Nathaniel Sargent in 1849. By 1916, Sargent's sons Frank and Foster were turning out more than 75,000 chairs a year. This photograph is by Don Ryder. (Courtesy of Ed Fynmore.)

In 1824, Owen built a tannery on Mill Creek between Jillson's gristmill and Tuttle's sawmill. The tannery passed through several hands before 1849 when Samuel Johnson, pictured here, purchased it. With the Black River Canal in place by 1850, he did a thriving business, importing raw hides from Latin America and exporting tanned hides to Boston. (Author's collection.)

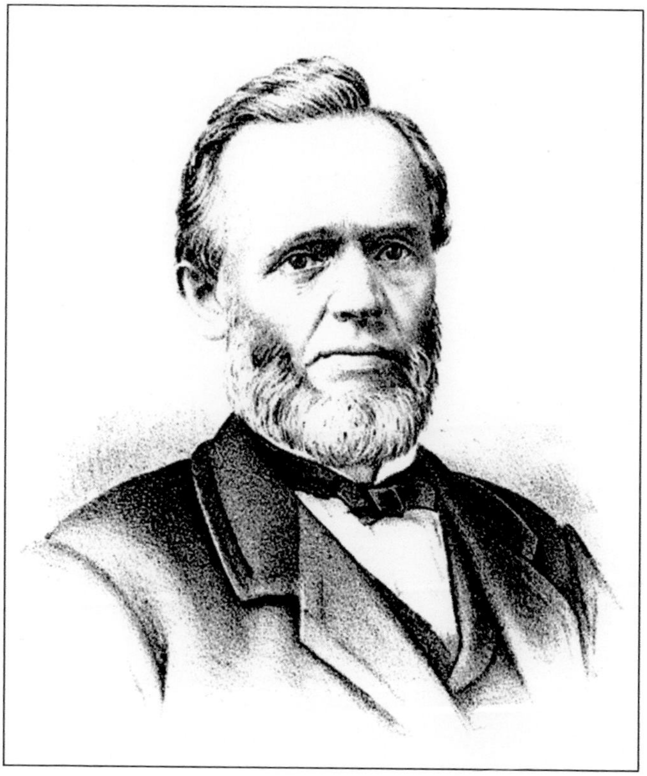

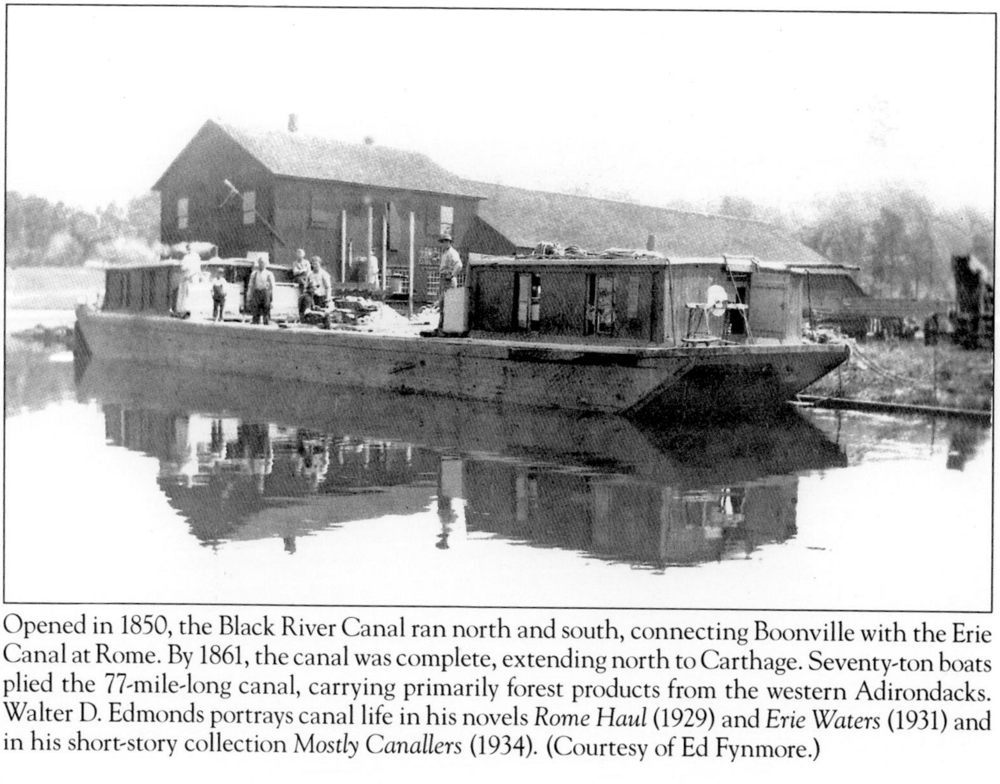

Opened in 1850, the Black River Canal ran north and south, connecting Boonville with the Erie Canal at Rome. By 1861, the canal was complete, extending north to Carthage. Seventy-ton boats plied the 77-mile-long canal, carrying primarily forest products from the western Adirondacks. Walter D. Edmonds portrays canal life in his novels *Rome Haul* (1929) and *Erie Waters* (1931) and in his short-story collection *Mostly Canallers* (1934). (Courtesy of Ed Fynmore.)

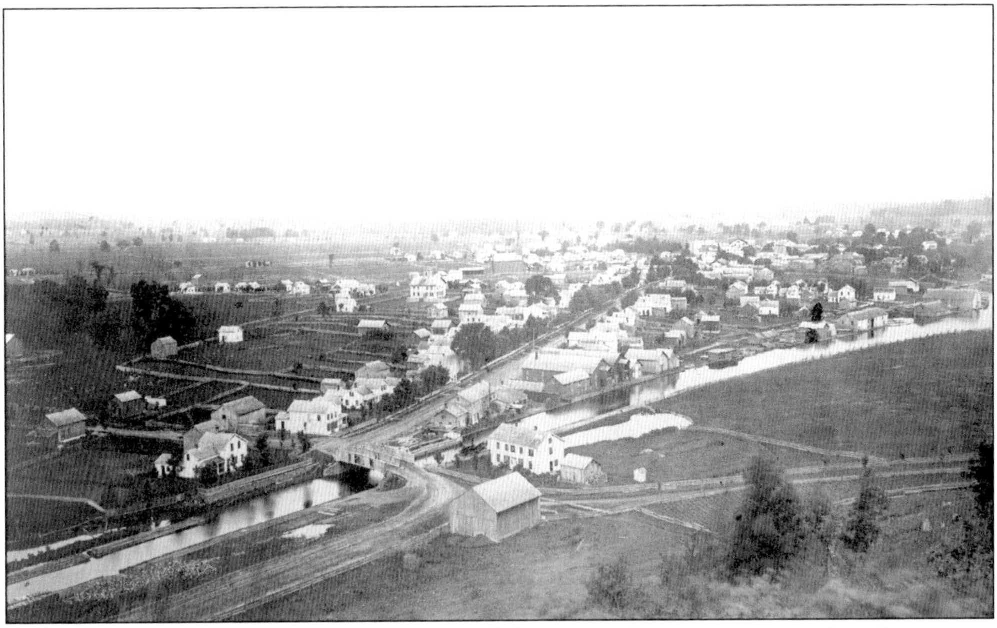

As traffic on the Black River Canal increased, businesses began to appear along its western bank. This view of the canal dates from 1866 when Boonville (population 1,500) was the largest town between Utica and Watertown. R. Fred Bowdish shot this photograph from Brinkerhoff's Mountain (later Park Hill). The site was named for Gilbert Brinkerhoff, who owned the property and ran a store next to the canal. (Courtesy of Ed Fynmore.)

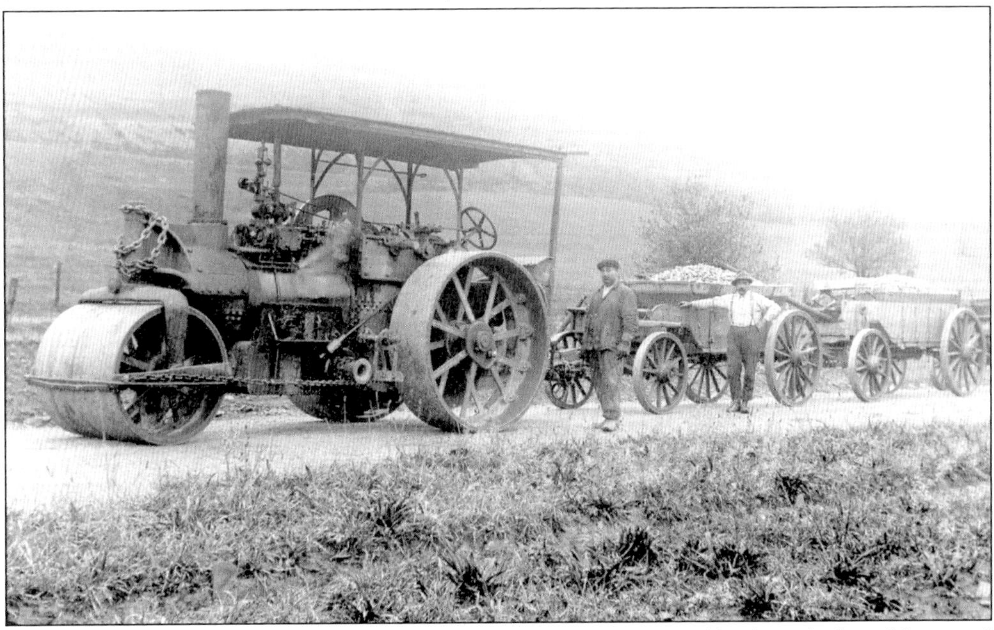

Main Street was once part of New York State Route 12, the principal highway linking Utica and Sackets Harbor. Beginning in 1817, it was operated as a turnpike but became a toll-free plank road in 1849. Around 1913, the highway was widened to 16 feet and macadamized, and in the early 1930s, it was widened again and paved with reinforced concrete. (Courtesy of Woodgate Free Library.)

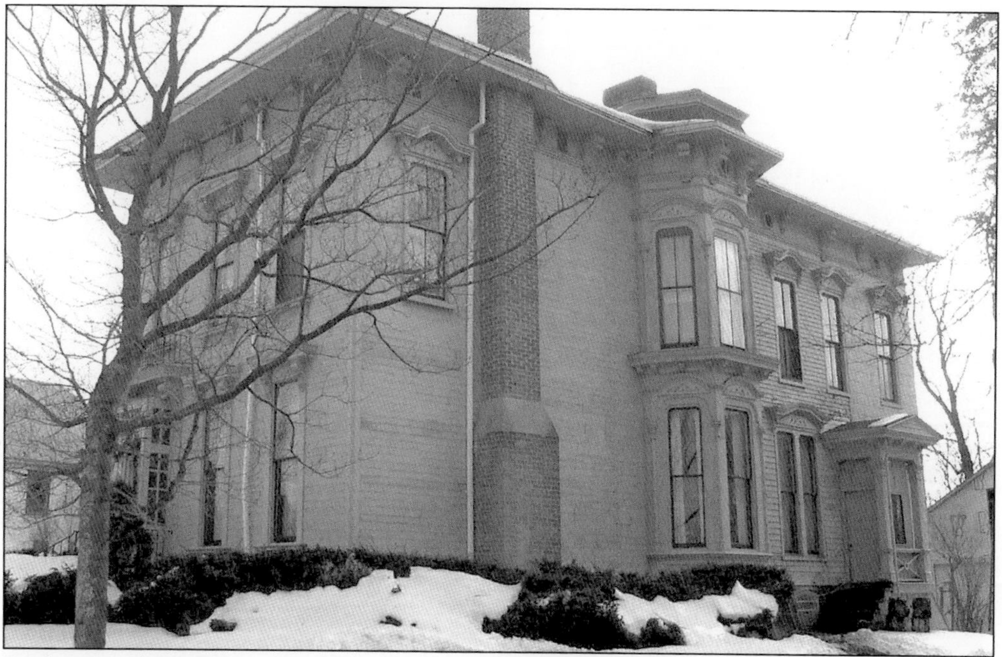

Banker Joseph R. Tharratt had this house built in 1876. The structure, located on Main Street just southeast of the Comstock Livery, replaced one built around 1830. Dr. S. Clay Markley, a clairvoyant physician, set up practice across the street in the early 1900s, using "spiritual vision" to diagnose illnesses and treat patients. (Author's collection.)

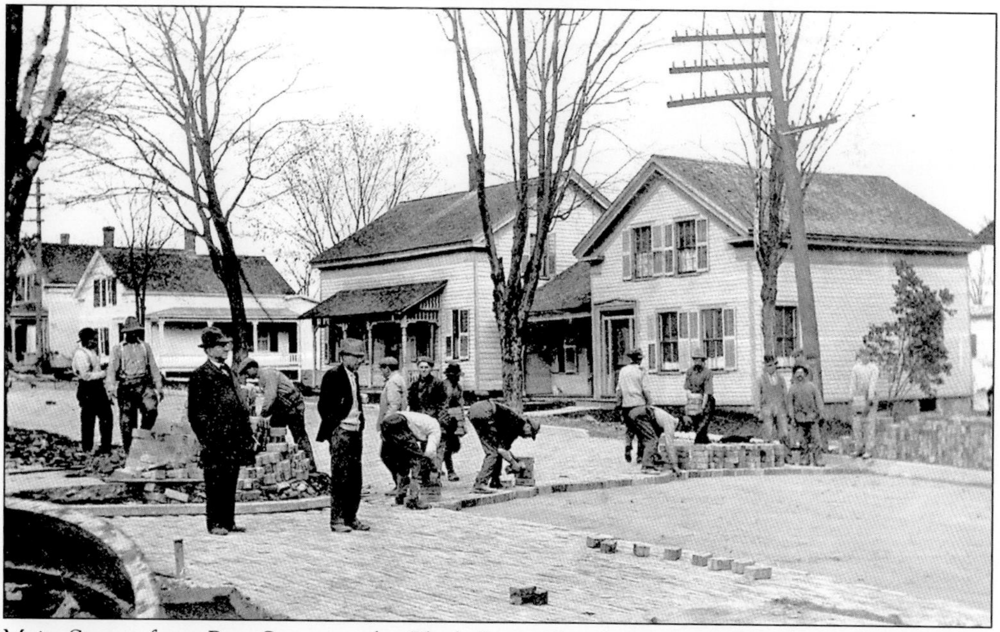

Main Street, from Post Street to the Black River Canal, was curbed and paved with bricks in 1912. This photograph shows the street crew working near the corner of Main and Grove Streets. From about 1915 through the 1920s, the village paved one or two streets each year and eventually retired the sprinkler wagon that had been used to hold down summer dust. (Courtesy of Vincent T. Fitch.)

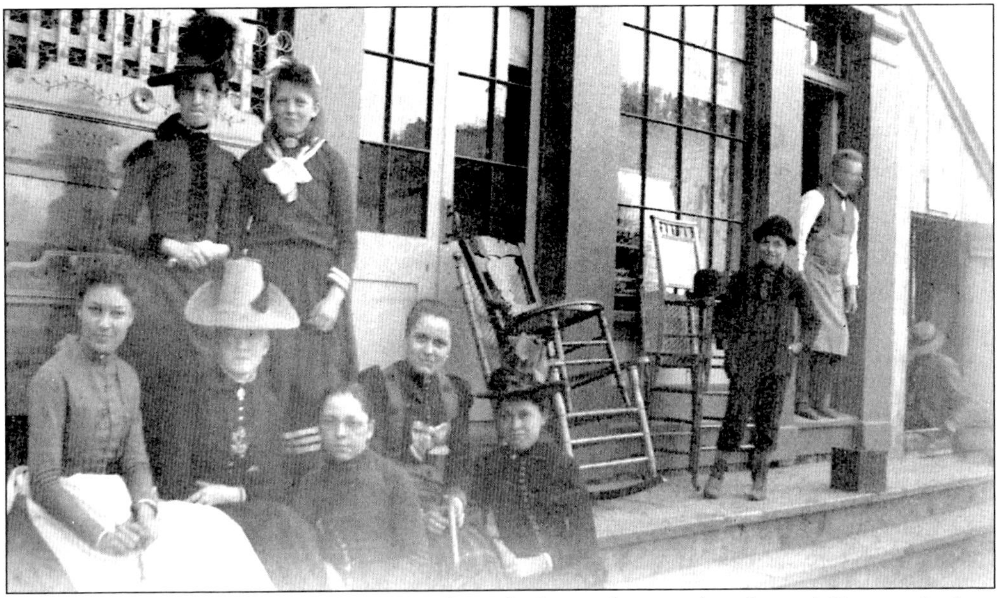

Irish émigré Thomas Watson (1820–1895) worked in cabinetmaker Samuel Bateman's shop opposite the Empire House (Methodist church). Later Watson maintained a furniture store near the corner of Academy and Main Streets. Pictured are (first row) Anna Ward, Hattie Wolcott, Eda Vollmar, Frances Thompson, and Lizzie Davis; (second row) Grace Traffarn and Grace Dewey. The boy is Bobby Roberts, and Thomas Watson is standing in the doorway. (Courtesy of Erwin Library.)

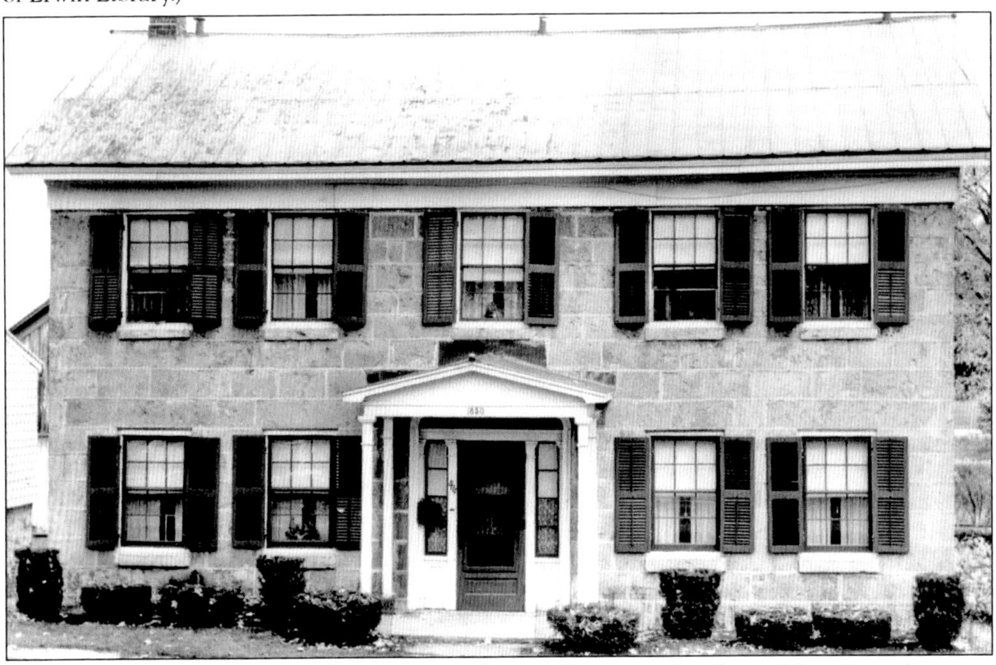

Some of the earliest residential development in Boonville occurred on lower Main Street between the business district and the canal. In 1851, stonemason Reese Davis built his house from limestone taken from the Rock Cut Quarry south of the village. The house is located near the canal on the west side of lower Main Street. (Courtesy of Oneida County Historical Society.)

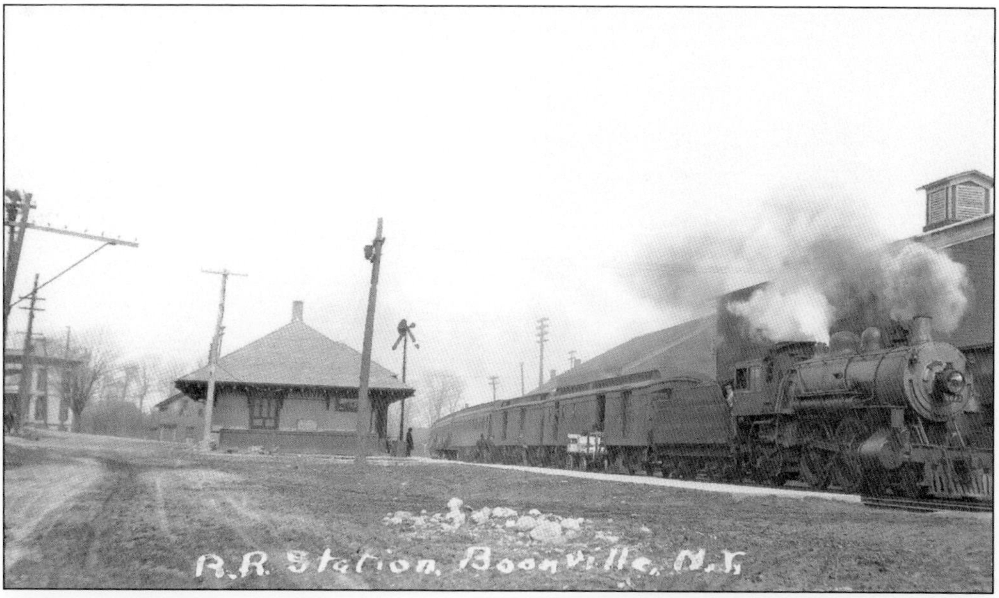

Work on the Black River and Utica Railroad began in August 1853, supervised by chief engineer Daniel C. Jenne. The railroad reached Boonville in December 1855, five years after the canal opened. President of the railroad that year was John Butterfield, a principal in steamship and stagecoach lines as well as a founder of the American Express Company (1850) and the Overland Mail Company (1858). (Courtesy of Jerry Putnam.)

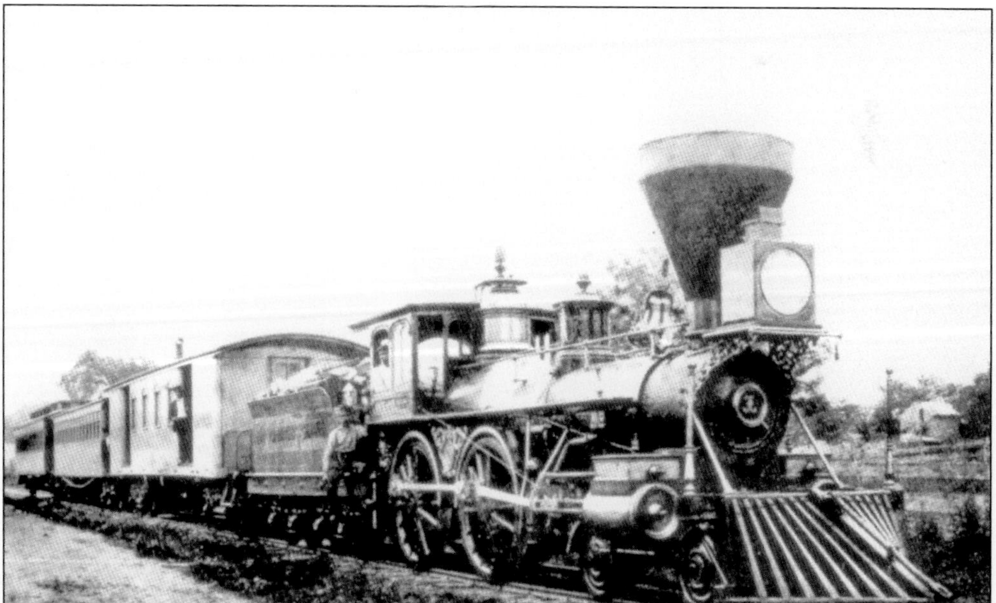

The 20-ton *John Butterfield* was the first locomotive to arrive in Boonville. Known affectionately as the "Butterfly," the locomotive was broken down at Rome and floated to Boonville on the canal. There it was put to use in constructing the northern section of the route. This photograph documents the first train on Thomas Durant's North Creek and Saratoga Railroad in 1865. The locomotive closely resembles the *John Butterfield*. (Courtesy of Ed Fynmore.)

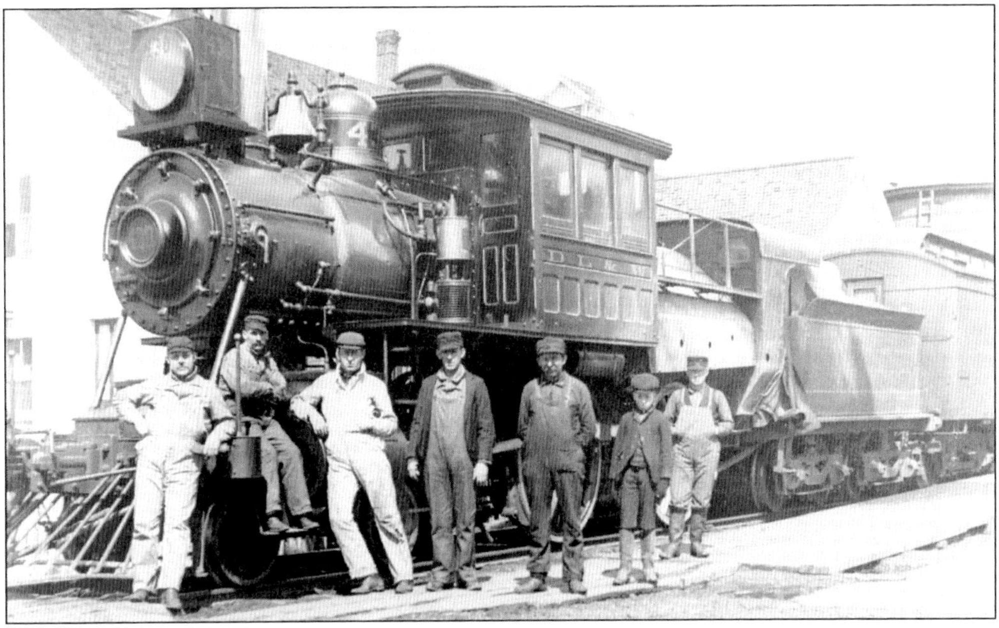

The Utica and Black River Railroad was leased to the Rome, Watertown, and Ogdensburg Railroad in 1886 and five years later became part of the New York Central Railroad system. Above, a Delaware, Lackawanna and Western Railroad locomotive parks in front of what was once Sam Ferguson's canal store (1863). By 1874, the site was home to the Railroad House, later known variously as Temperance Hotel, Nelson House, and Domenico's Hotel. (Courtesy of Ed Fynmore.)

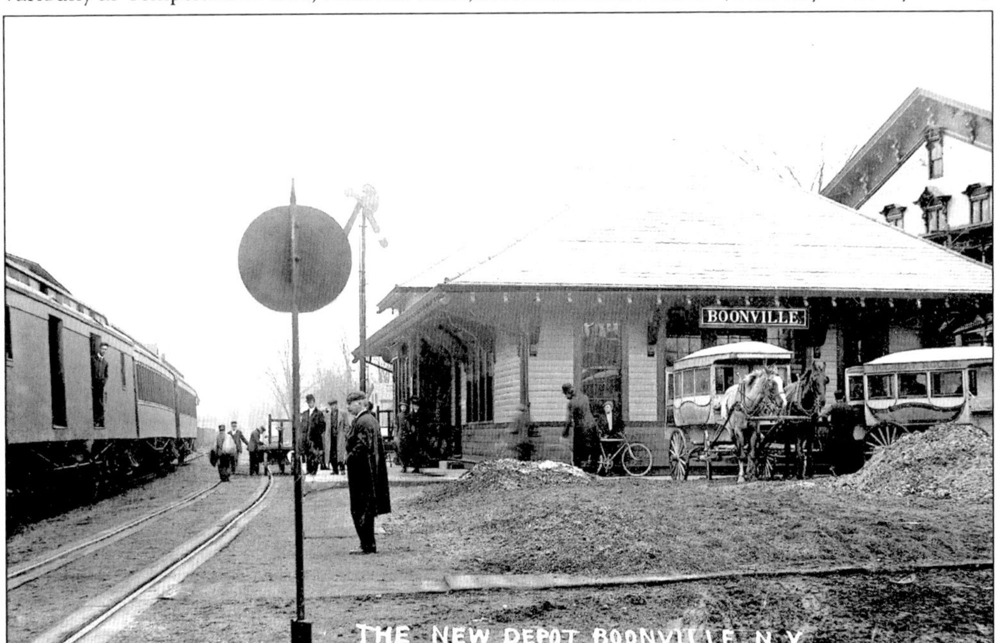

When the railroad was extended north in 1867, the tracks were repositioned along the west bank of the canal, and part of the old depot was moved from Post Street to Canal Street (later renamed Water Street). A new depot, pictured here, was built on the site in 1910. (Courtesy of Larry Myers.)

George A. Jackson was the first stationmaster in Boonville. James Doig was the second, assuming the position in 1857. When Doig died in the early 1860s, his son J. Howard Doig, pictured here, became stationmaster and held the position until he retired in 1910. He was a celebrated painter of trout, and in May 1897, he exhibited some of his works at the station. (Courtesy of Erwin Library.)

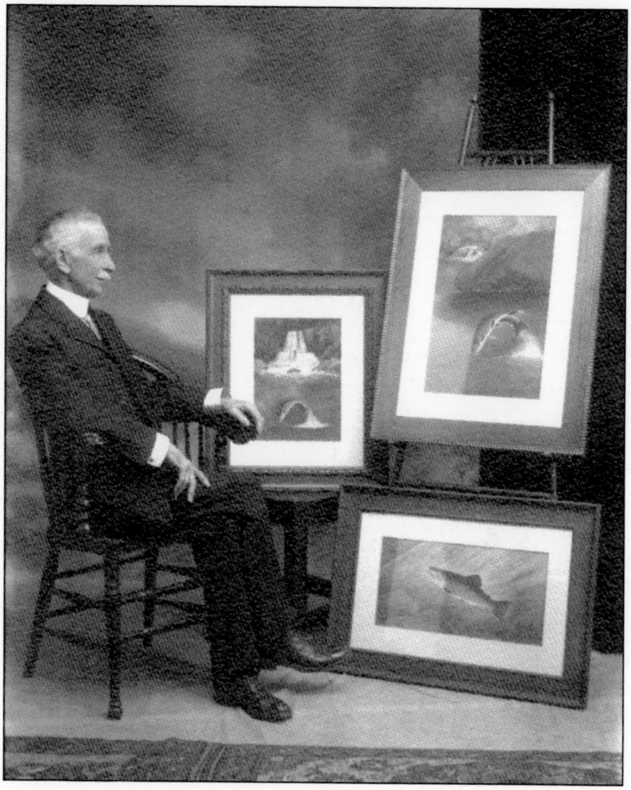

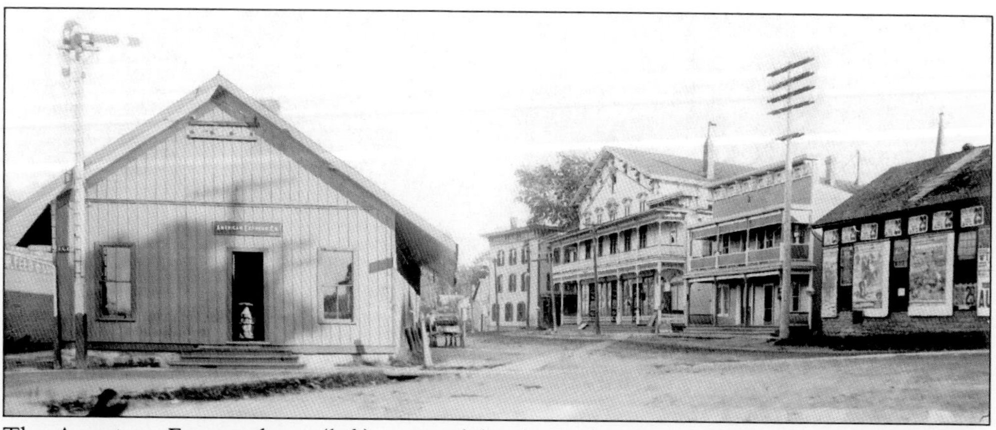

The American Express depot (left) received freight at the corner of Canal and East Schuyler Streets. To the right are the American Hotel (about 1868), Comstock Opera House (1886), Water Street Hotel (1853), and the U-Bet Blacksmith Shop of John Watts. In a 1924 letter to the *Boonville Herald*, J. Howard Doig recalled that, when he was a youth, children would ask Watts to fashion skate blades from old steel files. (Courtesy of Larry Myers.)

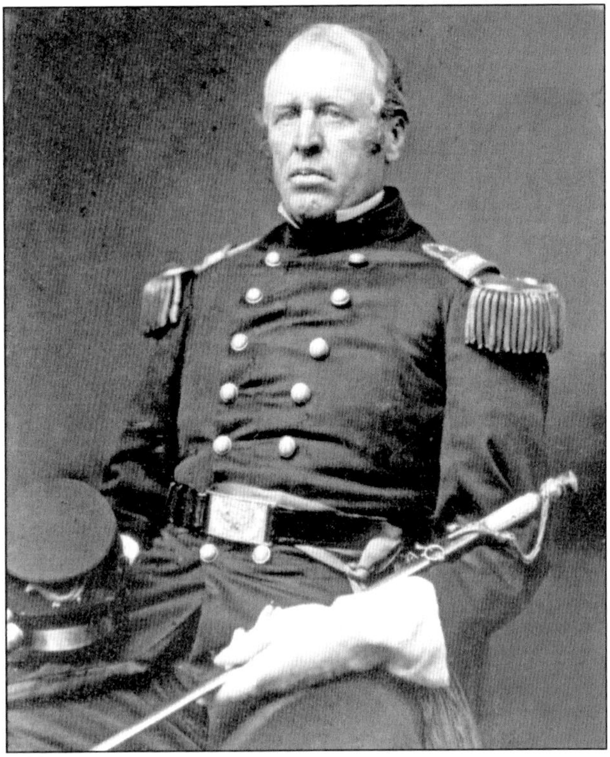

Following the Union's decisive defeat at the First Battle of Bull Run in 1861, Col. Charles Wheelock, local purveyor and militia leader, was instructed to recruit men for the 97th New York Volunteer Infantry, known as the "Conkling Rifles." The initial cost of supporting the regiment was largely borne by Wheelock. The infantry trained in vacant fields on the eastern side of the canal and quartered in Peter Post's warehouse. (Courtesy of Ed Fynmore.)

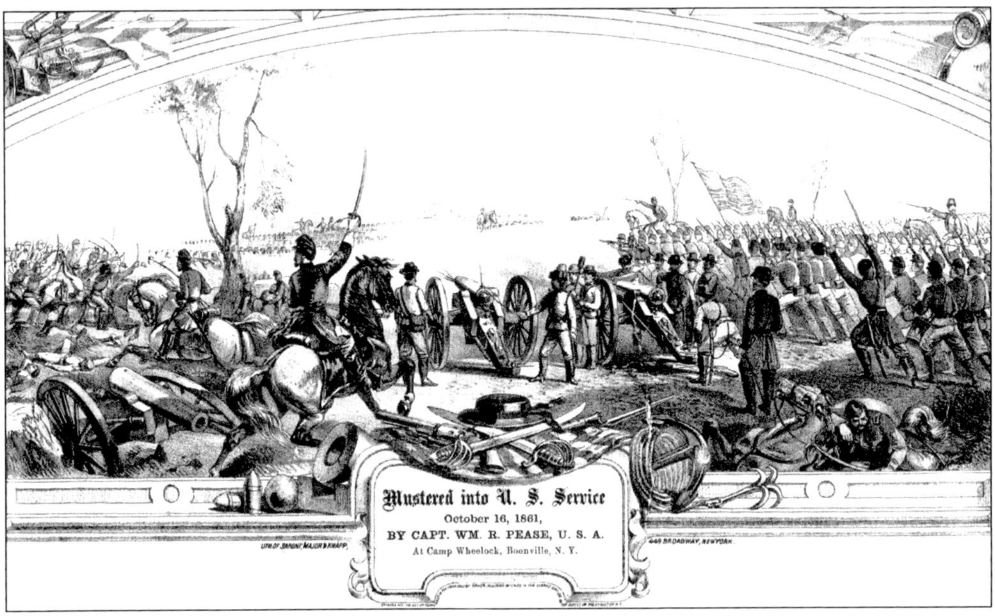

On March 12, 1862, in the middle of a blizzard, two engines departed Boonville pulling 16 bright yellow coaches. The train carried 928 soldiers bound for Washington, D.C. That August, the 97th New York Volunteer Infantry saw action at Cedar Mountain. The regiment fought in many of the bloodiest battles of 1862 and 1863, including the Second Battle of Bull Run, Antietam, Fredricksburg, Chancellorsville, Gettysburg, Wilderness, Cold Harbor, Spotsylvania, and Petersburg. (Courtesy of Ed Fynmore.)

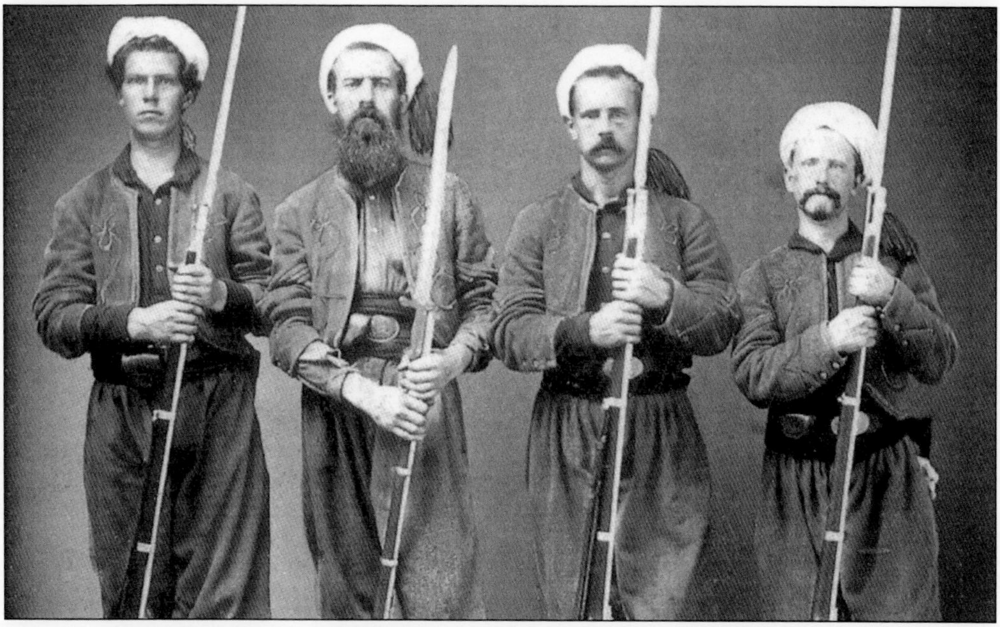

Many local men also joined the 146th New York Volunteers, known as "Garrard's Tigers." In 1863, the regiment was outfitted in light blue Zouave uniforms, modeled after those worn by French troops in Algeria. At the battle of Gettysburg, the 146th was instrumental in taking Little Round Top, securing the high ground for the Union. The regiment suffered heavy casualties in the Appomattox Campaign, most notably in the Battle of the Wilderness. (Author's collection.)

James G. Grindlay of Hawkinsville enrolled in the 146th New York Volunteers and soon rose to the rank of colonel. At Five Forks on April 1, 1865, Grindlay assumed command in the middle of battle and, leading his Zouaves against an entrenched enemy, prevailed in savage hand-to-hand fighting. His leadership was pivotal in forcing Gen. Robert E. Lee to abandon Petersburg. Grindlay received the Medal of Honor for conspicuous bravery. (Courtesy of Rome Historical Society.)

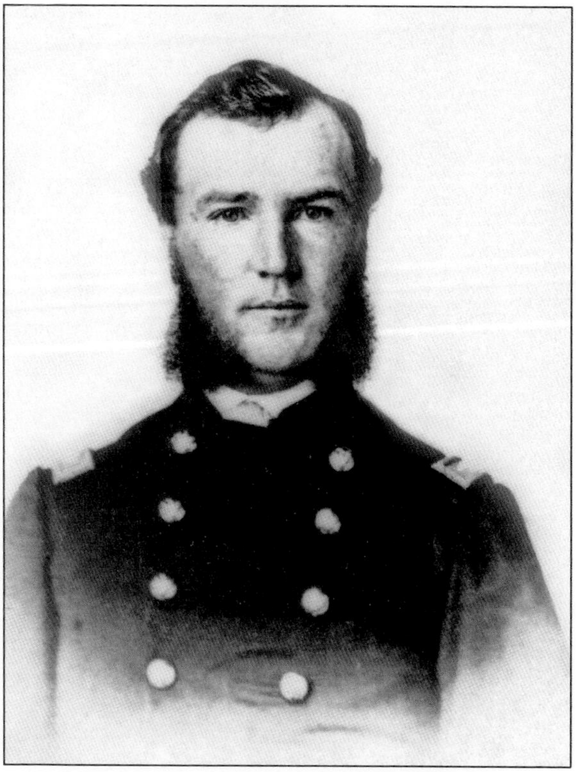

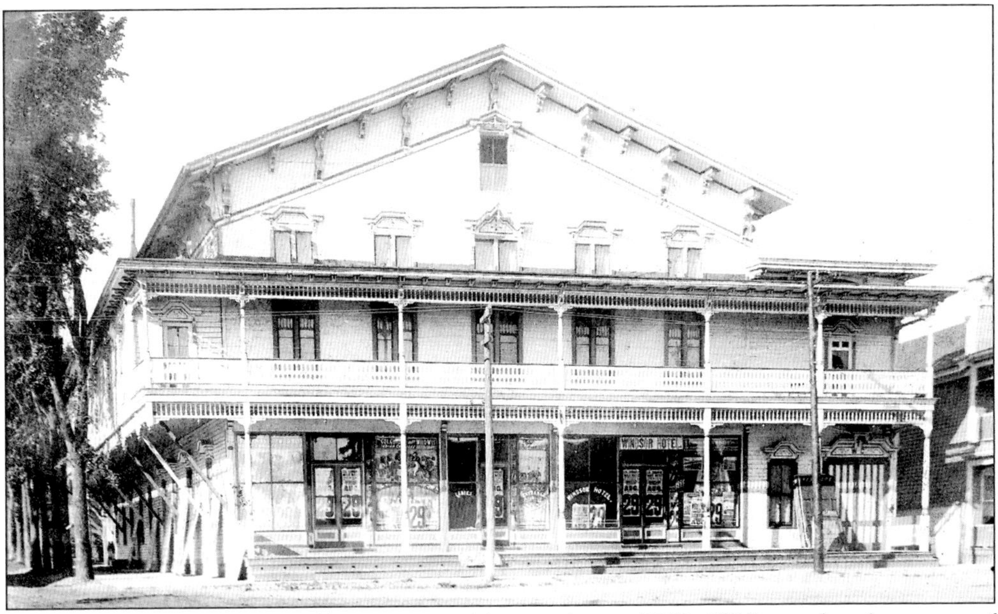

Painted in patriotic colors, William Comstock's opera house (1883–1886) stood at the corner of Canal and Ann Streets. The first floor housed the Windsor Hotel, which catered to traveling entertainers. The upper floors hosted minstrel shows, theatrical productions, silent movies, concerts, political meetings, boxing matches, and high school graduations. Frank Traffarn purchased the opera house in 1908. (Courtesy of Larry Myers.)

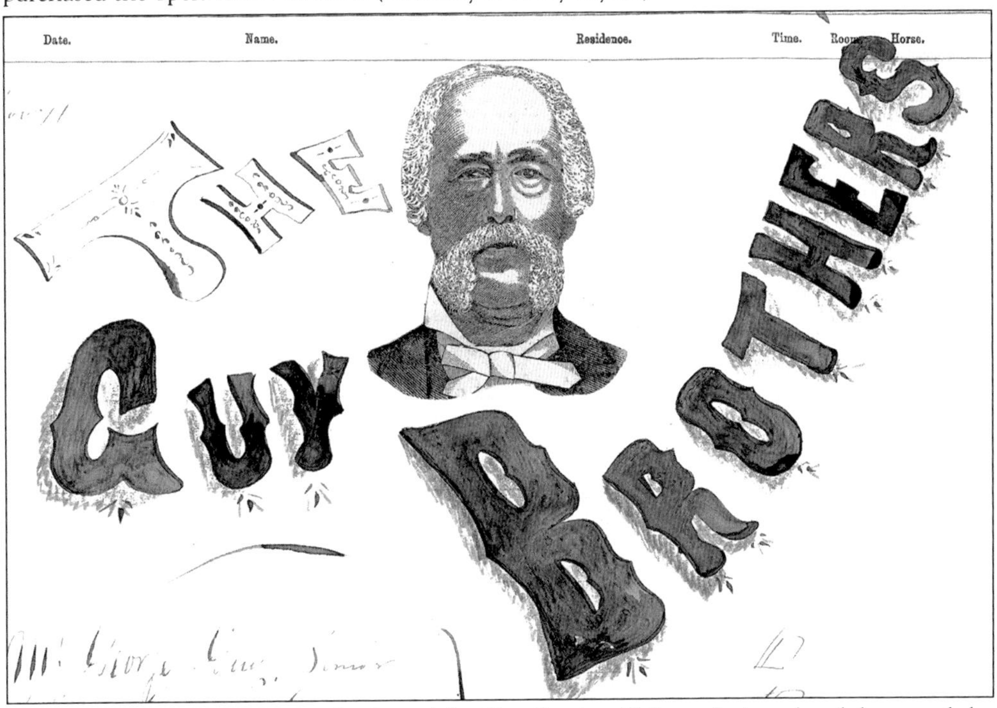

On November 11, 1887, George R. Guy of the Guy Brothers' Minstrels signed and decorated the register at the Windsor Hotel, owned by Charles Williams. The Guy Brothers continued to travel for another three decades, typically with 10 acts and 30 performers. (Courtesy of Jerry Putnam.)

Four

ERWIN PARK

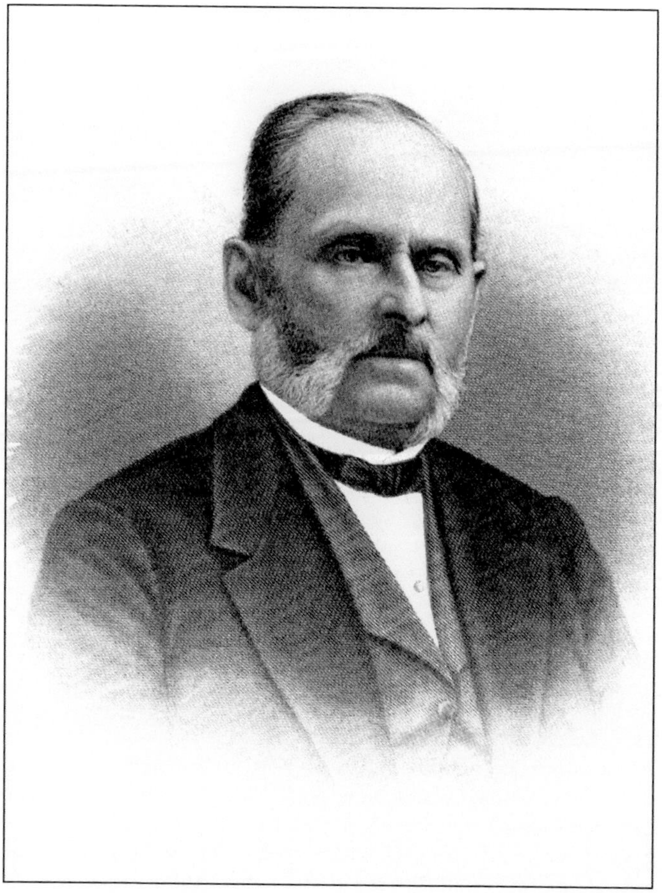

The son of local shoemaker Peter Erwin, Cornelius Bulkley Erwin (1811–1885) was a partner in the immensely successful Russell and Erwin Lock Company of New Britain, Connecticut. Predeceased by his wife and having no children, Cornelius made a number of bequests to his hometown, one of which was $20,000 to purchase land for a public park. (Author's collection.)

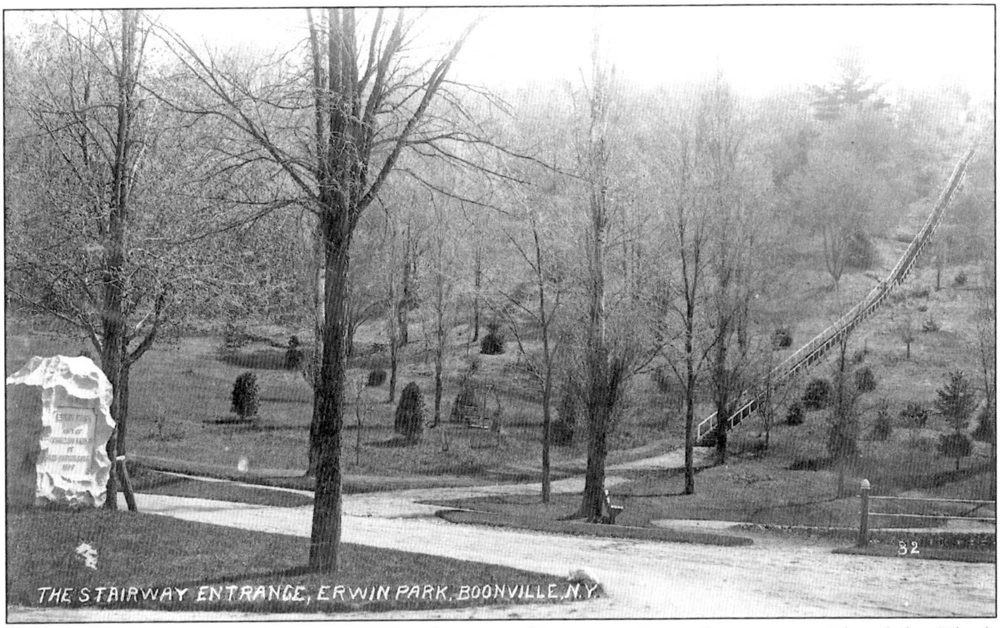

In the summer of 1890, citizens voted to locate a 40-acre park on the eastern side of the Black River Canal. Cornelius Bulkley Erwin's bequest is memorialized by a large granite monument (1909) near the south entrance to the park. (Courtesy of Larry Myers.)

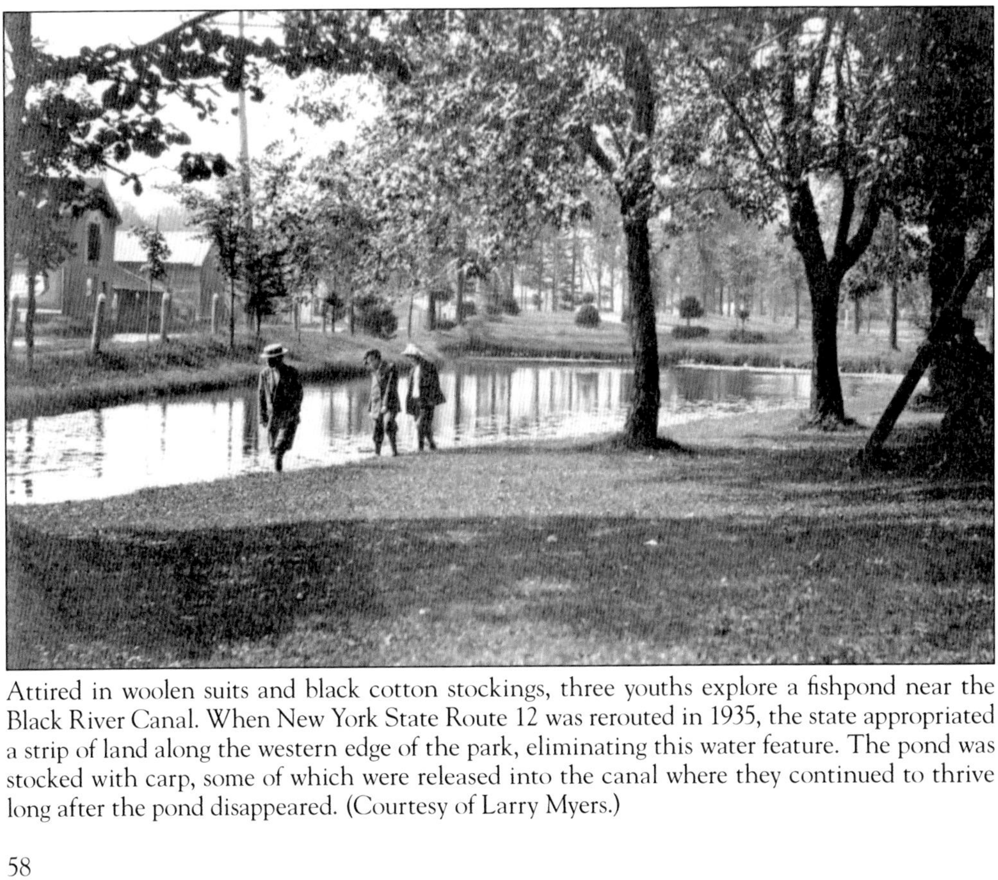

Attired in woolen suits and black cotton stockings, three youths explore a fishpond near the Black River Canal. When New York State Route 12 was rerouted in 1935, the state appropriated a strip of land along the western edge of the park, eliminating this water feature. The pond was stocked with carp, some of which were released into the canal where they continued to thrive long after the pond disappeared. (Courtesy of Larry Myers.)

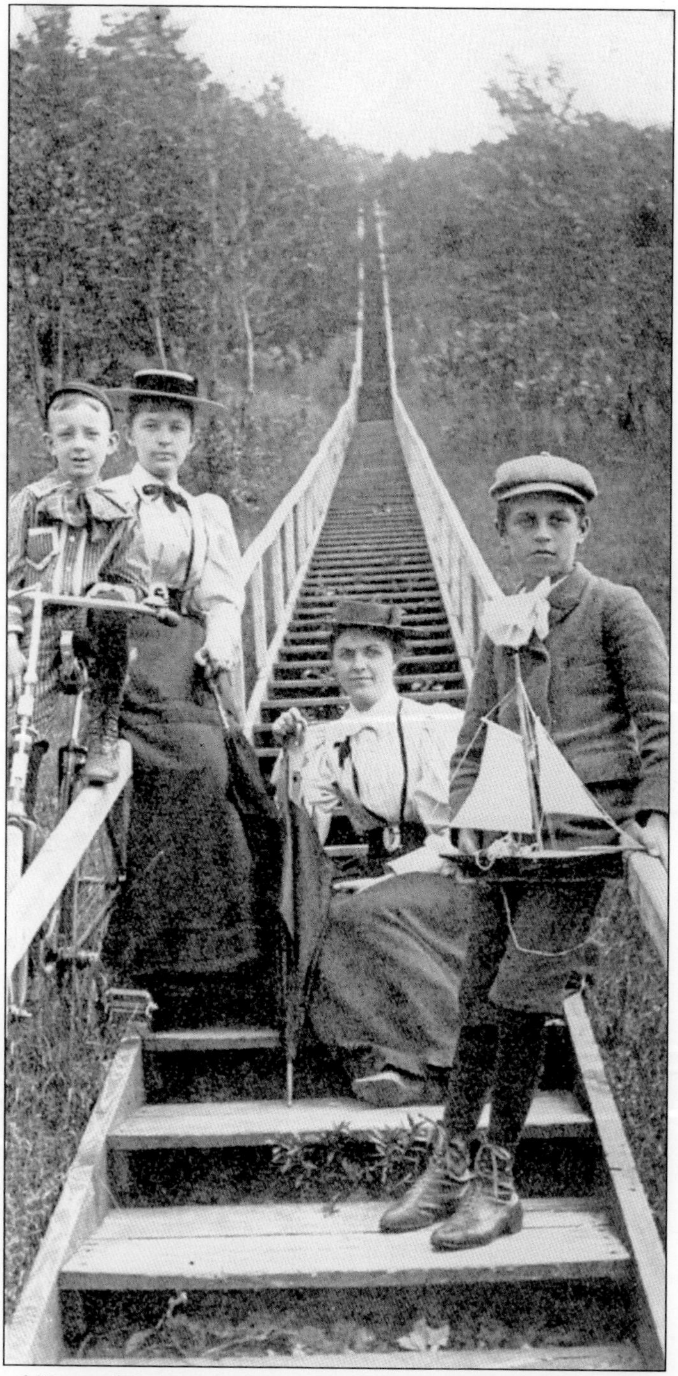

A flight of some 300 wooden stairs led to a sylvan glade and pavilion at the top of Park Hill, elevation 1,309 feet. By the early 1920s, the stairs became decrepit and were eventually dismantled. In 1902, the *Boonville Herald* suggested establishing a permanent deer herd in Erwin Park. This never came to pass, but in the second decade of the 20th century, the park boasted a small zoo. Located at the foot of Park Hill just west of Boonville Cemetery, the zoo featured a number of local animals, including bear cubs and a golden eagle. (Courtesy of Ed Fynmore.)

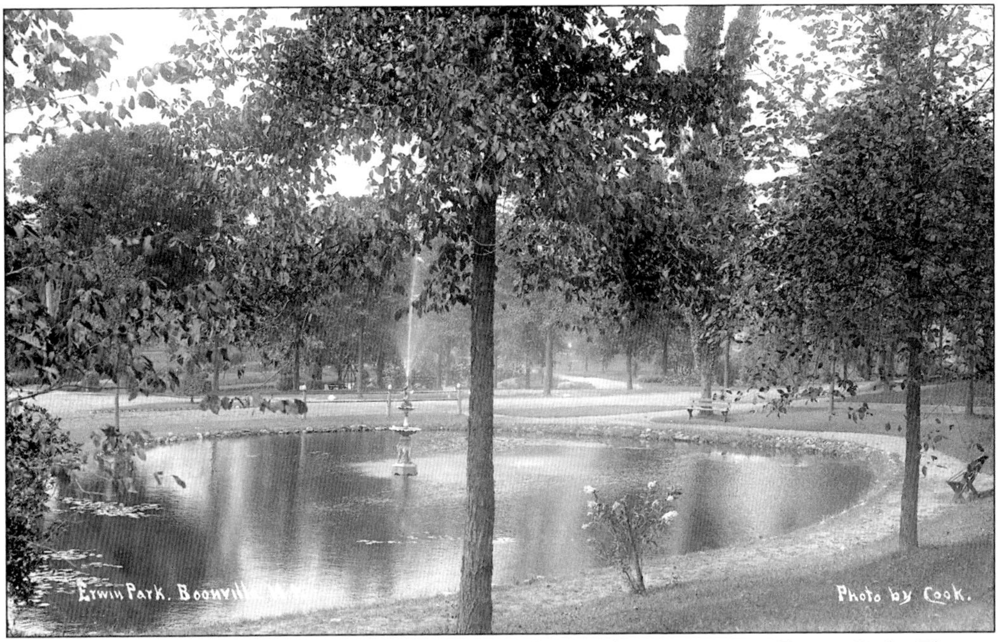

A footpath encircles the fountain and pool at the south entrance to Erwin Park. Elegant American elms and Lombardy poplars line the roads. Water from the boat basin was pumped to the top of Park Hill and then distributed to the fountains and the fishpond. The Boonville Fish and Game Club (1916) used this pool to raise fingerling brook trout. (Courtesy of Larry Myers.)

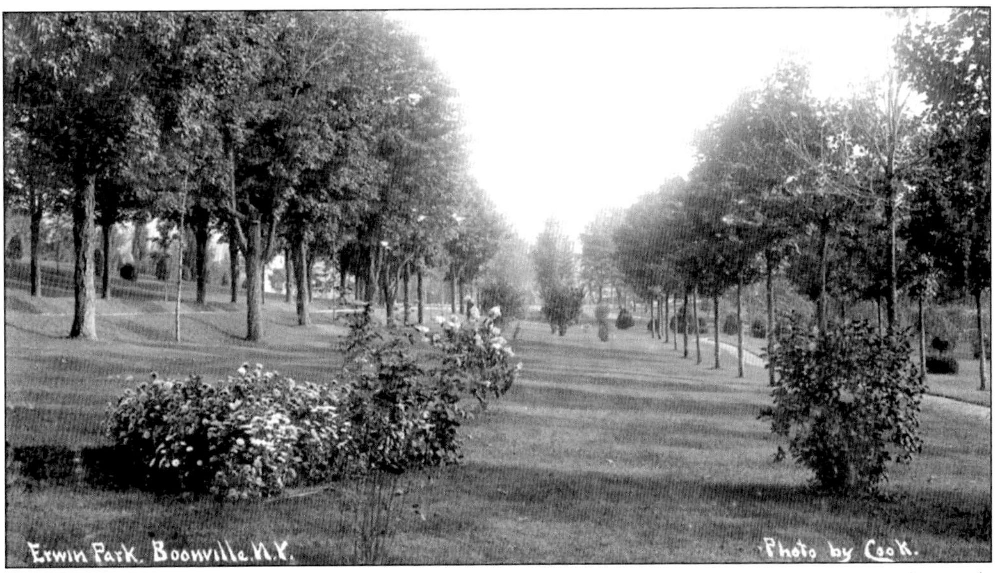

Parallel rows of maples run east and west along Cemetery Road (left) and a gravel footpath (right). The open area is dotted with ornamental shrubs. Between about 1915 and the early 1920s, tents were set up in the park for week-long Chautauqua meetings, featuring music, readings, and lectures. The photograph is by Walter L. Cook. (Author's collection.)

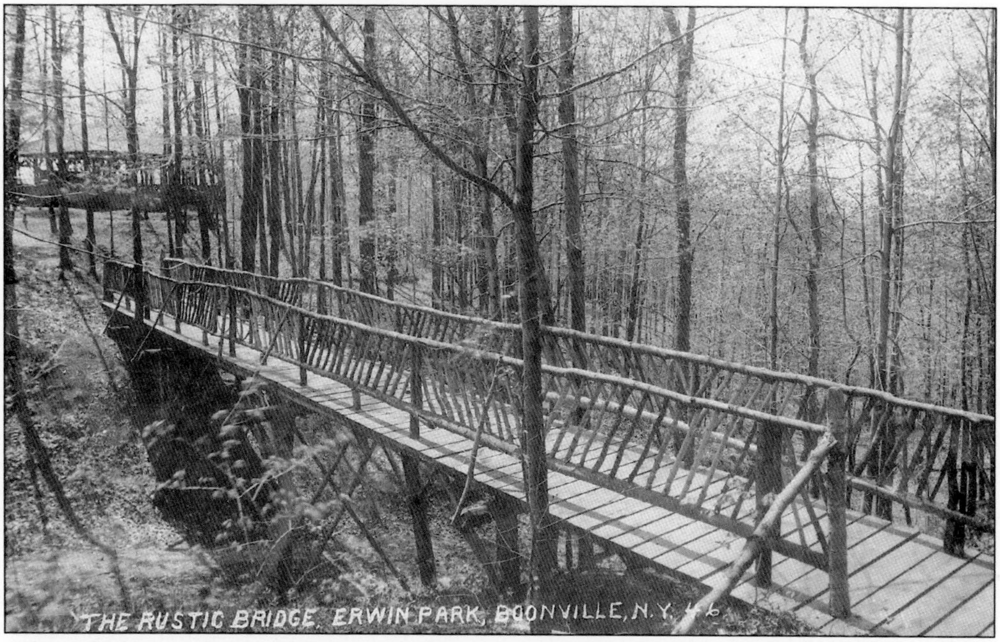

"Through the woods which cover the hillside, several miles of winding paths have been graded," the *Boonville Herald* wrote in 1891. "They are typical lovers' walks, which lead to many shaded and secluded nooks." One of these paths led across a rustic bridge to a pagoda, or picnic pavilion, at the summit of Park Hill. (Courtesy of Larry Myers.)

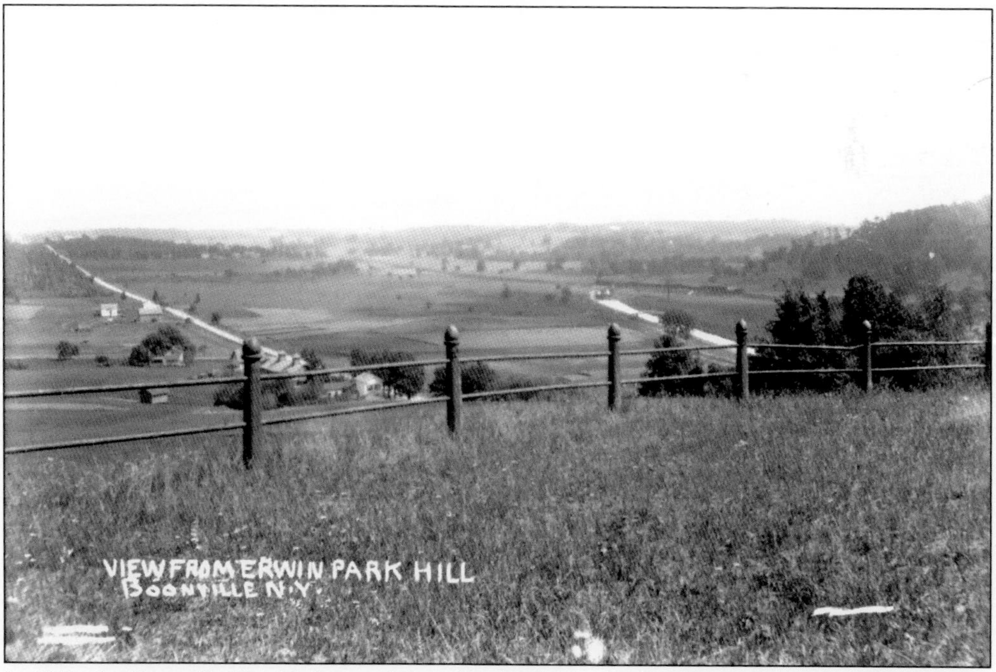

In 1891, the *Boonville Herald* observed that the chief attraction of the new park was "the summit which is skirted by an ornamental fence . . . Through the valley at the base of the hill, trains on the railroad seem to crawl along, while boats on the black bosom of the canal seem motionless." (Courtesy of Ed Fynmore.)

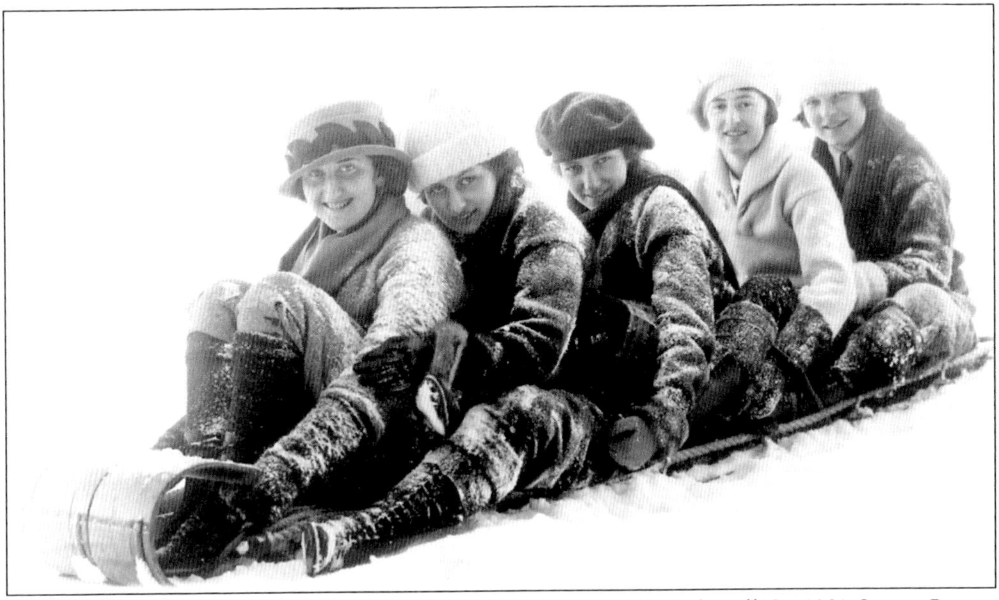

Louise Barlett (left) and friends enjoy a day of tobogganing on Park Hill. In 1921, Lewis Sperry surveyed and staked out a 10-foot-wide toboggan run on the north side of Erwin Park. That same year, a group of some 50 high school students formed the Outdoor Sports Club. (Courtesy of Erwin Library.)

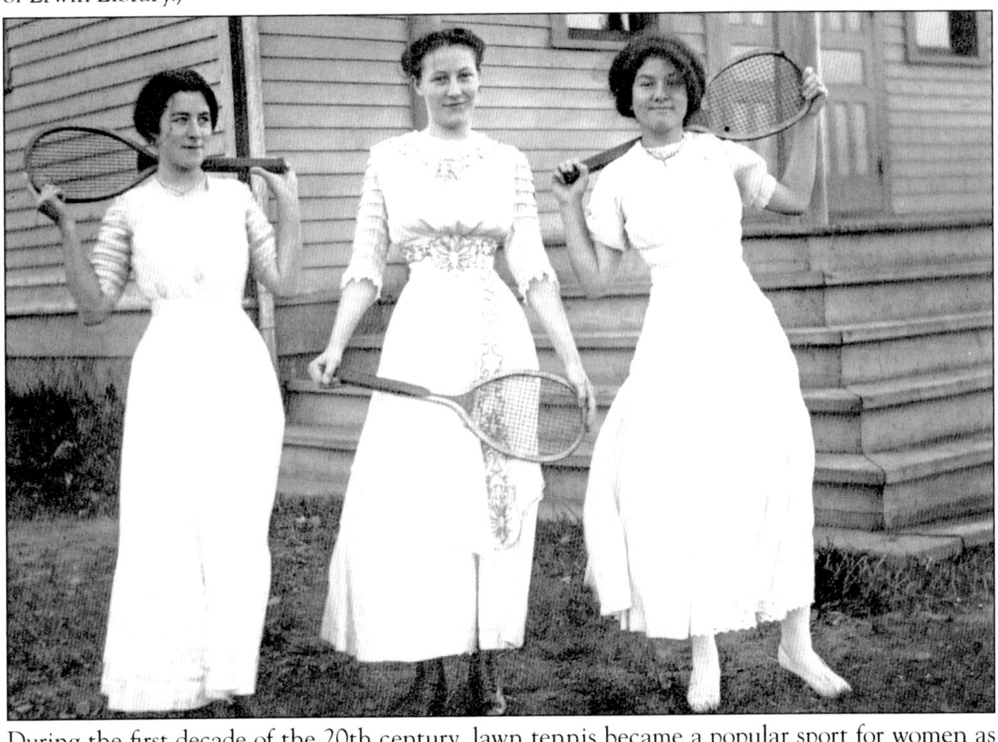

During the first decade of the 20th century, lawn tennis became a popular sport for women as well as men. By the next decade, Erwin Park featured public tennis courts. The tennis courts were paved in 1921 and enlarged in 1928. The young women above were photographed in front of the Port Leyden Methodist Church. (Courtesy of Larry Myers.)

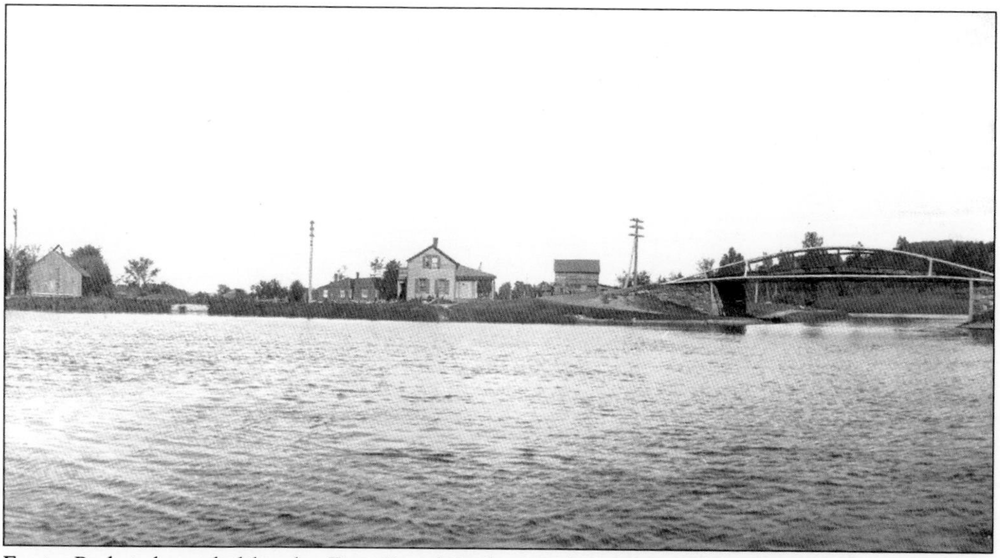

Erwin Park is bounded by the Erie Canal feeder on the north. This photograph, which looks east, shows the Boonville boat basin, a small harbor formed at the junction of the feeder canal and the Black River Canal. In the late 1850s, the feeder was flooded each winter to create a three-quarter-mile track for a week of horse racing. These popular contests filled local hotels, and saloons were transformed into betting parlors. (Courtesy of Larry Myers.)

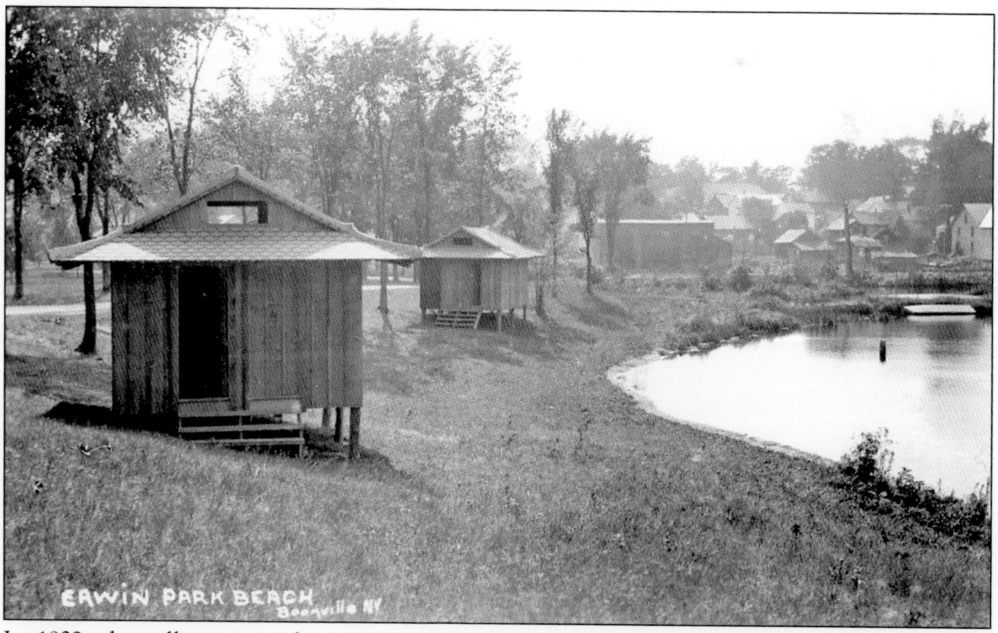

In 1932, the village created a swimming pool by erecting a berm on the south side of the feeder canal, thus sealing off the old turning basin. Erwin Beach (above) actually preceded the municipal pool. In 1920, sand was trucked in from the Draper pit, and several bathhouses were built. The following year, money was raised for shoot-the-chutes. In winter, the pool served as an ice-skating rink. (Courtesy of Vincent T. Fitch.)

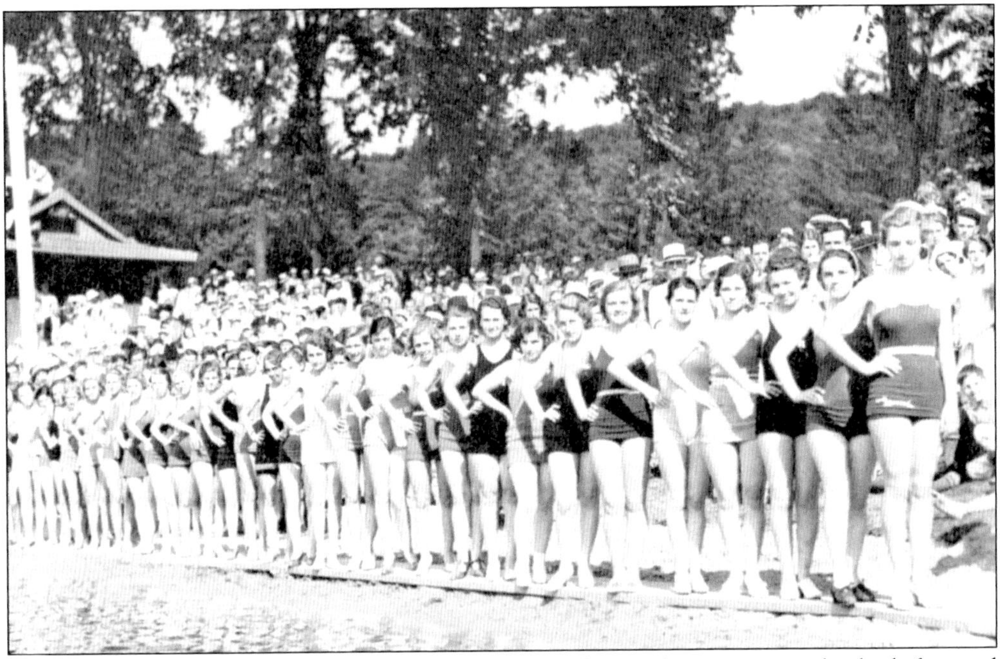

On July 4, 1933, over 6,000 people attended the second-annual water carnival, which featured tub races, canoe tilting, and various aquatic games. The highlight was a beauty contest with 29 entrants. Doris Shedd of Boonville (far right) and Dorothy Rivette of Lyons Falls (fourth from right) shared the first-place prize of $40. (Courtesy of Ed Fynmore.)

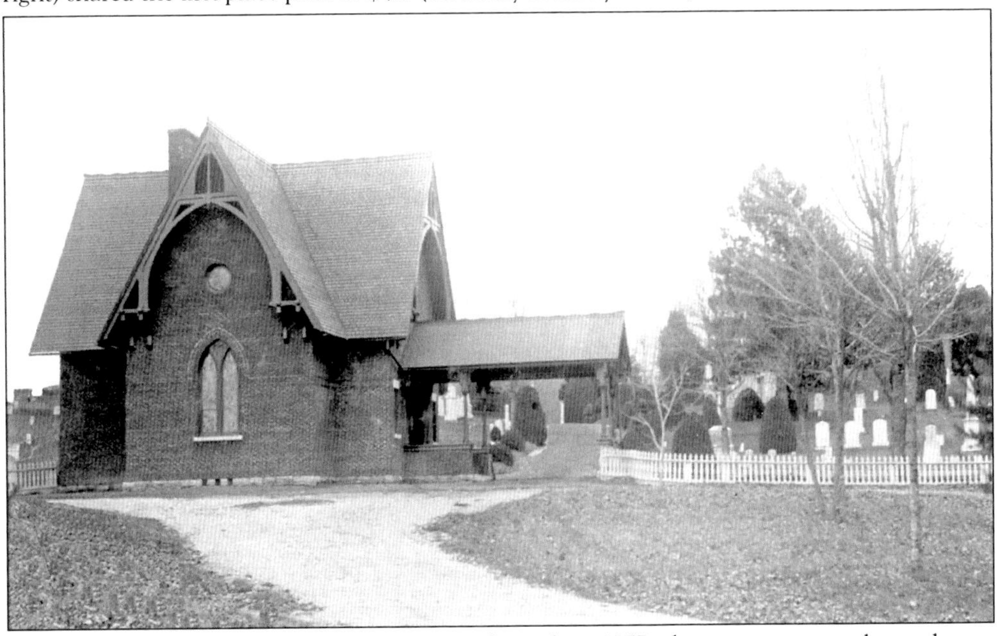

When the Boonville Cemetery Association formed in 1857, the cemetery was located near the junction of Canal and Schuyler Streets. To make way for the northern extension of the railroad in 1867, the association exhumed some 500 bodies and transferred the remains to a new cemetery on Park Hill. In 1885, Cornelius Bulkley Erwin bequeathed $10,000 to the association for maintenance as well as $2,500 for a chapel. (Author's collection.)

Five

AROUND TOWN

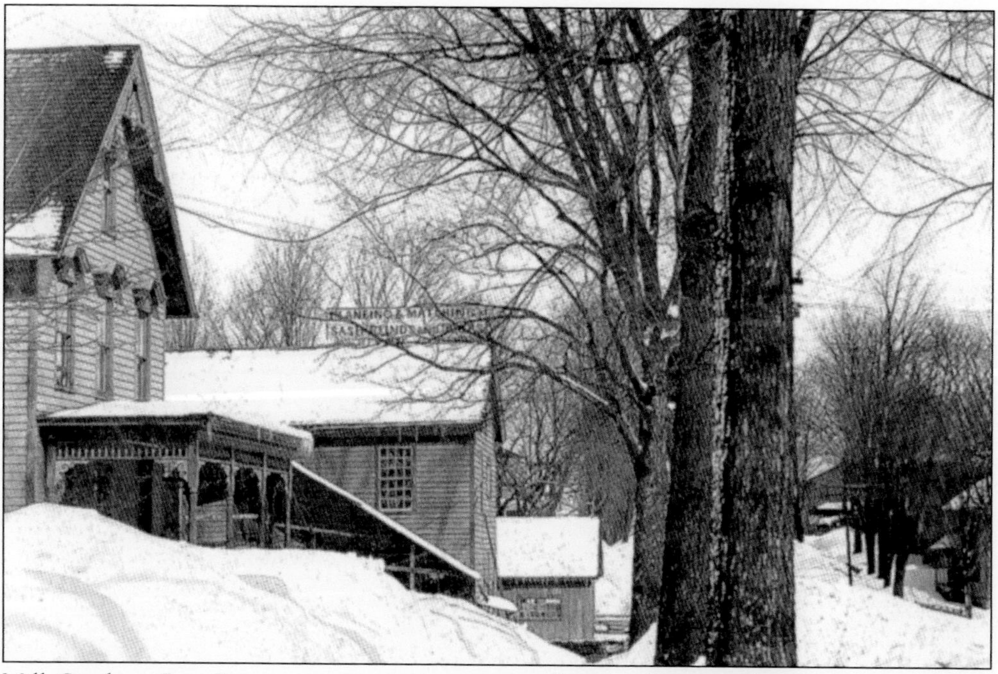

Mill Creek at Post Street was an active commercial scene for more than 100 years. Martin Southwell erected a cider mill on the west side of the street sometime before 1810. C. H. Jillson later built a foundry on the site, and at mid-century, John M. Fisk operated a sash and blind factory there. Purchased by Charles and George Rice in 1868, the factory evolved into the Boonville Lumber Company, a going concern until about 1932. (Courtesy of Ed Fynmore.)

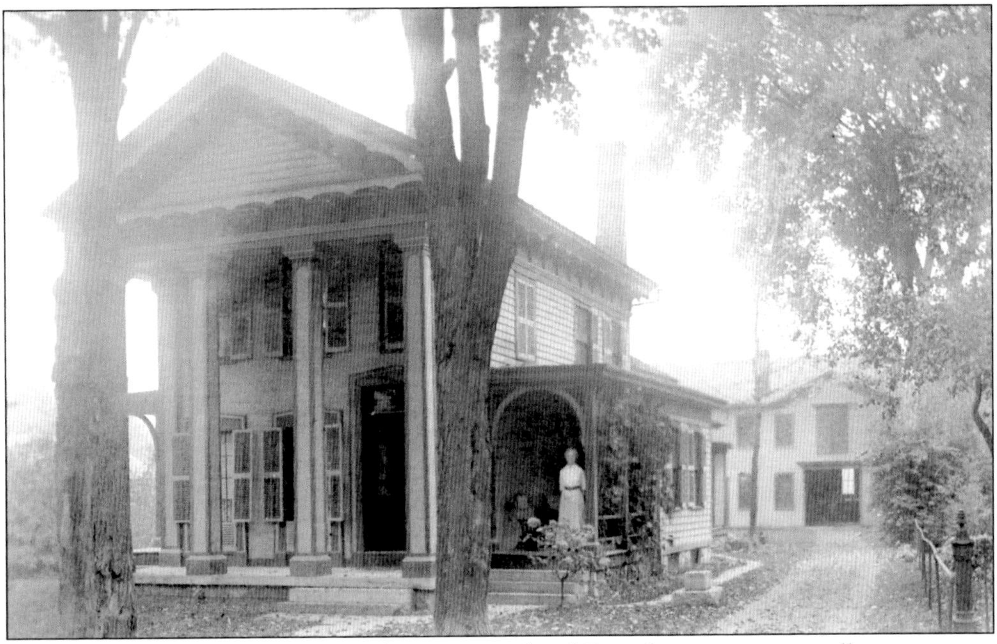

This Greek Revival structure on the eastern side of Post Street was originally a one-story residence. In 1864, Edwin S. Thompson purchased the house and in 1880 added a second story. In the mid-1890s, dry goods merchant Jesse P. Babcock purchased the house. Standing on the side porch is Anna Stimson Babcock. (Courtesy of Jerry Putnam.)

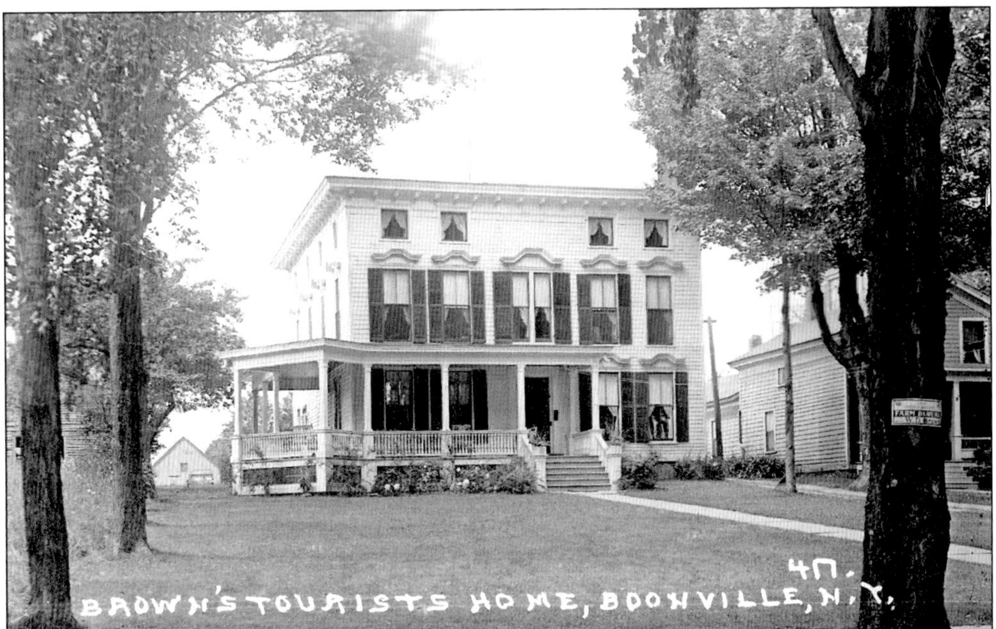

As automobiles proliferated, tourist homes offered an alternative to hotels in the business district. Wallace D. Brown's Tourist Home, pictured here, was on the west side of Post Street. In accordance with a deed restriction, the residential set-back from the street is the same as that of the original Post house. This photograph was taken about 1926. (Courtesy of Ed Fynmore.)

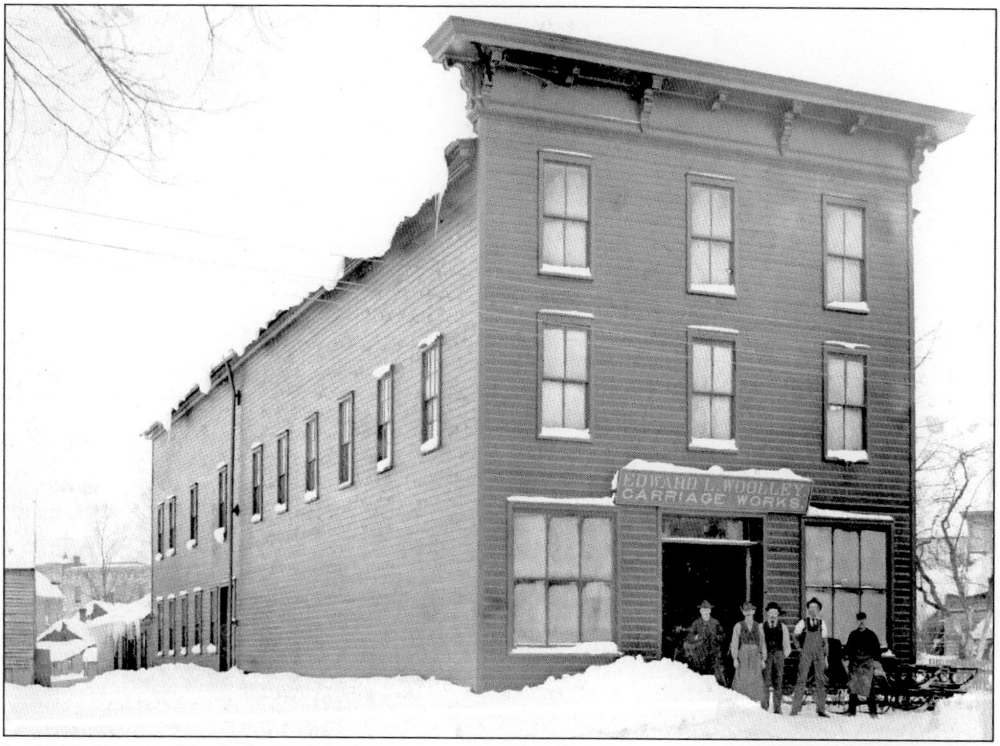

In 1830, Burton Tuttle built this three-story carriage factory on the south side of East Schuyler Street. Although Tuttle died in the cholera epidemic of 1832, his sons carried on the trade. The firm passed into the hands of John M. Fisk, who in 1857 sold it to Emanuel G. Woolley and William R. Tannery. The Central Hotel is visible in the distance (left). (Courtesy of Erwin Library.)

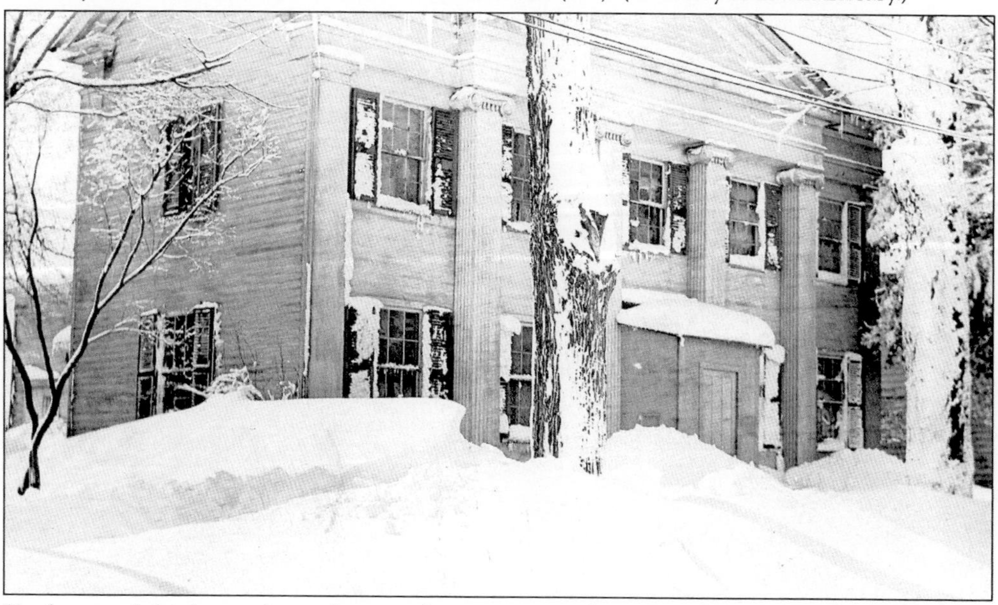

Tuttle owned this house, located next to his carriage works on East Schuyler Street. He built the rear section of the house around 1820, and son Noyes Tuttle, a carpenter, added the front section in 1830 and carved the six butternut pilasters and Ionic capitals. (Courtesy of Larry Myers.)

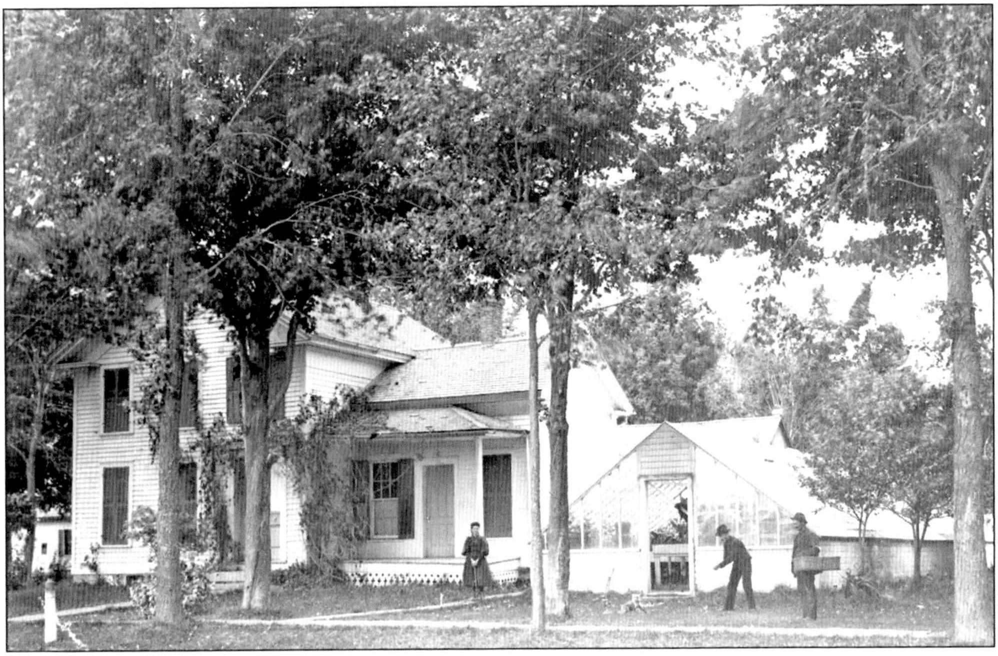

The Edward B. Snow residence sits at the northeast corner of Schuyler and Summit Streets. Pictured from left to right are Mary, Ted, and Edward B. Snow. The property was later sold to grocer Lewis B. Joslin. Edward, a florist, maintained a greenhouse on the eastern side of his house. This is long gone, but the hitching post still stands. (Courtesy of Jim Pitcher.)

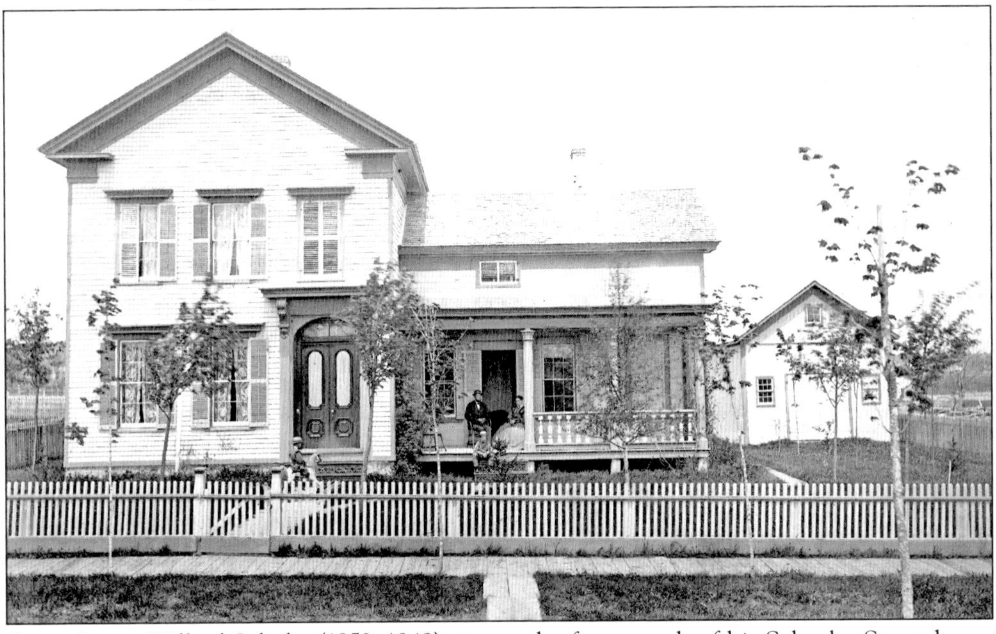

Young James Willard Schultz (1859–1949) sits on the front porch of his Schuyler Street home with his father Philemon "Bush" and mother Frances. Brother Frederick is on the hobby horse. In partnership with Lemuel Joslin, Bush Shultz owned a prosperous warehouse and forwarding business on the Black River Canal. Note the plank sidewalk. The photograph by R. Fred Bowdish dates from about 1865. (Courtesy of Erwin Library.)

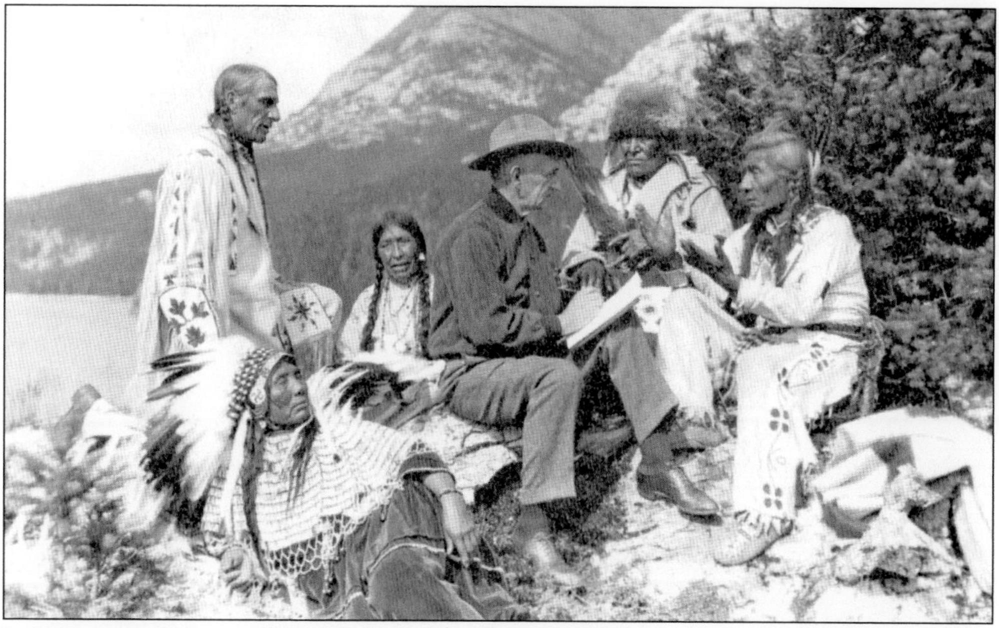

In 1877 at age 18, James Willard Schultz left Boonville and set out for northern Montana, where he took up residence with the Blackfoot Indians. In 1907, he published My *Life as an Indian*, the first of 37 books issued in his lifetime. His adventure stories appeared regularly in popular magazines between 1880 and 1937, and another five books were published posthumously. This 1931 photograph was taken in Waterton Park, Alberta. (Courtesy of Erwin Library.)

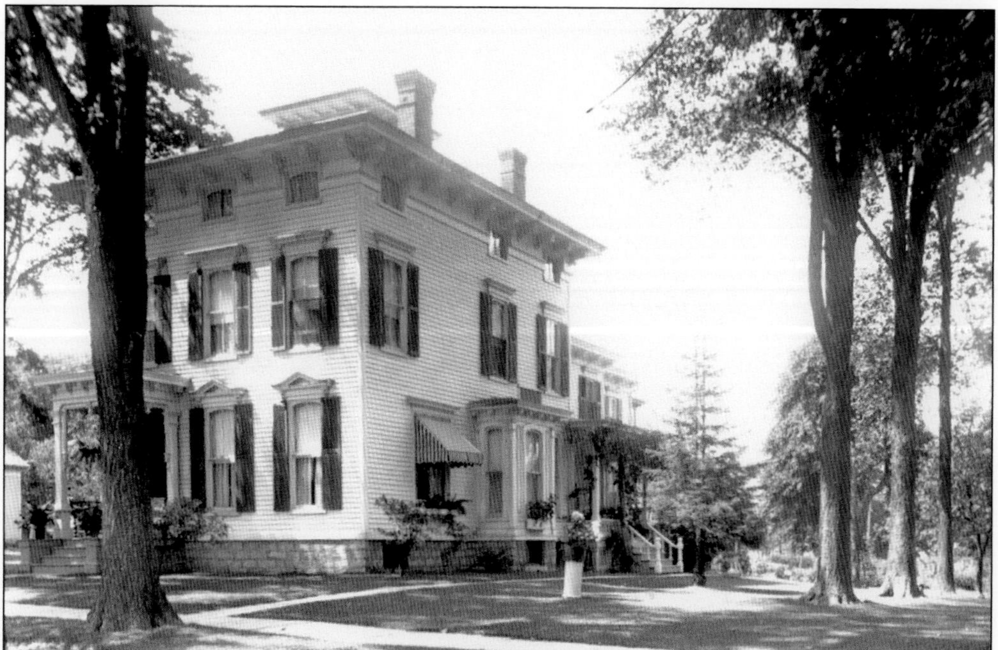

In 1872, Edwin S. Thompson built this residence near the summit of Schuyler Street. The following year, he sold the house to his parents, Schuyler C. and Verlona Thompson. Hardware merchant Henry D. Ryder bought the house in 1908. (Courtesy of Erwin Library and Jerry Putnam.)

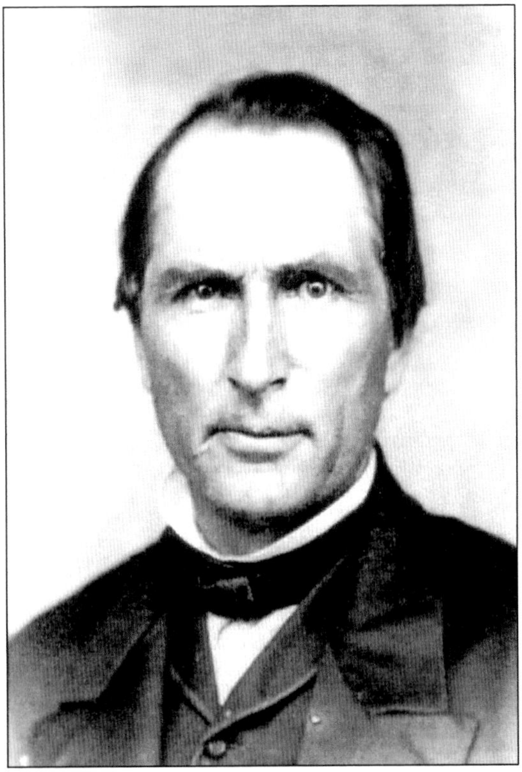

Schuyler C. Thompson (1811–1879) had his hand in many area enterprises. At Highmarket, he ran an oar and spar shop. After the Civil War, he established S. C. Thompson's National Bank in Constableville and in 1872 moved the bank to Boonville. He purchased the Port Leyden Iron Company in 1876. The following year, he opened Thompson's Grist and Flouring Mill on the west bank of the Black River Canal in Boonville. (Courtesy of Jerry Putnam.)

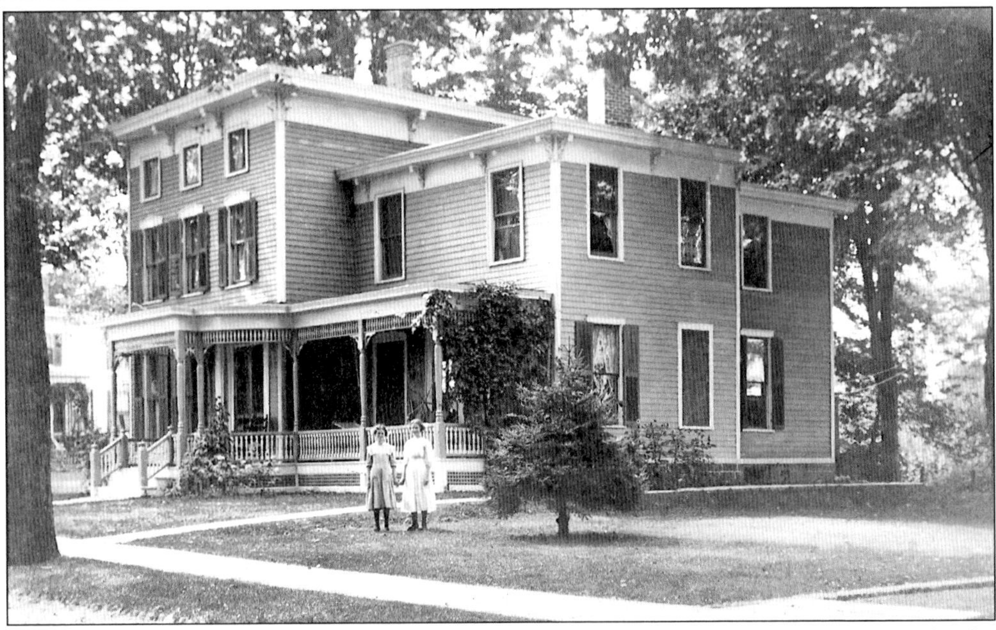

Stephen Albert Johnson had this Italianate Revival house built on the north side of Schuyler Street in 1869. While serving in the 3rd Pennsylvania Regiment, Johnson was severely wounded at Antietam and honorably discharged. In 1866, he married Thompson's daughter Emeline and, beginning in 1867, worked as a cashier in S. C. Thompson's National Bank. In later years, dry goods merchant Lincoln Perry occupied the house. (Courtesy of Larry Myers.)

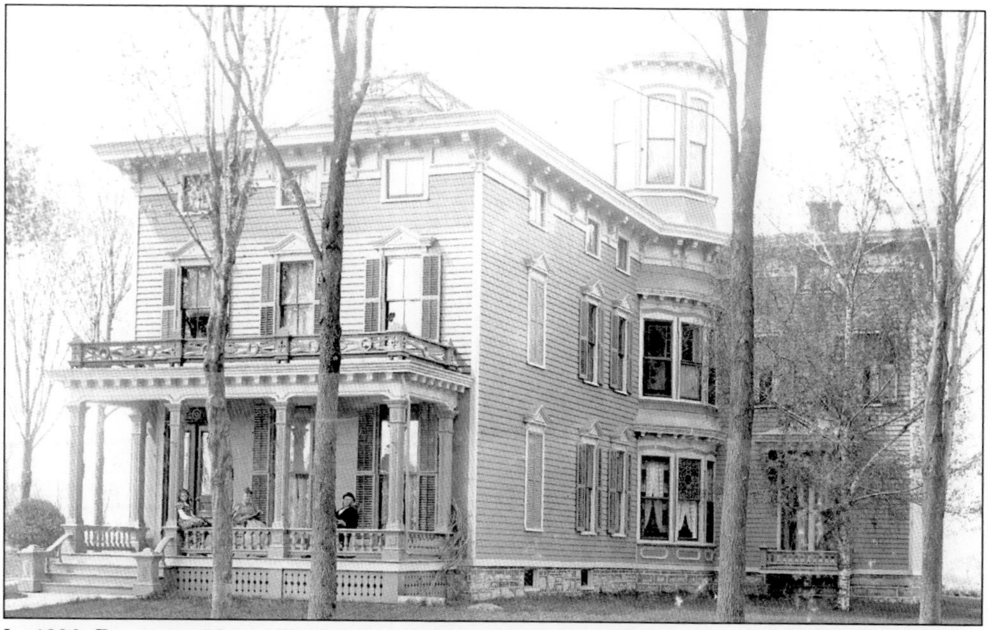

In 1890, Democrat Henry W. Bentley (1838–1907) defeated Republican "Sunny Jim" Sherman for a seat in the House of Representatives. Bentley was vice president of the First National Bank and maintained a law office on the second floor of that building. His residence, above, was on the north side of Schuyler Street. Pictured are daughter Eleanor Bentley, wife Mary D. Bentley, and the Honorable Henry Bentley. (Courtesy of Erwin Library.)

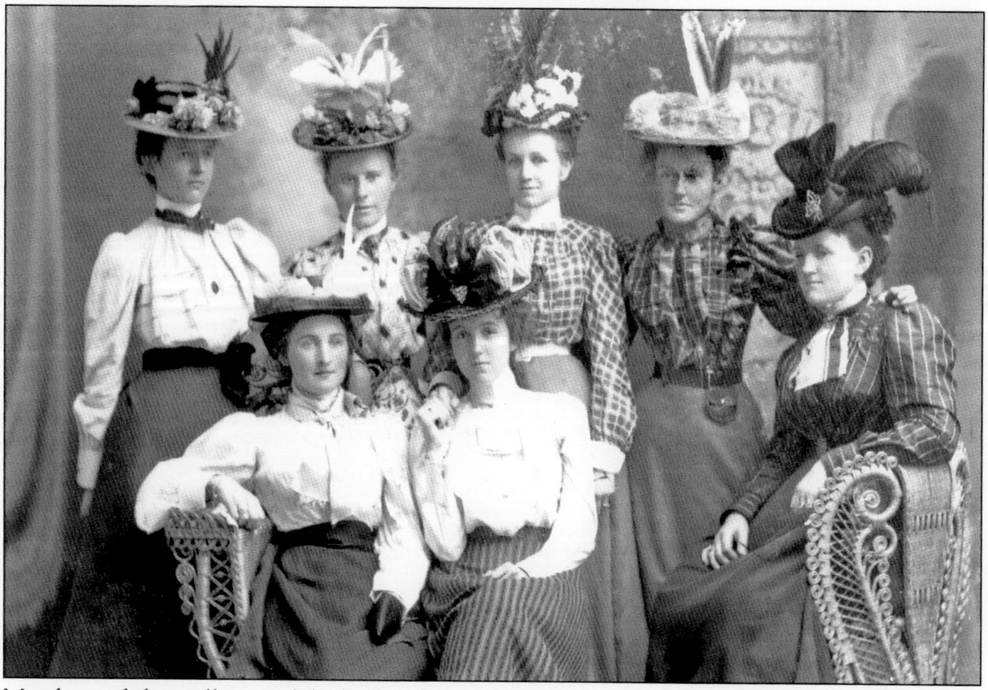

Members of the millinery club display their creations. In the early 1900s, hat materials were available at shops run by Miss M. J. Farley, Lucy Nellis, George Birdseye, and Georgiana Sears. (Courtesy of Ed Fynmore.)

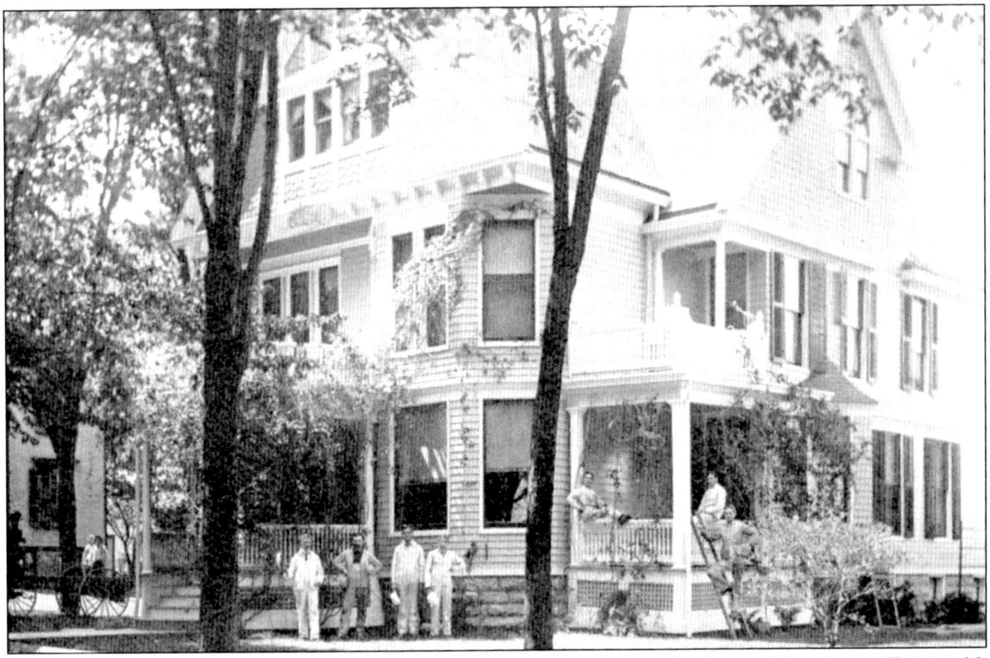

In 1891, Garry Willard succeeded his father, Harvey, as owner and editor of the *Boonville Herald*. In this 1909 photograph, Willard's Queen Anne home on Schuyler Street receives a new coat of paint. The painters, from left to right, are Darwin Byron Olney, Charles Blakeman, John O. Kent, Clyde Burris, Arch Tuttle, Eva Olney, and Fred Olney. (Courtesy of Ed Fynmore.)

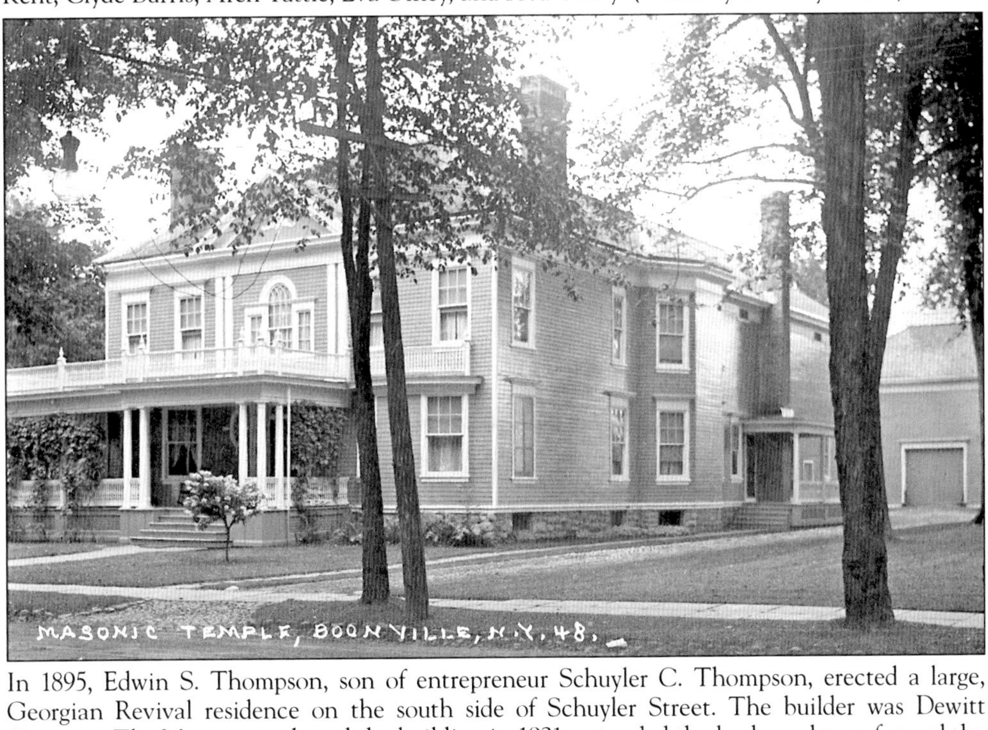

In 1895, Edwin S. Thompson, son of entrepreneur Schuyler C. Thompson, erected a large, Georgian Revival residence on the south side of Schuyler Street. The builder was Dewitt Grosjean. The Masons purchased the building in 1921, extended the back, and transformed the structure into a lodge. (Courtesy of Ed Fynmore.)

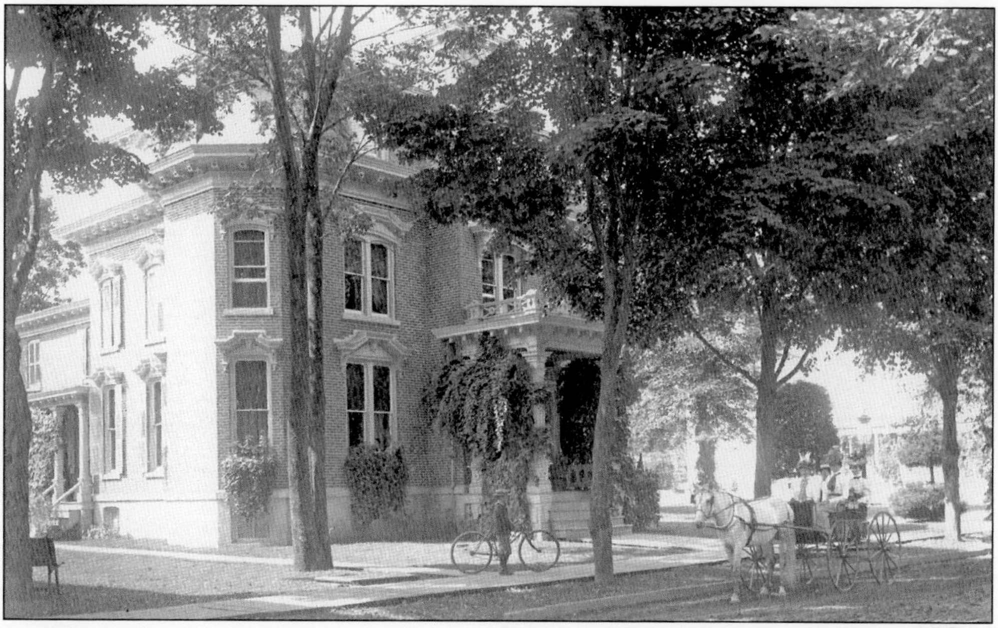

In 1875, banker Clark Dodge built this brick house on the south side of Schuyler Street. Charles W. Pratt (1854–1934) purchased the house in the 1890s. After achieving success in western mining and Pennsylvania oil, Pratt acquired vast acreage in the Adirondacks and became a principal in the Gould Paper Company (1892). The photograph dates from 1905. (Courtesy of Dodge-Pratt-Northam Center.)

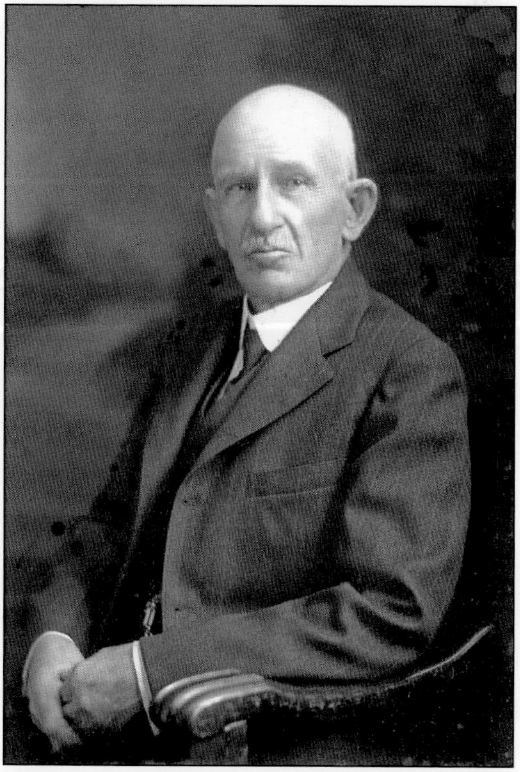

In 1898, Pratt (pictured here) organized the Island Paper Company in Carthage. His son C. Walter Pratt (1888–1961) joined him in business after serving as an ambulance driver in World War I. Disaffected with Franklin D. Roosevelt's election, the Pratts closed the Island Paper Company in 1932, vowing not to reopen until a Republican returned to the White House. When Dwight Eisenhower was elected in 1952, however, reopening was no longer practical. (Courtesy of Dodge-Pratt-Northam Center.)

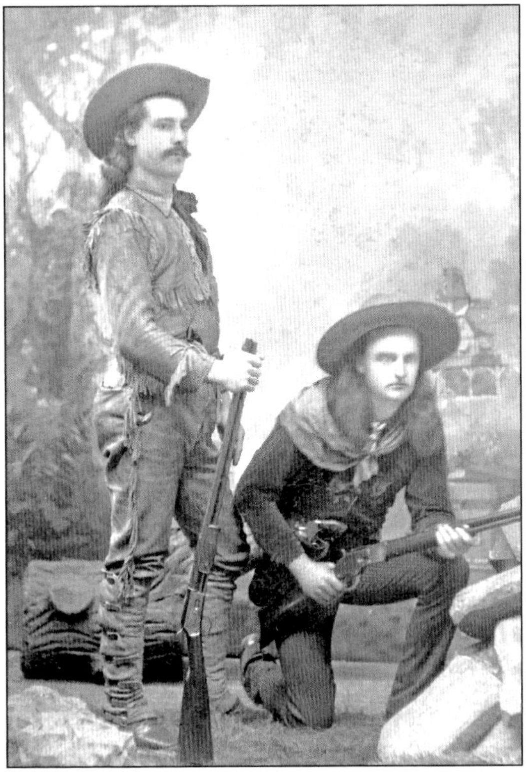

Leaving home around 1883, George Oliver Capron (left) toured as a horse rider, sharpshooter, and stage performer in various Wild West shows for nearly 25 years. He is shown here with Dan Sullivan—both members of Pawnee Bill's Wild West Show at the time. The photograph was taken in 1892. (Courtesy of Charlotte Capron Willoughby.)

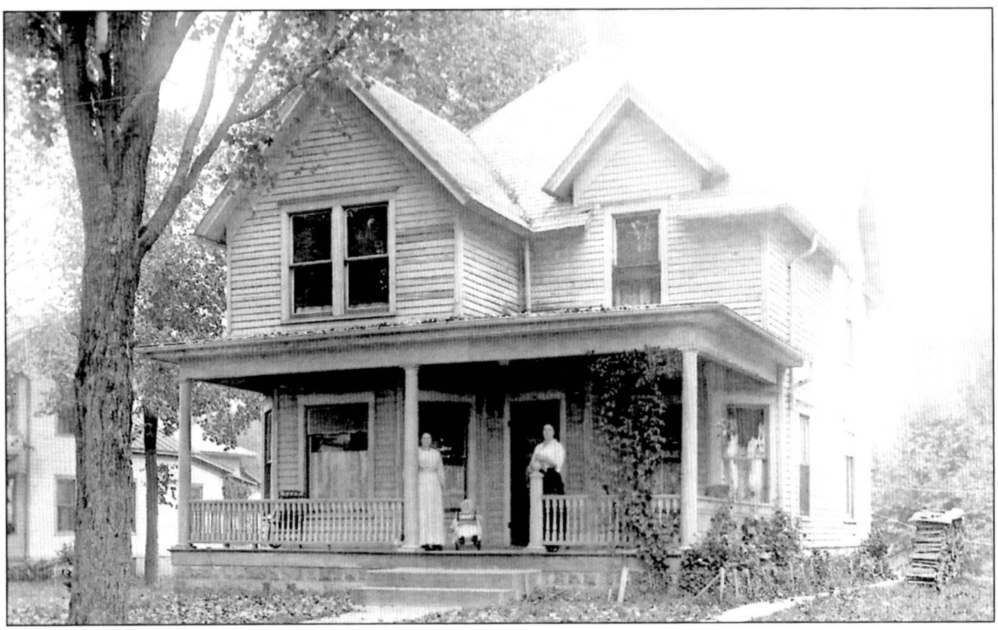

In 1908, Capron returned to Boonville and built this Sears and Roebuck house on Summit Street. In the summer, Capron worked locally as a stonemason. During the winter, he produced a superb line of handmade snowshoes in the barn behind his house, thereby continuing a Boonville tradition. In the early 1900s, C. Earl Phelps operated a snowshoe factory on Main Street, the only one in the country at the time. (Author's collection.)

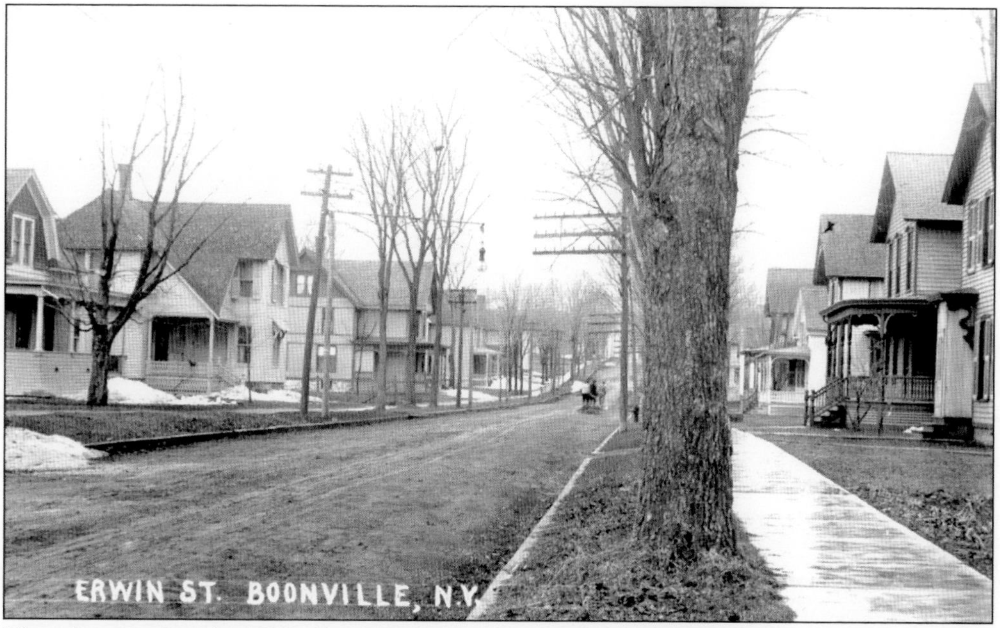

Though opened in the 1870s, Erwin Street was not graded and curbed until 1909. In August of that year, work was abruptly discontinued, rendering the street impassable. The *Boonville Herald* reported, "Crushed stone is piled up in front of Mayor Belknap's residence and he does not relish it a little bit . . . There are indications of lively times if the street is not put in better condition." (Courtesy of Ed Fynmore.)

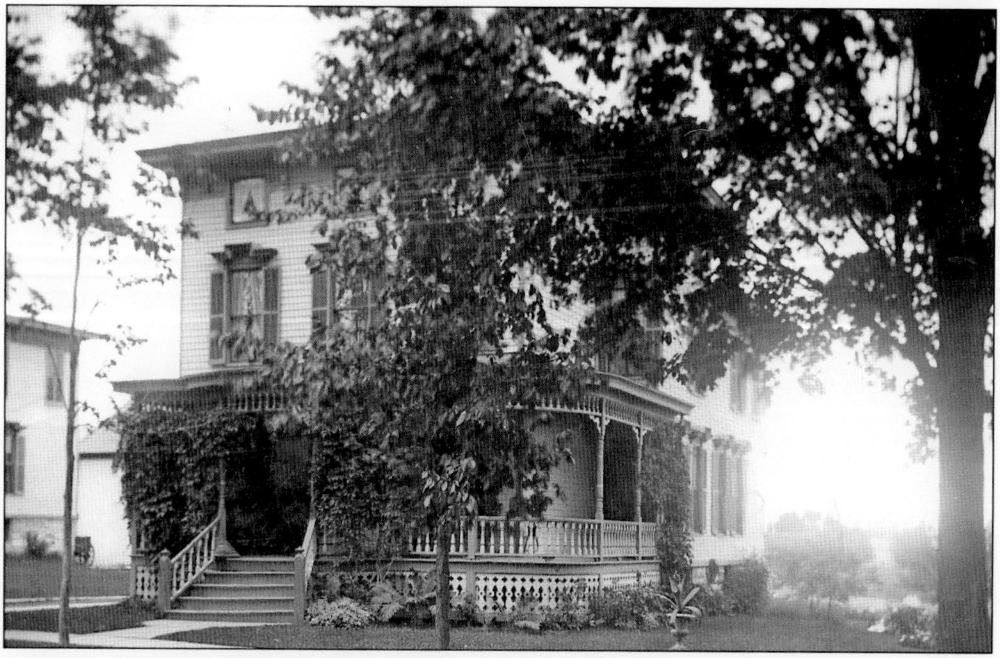

Swiss immigrant David Karlen (1842–1924) managed 22 local cheese factories, including one on Summit Street that specialized in Limburger. In the 1870s, he built three large houses on Erwin Street for his children. Automobile dealer Sam Karlen lived in the one pictured here. (Courtesy of Larry Myers.)

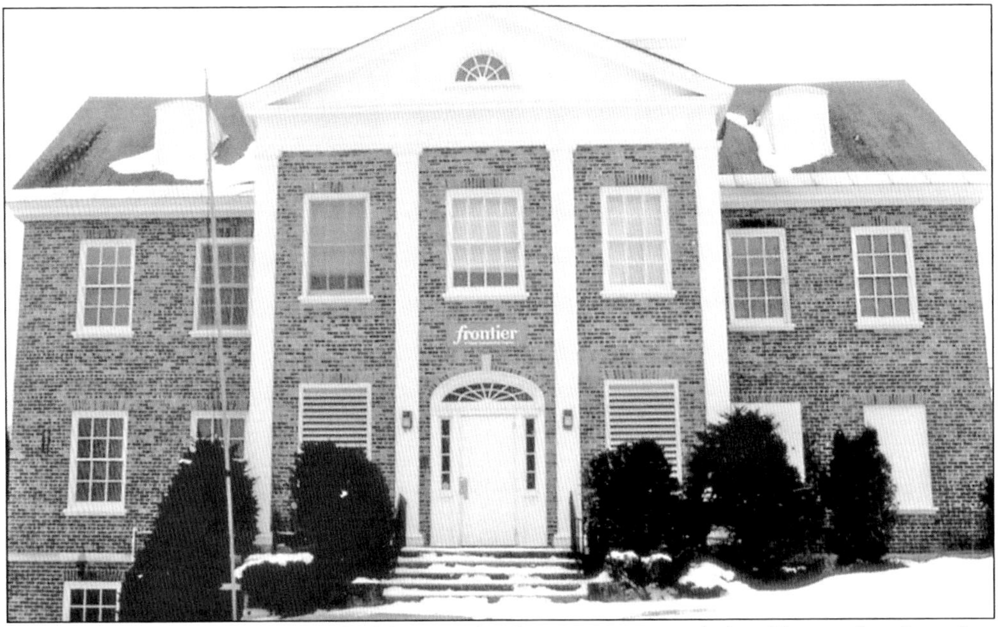

In 1927, Cassie E. Dodge bequeathed $40,000 for the construction of a local hospital and another $30,000 for its maintenance. The hospital board chose a site on Erwin Street, and construction began on a brick, three-story Colonial structure capable of accommodating at least 20 beds. Another $30,000 was needed to put the hospital into operation, but attempts to raise the start-up money were frustrated, in part, by the Great Depression. (Author's collection.)

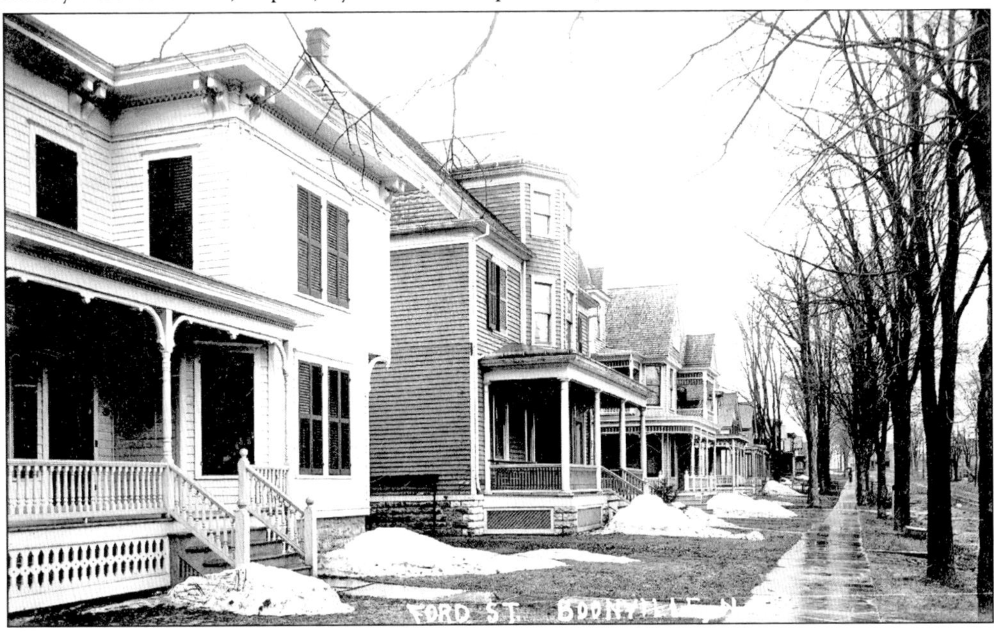

By 1910, handsome frame homes lined the south side of Ford Street (named for landholder Orrin Ford). When the village began laying a sidewalk on the north side of the street in 1923, residents on the south side protested vigorously. The new sidewalk would have a 30-inch setback from the curb, whereas the sidewalk on the south side had a nine-foot setback. The disparity, they felt, would give the street a woefully lopsided appearance. (Courtesy of Ed Fynmore.)

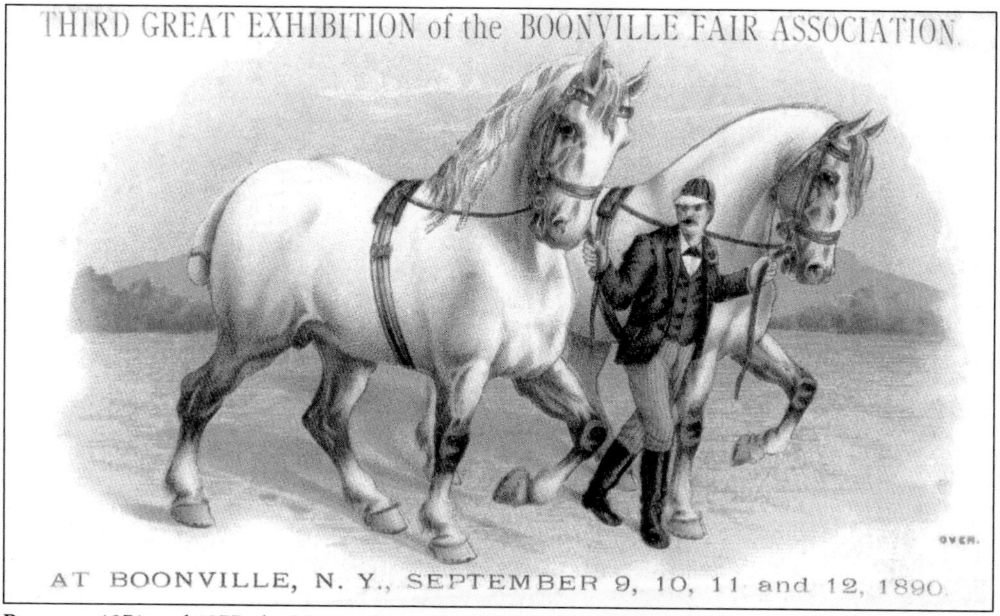

Between 1871 and 1877, the Union Agricultural Society held annual fairs on the 17-acre grounds of the Boonville Driving Park located west of Summit Street and south of Schuyler Street. With the formation of the Boonville Fair Association in 1888, annual fairs resumed and have continued to the present. The fair association leased the grounds from the Driving Association until 1905 when it purchased the land outright. (Courtesy of Jerry Putnam.)

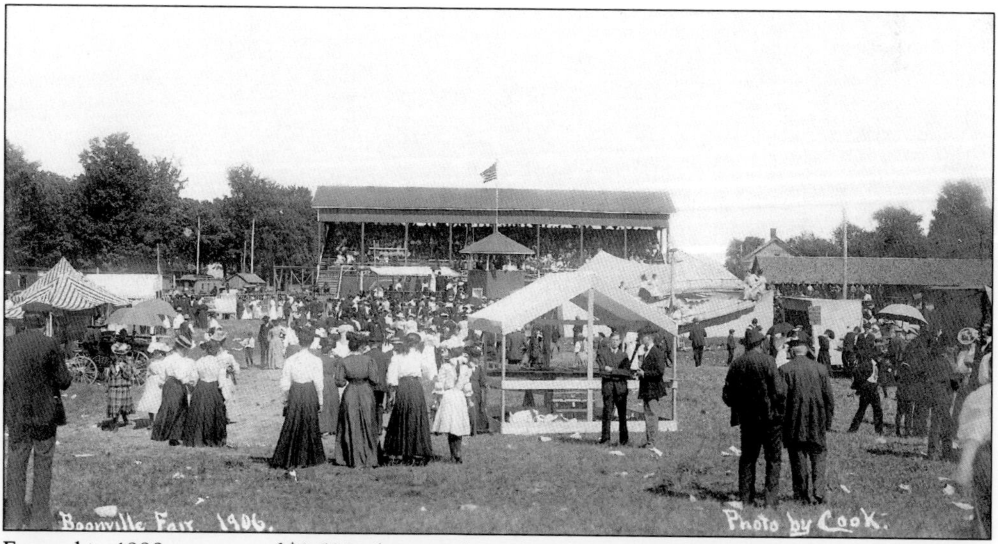

Erected in 1888 at a cost of $2,500, the grandstand measured 30 by 100 feet and could seat more than 1,200 people. The space beneath the seating served as a dining room. The structure was originally parallel to Summit Street and faced west. A featured speaker addressed the crowd each year, beginning in 1888, when the speaker was Belva Ann Lockwood, presidential nominee of the Equal Rights Party. (Author's collection.)

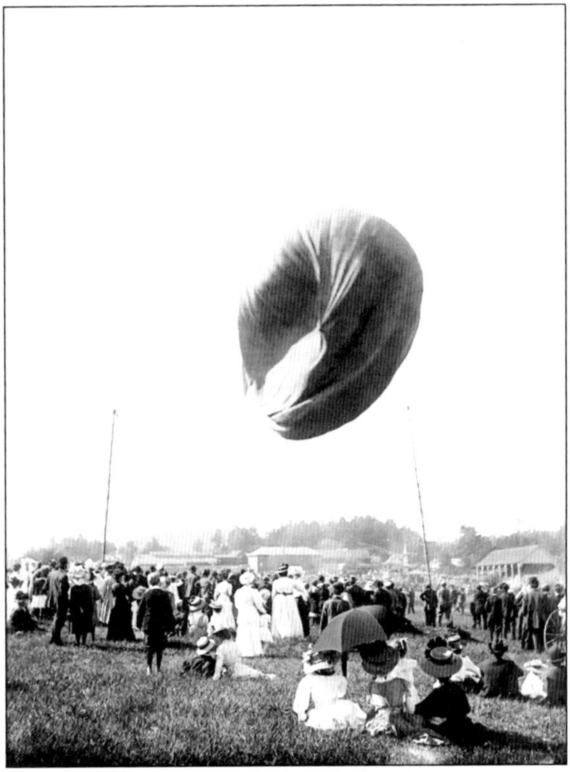

The balloon ascent, which followed the afternoon baseball game, was widely regarded as the highlight of the day. In 1888, some 8,000 spectators witnessed "Professor" Charles E. Slocum make the first ascent. The following year, a St. Bernard parachuted to earth. In 1903, a cornet player ascended, playing "Nearer My God to Thee." And in 1926, George Hatsell parachuted, becoming entangled in an elm tree near the Baptist church. (Courtesy of Ed Fynmore.)

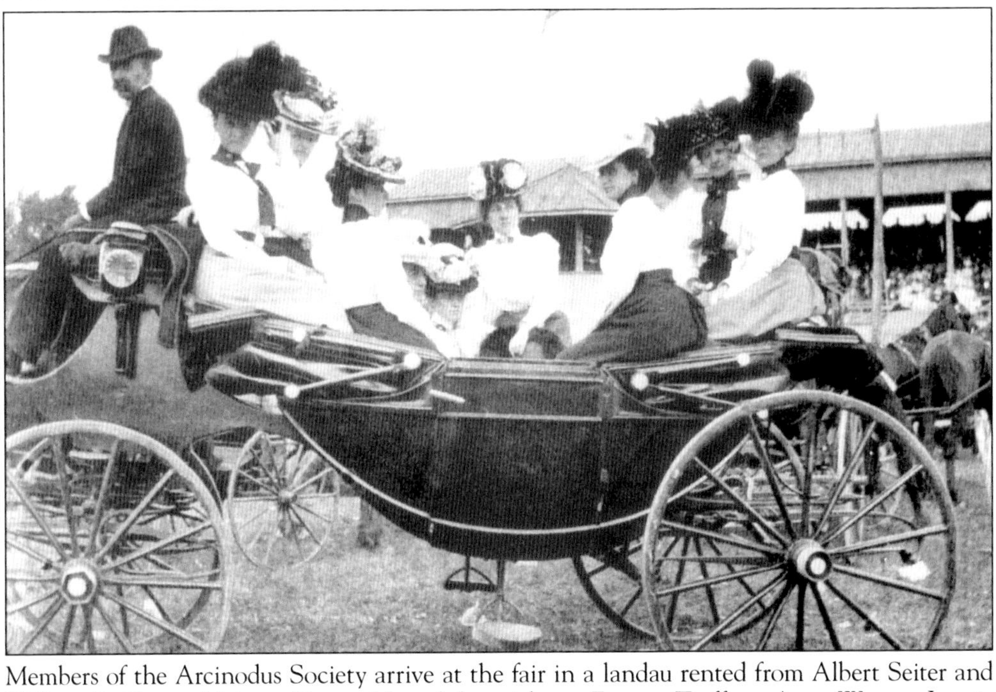

Members of the Arcinodus Society arrive at the fair in a landau rented from Albert Seiter and William B. Gleason's Livery. Pictured from left to right are Frances Traffarn, Anna Watson, Jennie Wentworth, Louisa Felshaw, unidentified, Florence Colton, Marie Utley, Irene Griffith, Maude Calen, and Edna Traffarn. The photograph dates from the 1890s. (Courtesy of Ed Fynmore.)

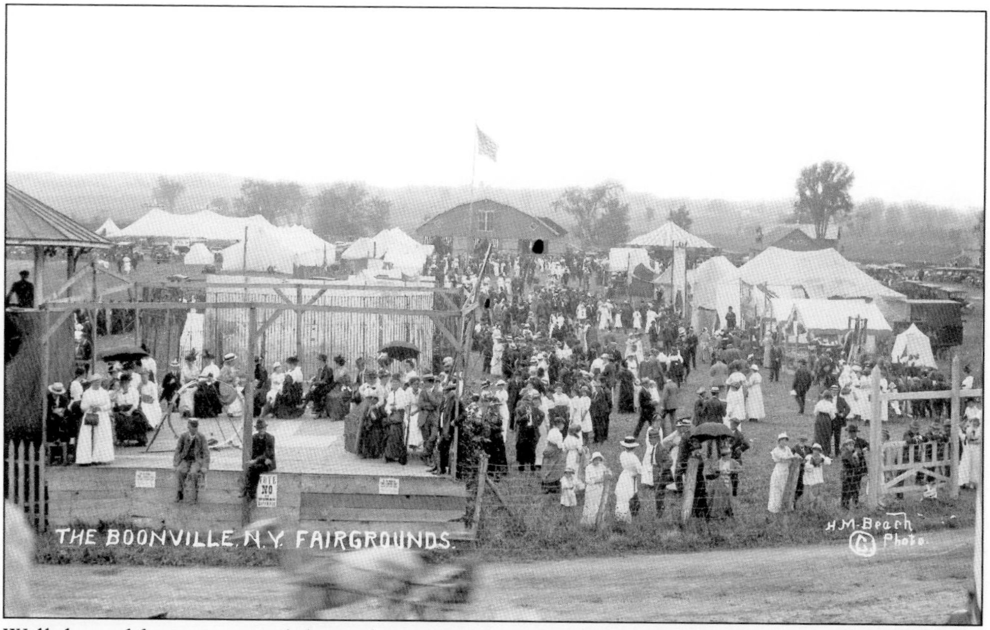

Well-dressed fairgoers crowd the midway around 1916. A flag marks the Floral Hall (1888), where exhibits in the domestic arts and agriculture were displayed. Beneath the three-pole marquis (in the distance at left), Ambrose C. Capron is showcasing Studebakers. In the foreground, a horse pulls a sulky around the original racetrack. A poster on the stage urges voters to reject women's suffrage. (Courtesy of Ed Fynmore.)

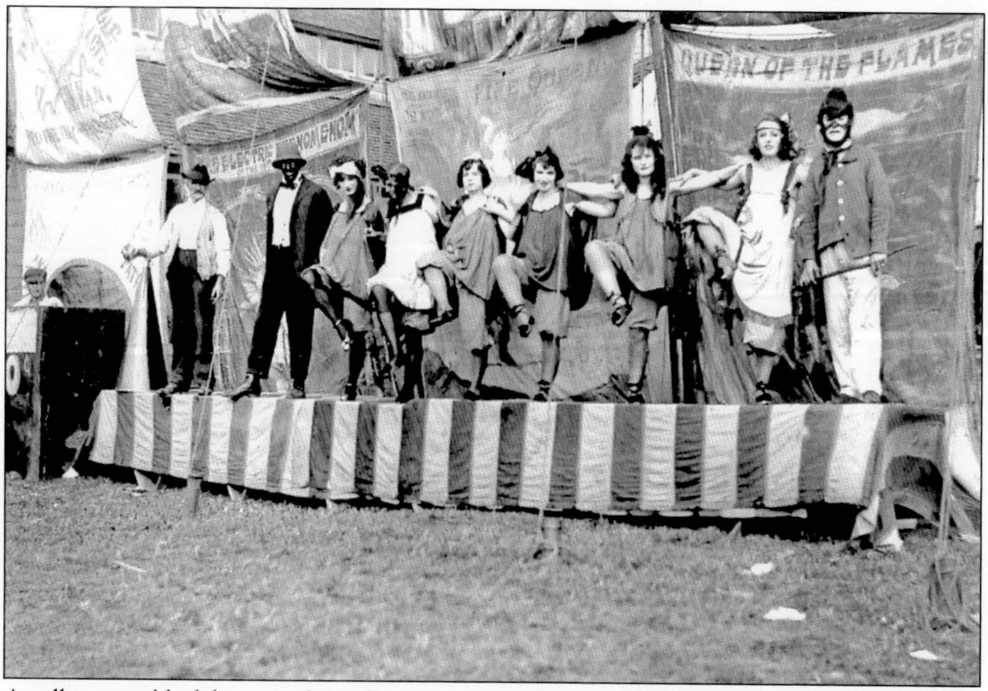

A talker, two blackfaces, and six dancing women try to arouse interest in Prof. G. W. Van's sideshow, billed as "A Magnificent Triumph to Amusement Lovers" and featuring Mlle Katamirea, the "Fire Queen." The price of admission was 10¢. (Courtesy of Ed Fynmore.)

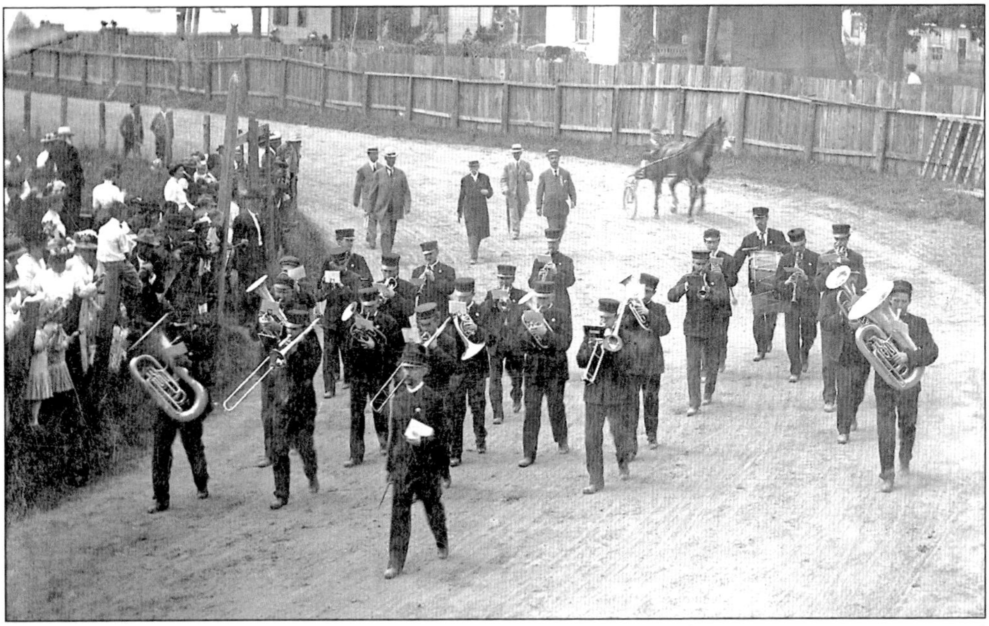

Evan Oldfield's military band honors Edward Payson Weston, the "Great Transcontinental Walker" on August 24, 1909. Weston began his walking career in 1861, when, at age 22, he walked 463 miles from Boston to Washington, D.C., to attend Abraham Lincoln's inauguration. At age 71, he trekked from Los Angeles to New York in 88 days, averaging 41 miles a day. Weston sometimes walked 550 miles in six-day walking contests. (Courtesy of Larry Myers.)

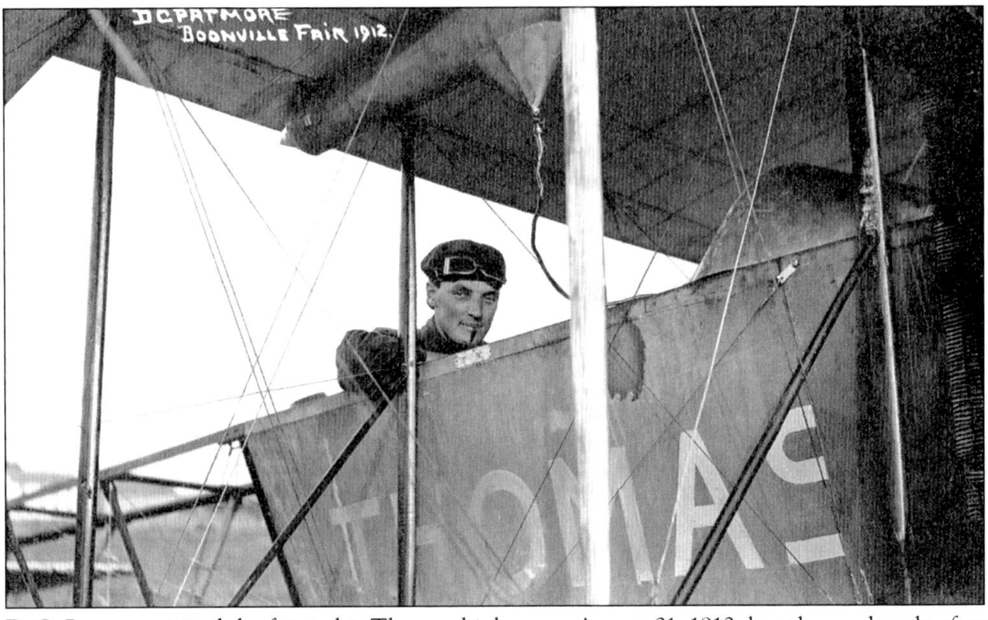

D. C. Patmore visited the fair in his Thomas biplane on August 21, 1912, less than a decade after the Wright brothers' successful flight at Kitty Hawk, North Carolina. Unfortunately, Patmore crashed his plane on arriving and, after making repairs, crashed it again the following day. In 1919, stunt pilot Lt. Stewart J. Davies put on an exhibition and offered rides in his plane at the rate of $1 per minute. (Courtesy of Larry Myers.)

Six

Churches and Schools

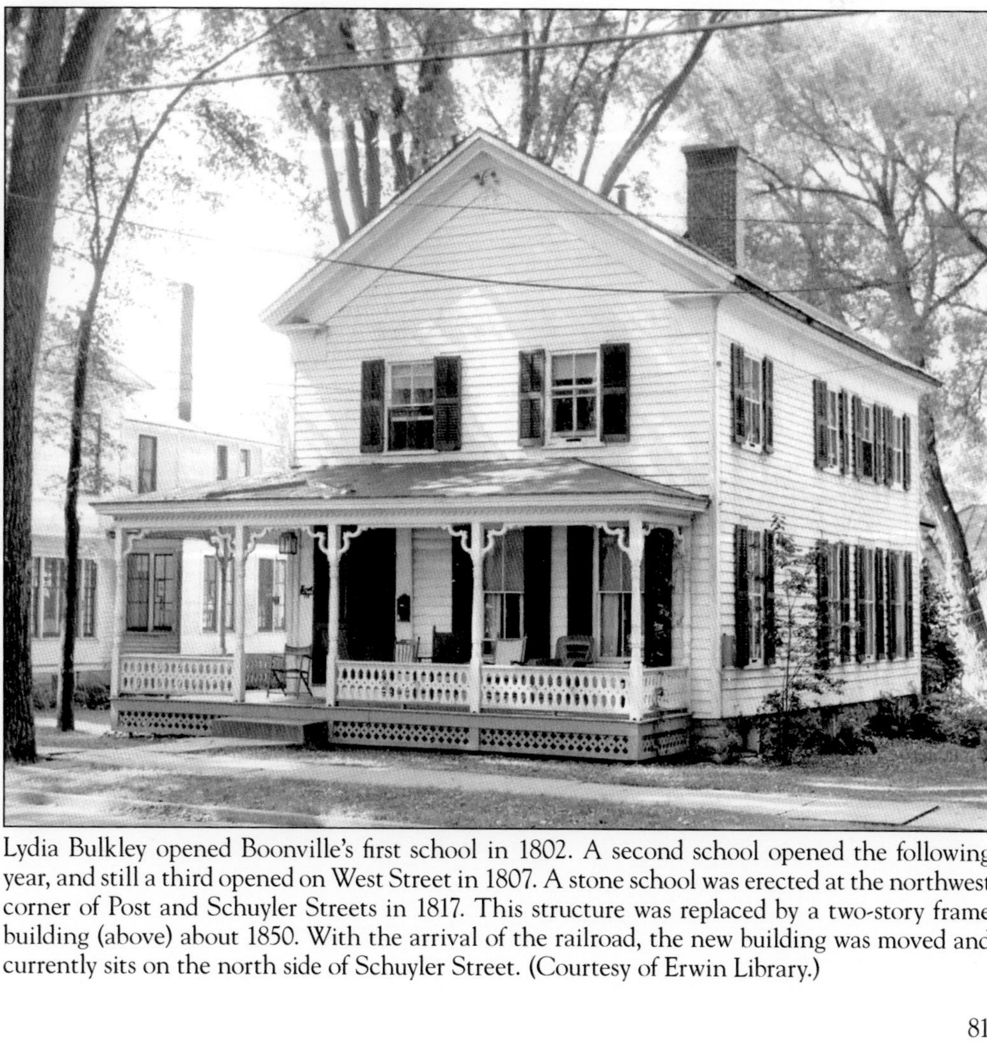

Lydia Bulkley opened Boonville's first school in 1802. A second school opened the following year, and still a third opened on West Street in 1807. A stone school was erected at the northwest corner of Post and Schuyler Streets in 1817. This structure was replaced by a two-story frame building (above) about 1850. With the arrival of the railroad, the new building was moved and currently sits on the north side of Schuyler Street. (Courtesy of Erwin Library.)

YOUNG LADIES' SCHOOL.

THE SUMMER TERM of the Young Ladies' School will commence

MONDAY, MAY 3D, 1858.

T E R M S .

Primary Department,	$3,00
Common English,	4,00
Astronomy, Algebra, Geometry, Philosophy, Botany, Rhetoric, History, etc., each extra,	,50
French, extra,	1,00
Drawing—Printing in Water Colors, and on Velvet, each extra,	3,00
Oil Painting, extra,	6,00
Lessons on Guitar,	6,00

In 1855, the Philleo sisters opened a finishing school in the Owens Block on Post Street. This advertisement appeared in an 1858 edition of the *Black River Herald*. In the late 1860s, the school became Duffys' Select Academy for Boys and Girls. At first, the academy excluded boys because it was thought boys' shoes were too loud on wooden floors. In time, the problem was solved by providing boys with slippers. (Courtesy of Jerry Putnam.)

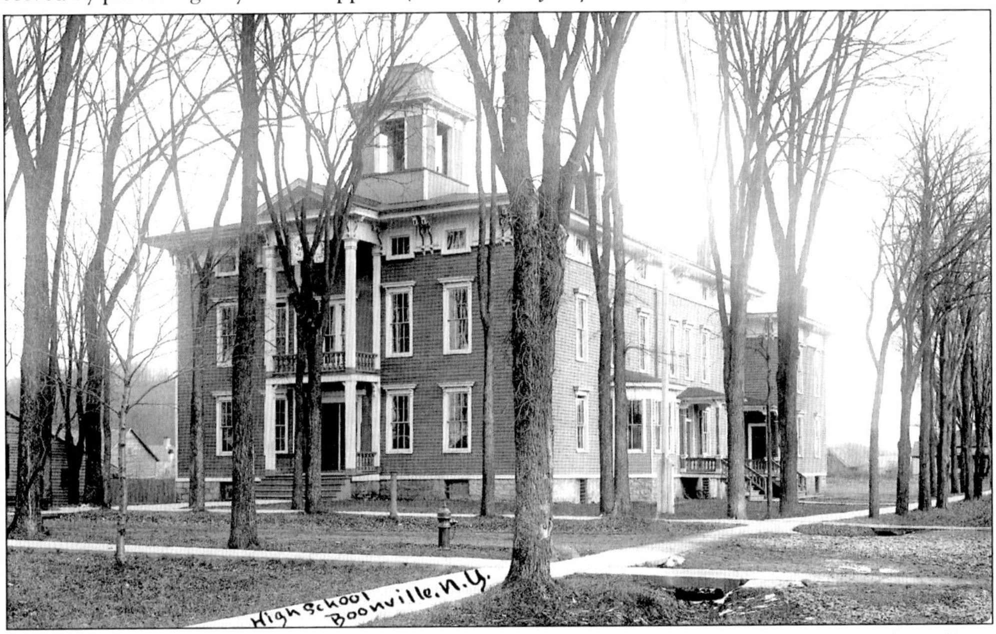

In 1855, under the leadership of Robert Bamber, Ela Kent, and Samuel Bateman, the village commissioned Dewitt Grosjean to build a public school at the corner of Academy and Charles Streets. In 1857, the school was officially named the Union Free School and Academy and, in 1867, renamed Boonville High School and Academy. The school was enlarged in 1876 and moved in 1879 to make room for a still larger school. (Courtesy of Larry Myers.)

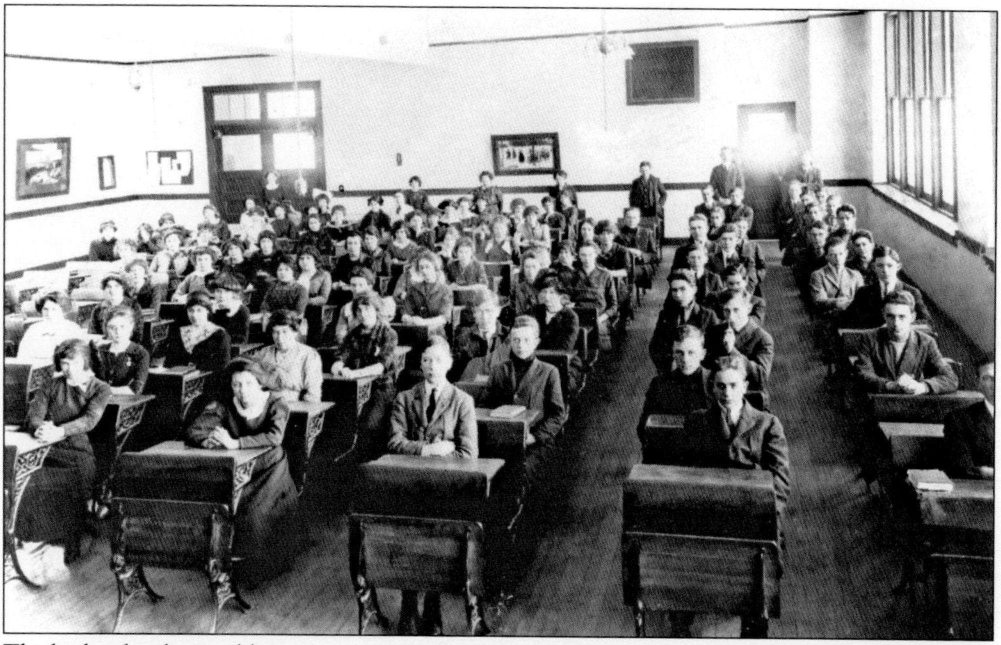

The high school assembly room accommodated over 100 students in fixed rows of detached desks, with girls on one side and boys on the other. By 1909, it had become apparent that a new school was needed to accommodate the growing number of students. Some taxpayers suggested forming a stock company to convert the old academy into a summer hotel. (Courtesy of Ed Fynmore.)

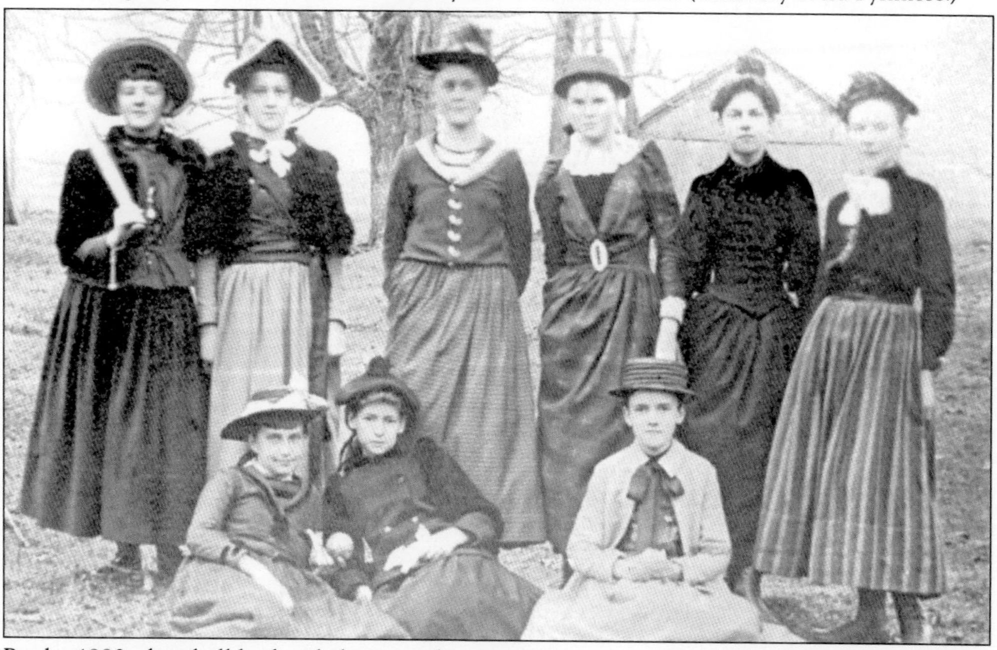

By the 1880s, baseball had truly become the national pastime. Here high school girls gather for a team portrait. Pictured are (first row) Mary Utley, Cora Belle Mitchell, and Louise Wentworth; (second row) C. Maude Calen, Florence Grosjean, Eugenia Ballou, Irene Griffith, Jennie Wentworth, and Clara Belle Lewis. The photograph was taken by Clinton W. Hough about 1889. (Courtesy of Erwin Library.)

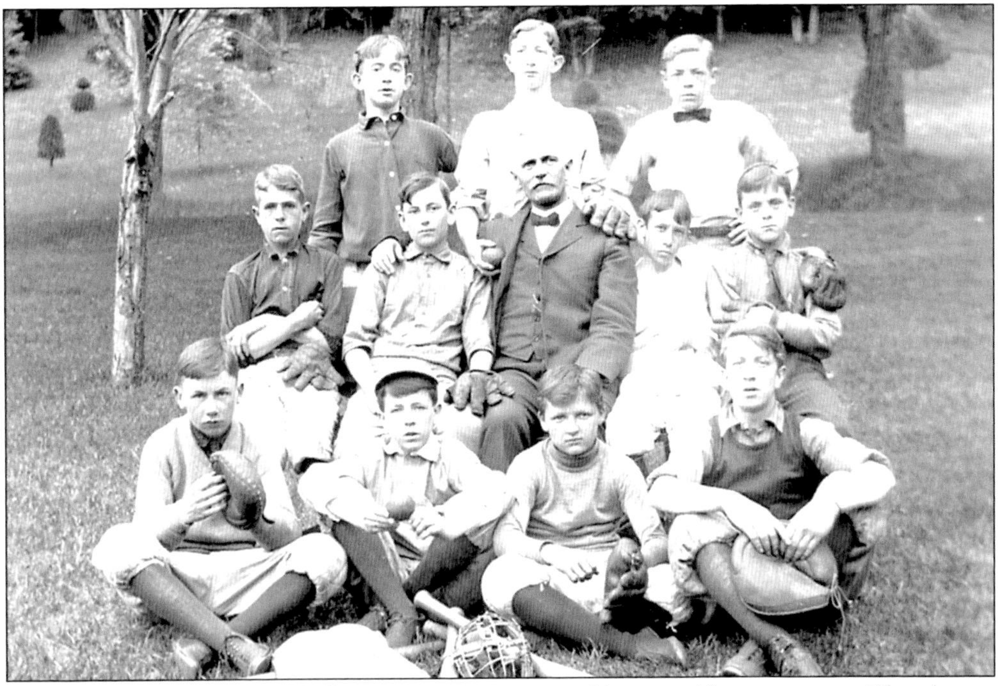

The 1908 junior varsity baseball team won 24 games and lost one 15-inning game. The players, from left to right, are (first row) Davidson, Barry, Hayes, and Noble; (second row) Johnson, Wood, Henry G. Grubel (manager), Richardson, and Newey; (third row) Lewis, Wood, and Glenn. (Courtesy of Vincent T. Fitch.)

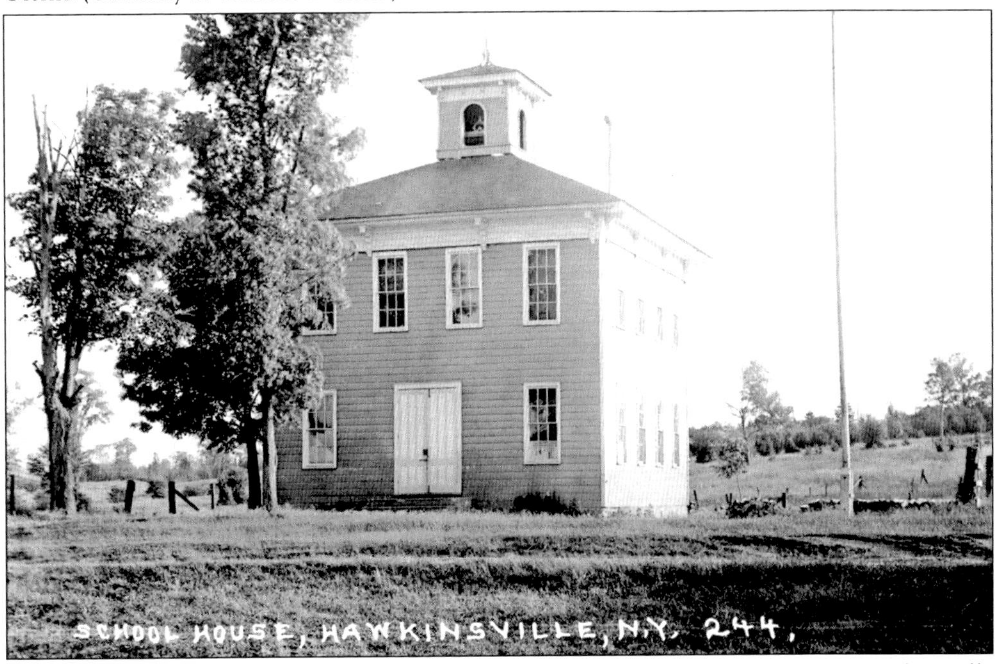

In 1907, the town of Boonville still had 17 district schools. The largest of these was at Hawkinsville where two teachers were employed. Schools in the township were centralized in 1944. (Courtesy of Larry Myers.)

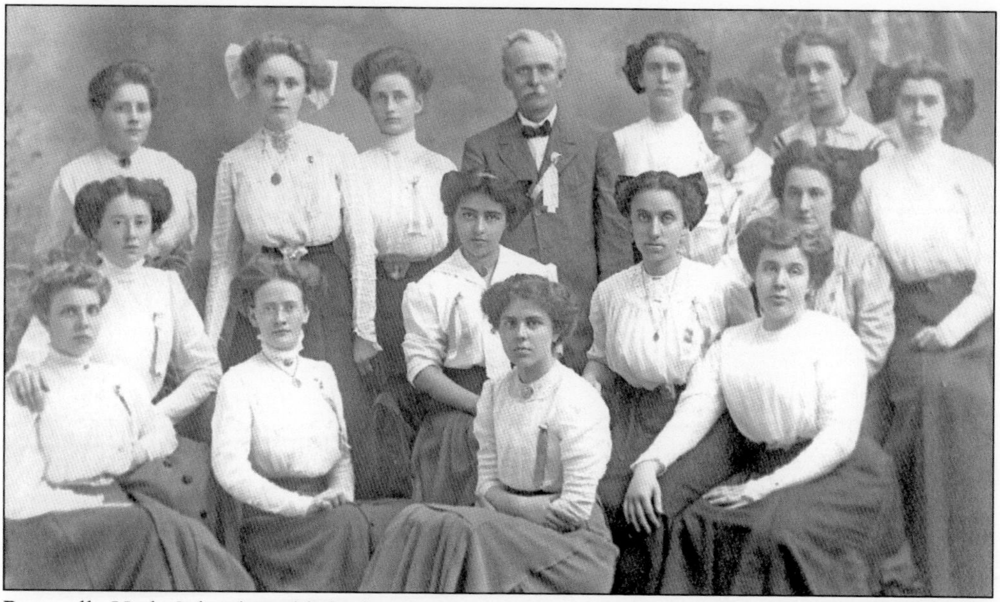

Boonville High School established a teacher training institute in 1885. Graduates could teach for up to three years in any rural school that did not maintain an academic department. In 1910, the graduating class included (first row) Anna Allport, Hazel Parkhurst, Florence Harvey, and Florence Allen; (second row) Edna Nelson, Collis Jones, Clara Tine, and Mae Clark; (third row) Laura Kenwell, Esther Lehr, Edith Nelson, Prof. Henry G. Grubel (instructor), Anna Howley, Olive Sanborn, Cecil Fardette, and Mary Haney. (Courtesy of Adirondack Central School.)

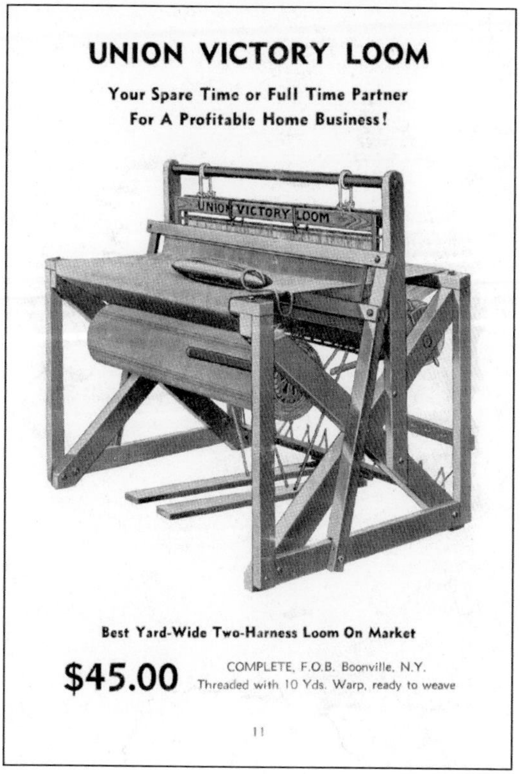

In 1911, John H. Elsaser transformed the old high school into the Union Specialty Works. In addition to grandfather clocks, furniture, and camper trailers, the firm manufactured looms for home weaving. These proved especially profitable, and in 1921, the firm changed its name to the Union Loom Company. By the late 1920s, the firm employed 160 workers. (Courtesy of Jerry Putnam.)

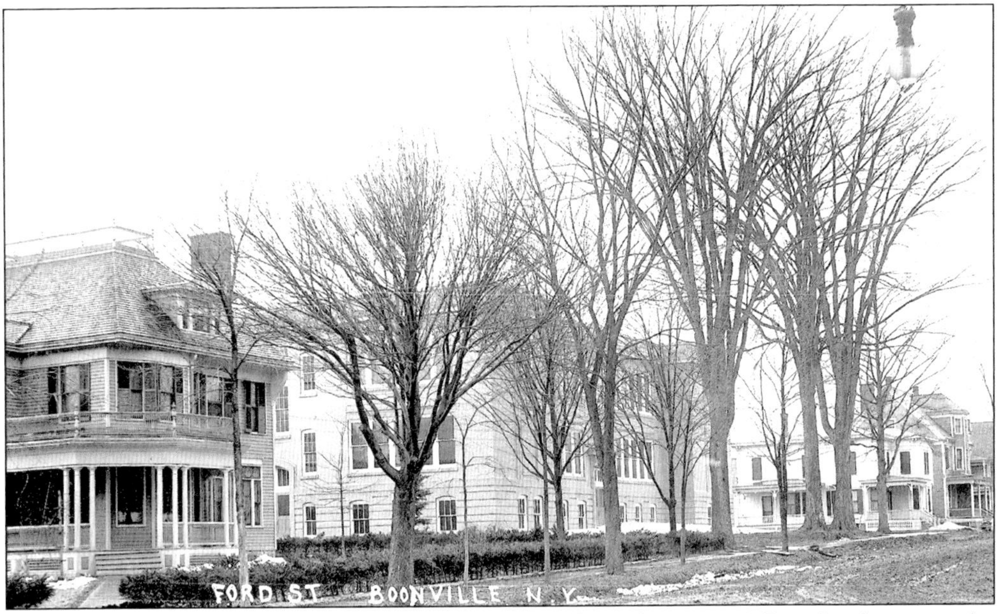

To accommodate the growing population of schoolchildren, the Byron I. Douglass home on the south side of Ford Street was razed in 1910, and a new $40,000 high school with a mission-style interior was erected. Designed by architect Wilson Potter of New York City, the new school opened on January 8, 1911, with separate entrances for boys, girls, and faculty. Samuel J. Neff was principal. (Author's collection.)

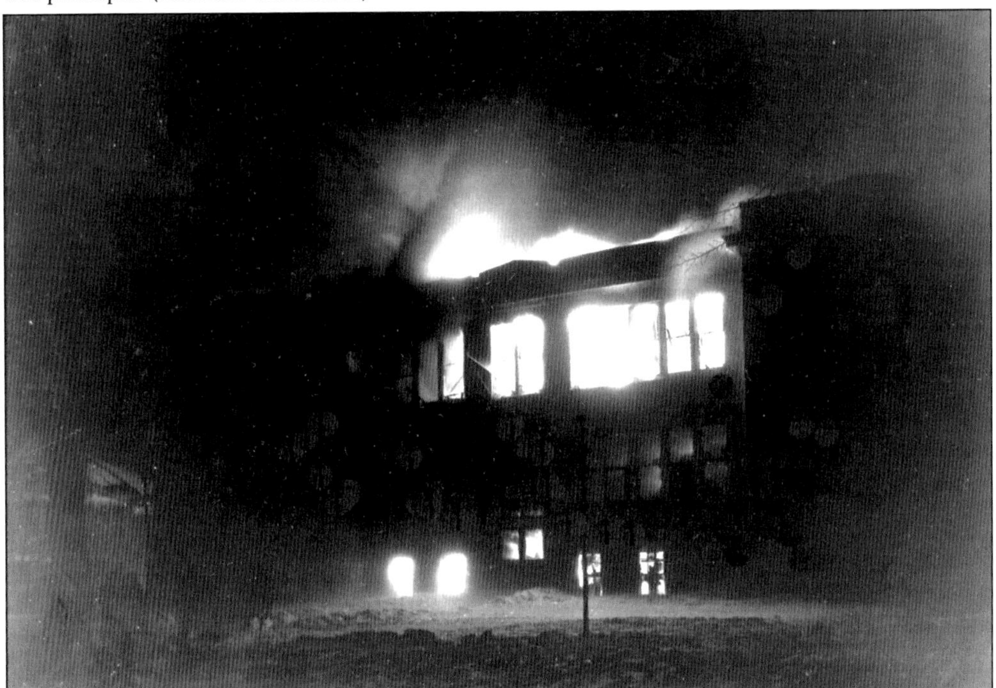
After only 11 years of use, the second high school burned down on the night of February 9, 1922. The fire department surmised that damp coal had ignited spontaneously. Insurance proved inadequate, covering only $17,000 of a $50,000 bond. (Courtesy of Ed Fynmore.)

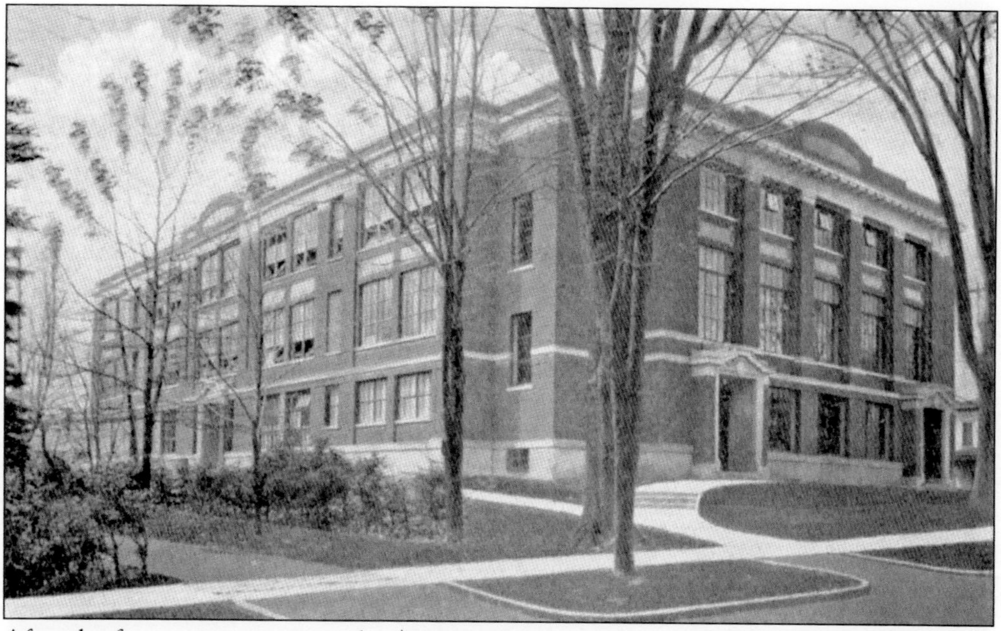

After the fire, taxpayers approved a $185,000 bond issue for a third Boonville High School, which opened in 1924 and was built on the site of the previous high school. Robert B. Searle was principal at the time. (Author's collection.)

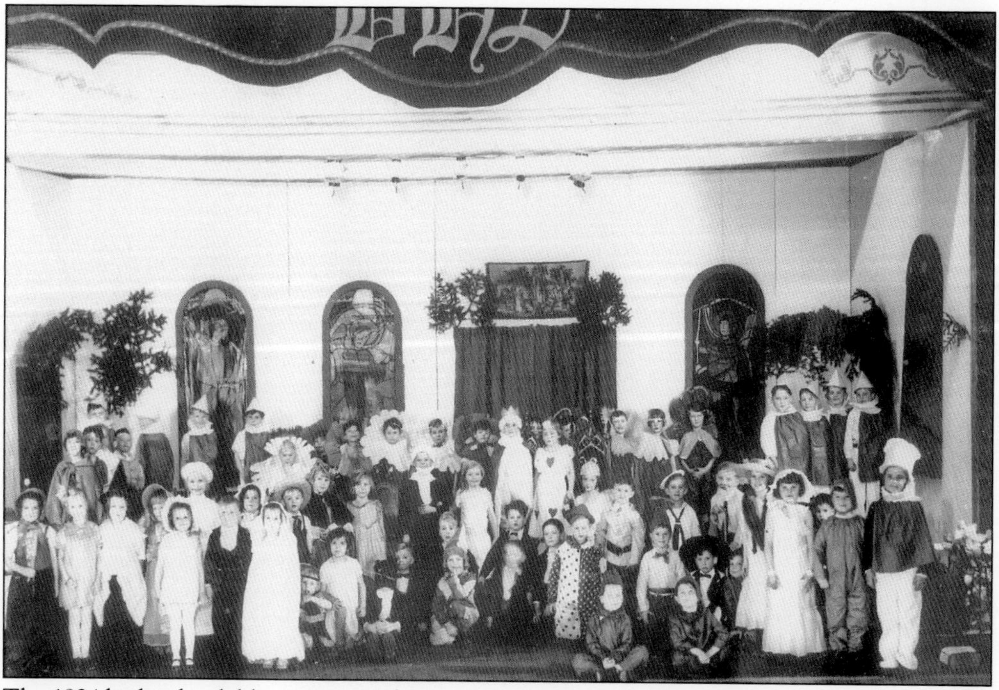

The 1924 high school, like its two predecessors, housed students in the elementary grades as well as those in grades 7 through 12. In the photograph above, costumed children pose for a group photograph on the high school stage. (Courtesy of Ed Fynmore.)

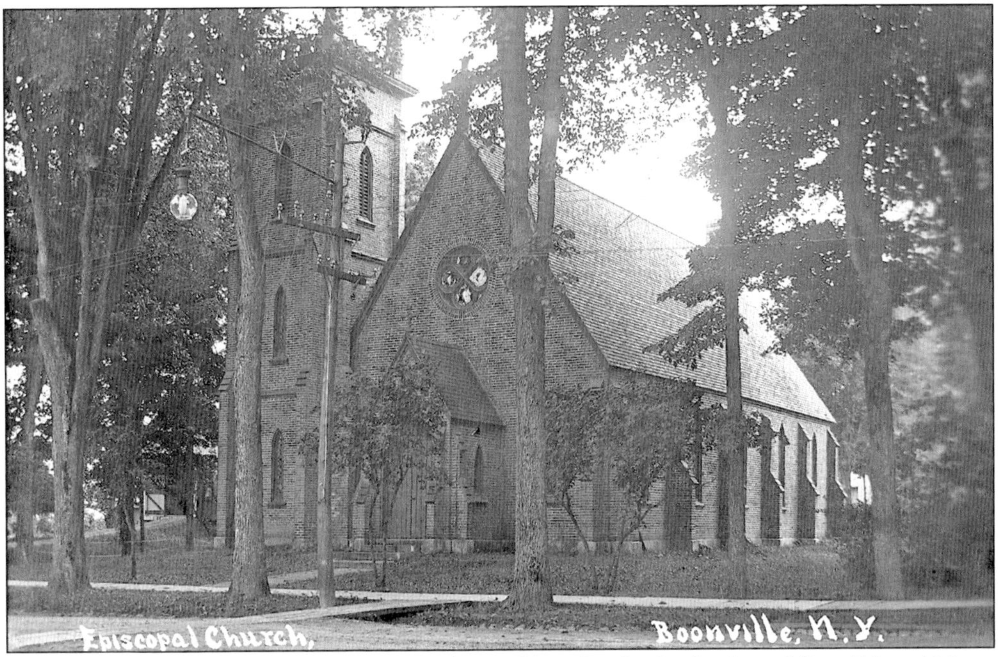

Trinity Episcopalian Church was organized in 1855 under the leadership of Rev. Edward Hurtt Jewett. Three years later, the congregation built a brick church on a Schuyler Street property donated by the Post family. The parish erected a wooden-frame rectory behind the church in 1911 and replaced it with a brick structure in 1927. (Courtesy of Larry Myers.)

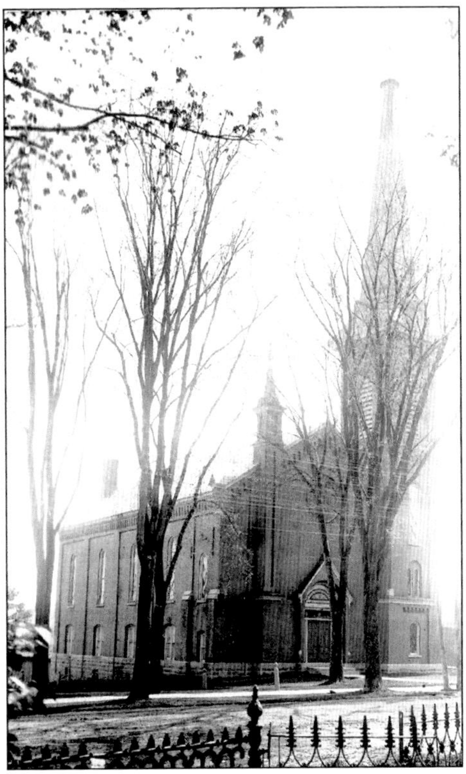

From the early to mid-1820s, Methodists held services in members' homes. Between 1827 and 1845, the congregation worshipped at the Union church on Post Street. After selling their interest in the Union church to the Congregationalists, the Methodists built a small church on the site of what would later become the Herald Building. They remained there until 1873, when they erected a $15,000 church on the site of the former Empire Hotel. (Courtesy of Larry Myers.)

The Presbyterians organized in 1805, holding services in private homes until 1827, when they began to worship at the Union church on Post Street. They continued to meet at the Union church until the structure was moved to make way for the railroad. In 1856, the Presbyterians built a church on the southwest corner of James and Church Streets. The land was donated by Joseph R. Tharrett. (Author's collection.)

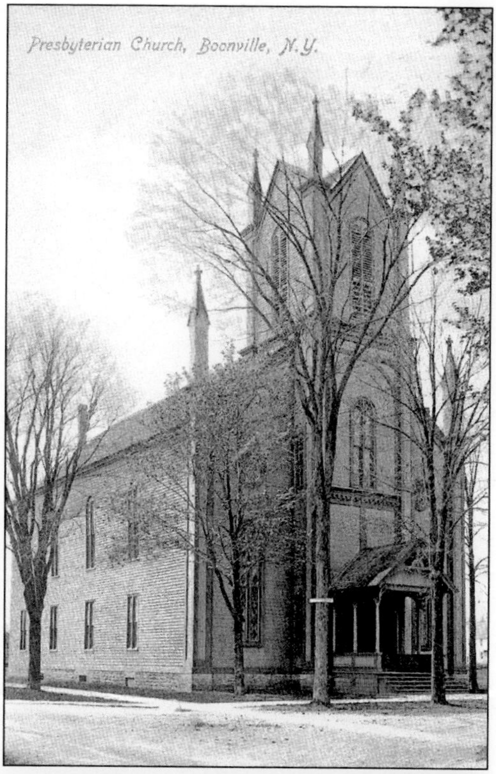

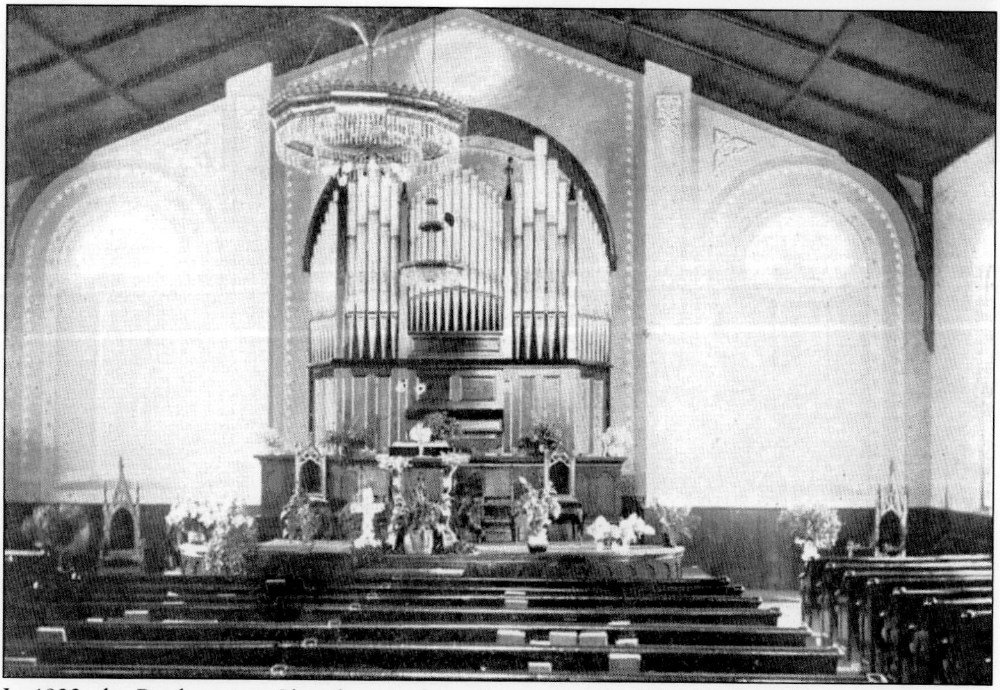

In 1923, the Presbyterian Church retired its pipe organ, which had served the congregation for 43 years. The new organ, pictured here, was built by C. R. Morey of Utica. The organist at the time was Frank V. Kent. (Courtesy of Larry Myers.)

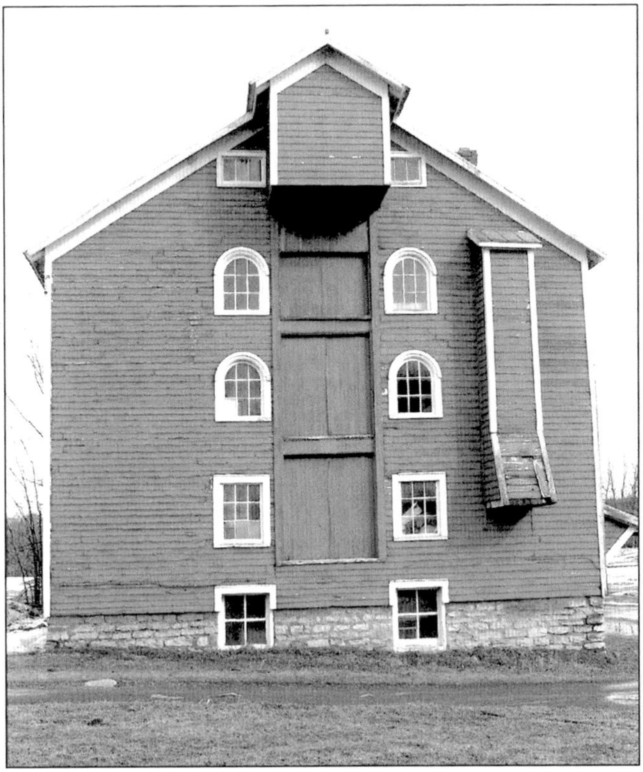

The German Lutheran Church was organized in 1869 under the leadership of Nicholas Schweinsberg, coal-and-feed merchant, and Jacob Jacobs, proprietor of the American Hotel. In 1872, the congregation built a house of worship on James Street, located two lots west of the Presbyterian church. Over time, membership declined, and in 1936, the church was moved to the B. O. Jackson farm, where it was converted into a chicken house. (Author's collection.)

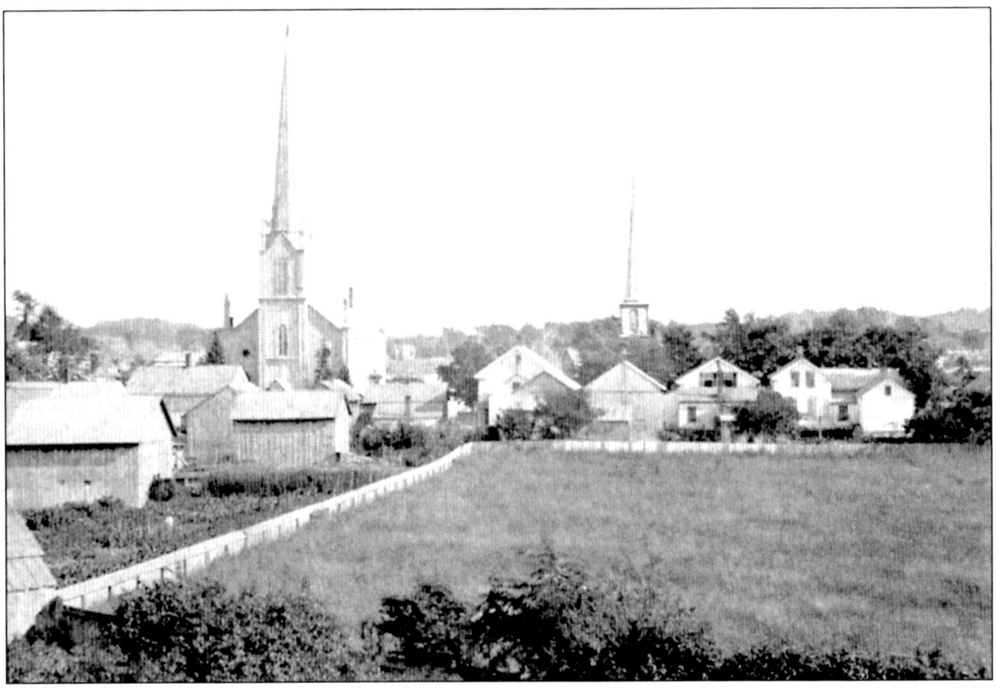

As this photograph from an Ackerman Brothers stereo card attests, the Presbyterian church (left) and German Lutheran church (right) once had steeples. The Presbyterian spire was removed in 1925. The photograph dates from the 1870s, and the view is to the south. (Author's collection.)

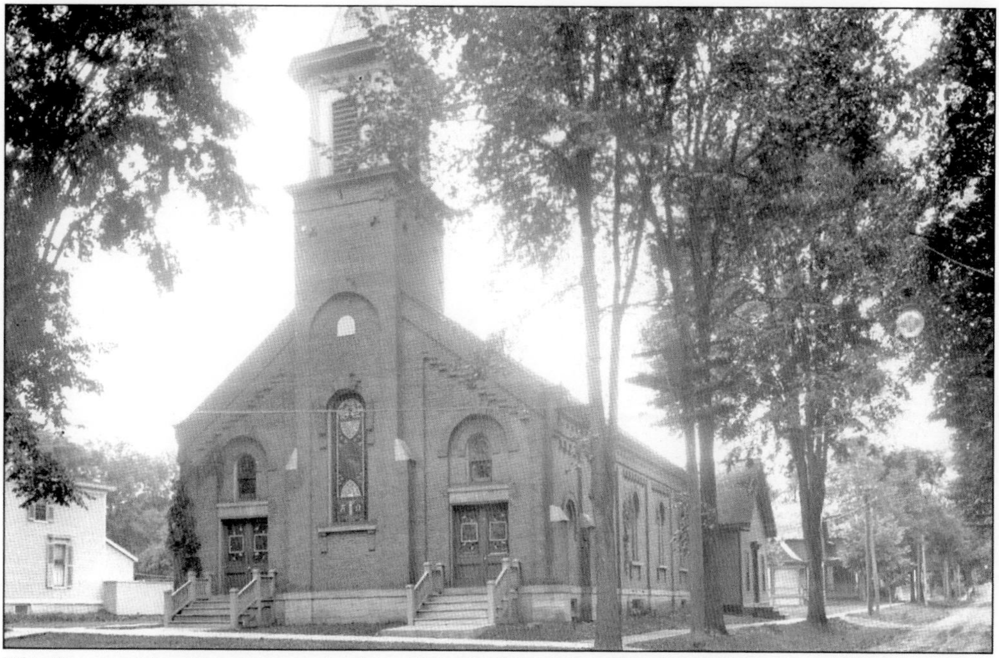

The Baptist Church was organized in 1810 by Elder John Upfold. Services were held in private homes until 1826, when members built a church at the intersection of Post Street and East Road. In 1866, the congregation erected a church at the southwest corner of Post and Erwin Streets. A section of the original railroad station was converted into a church annex (visible at rear right). (Courtesy of Larry Myers.)

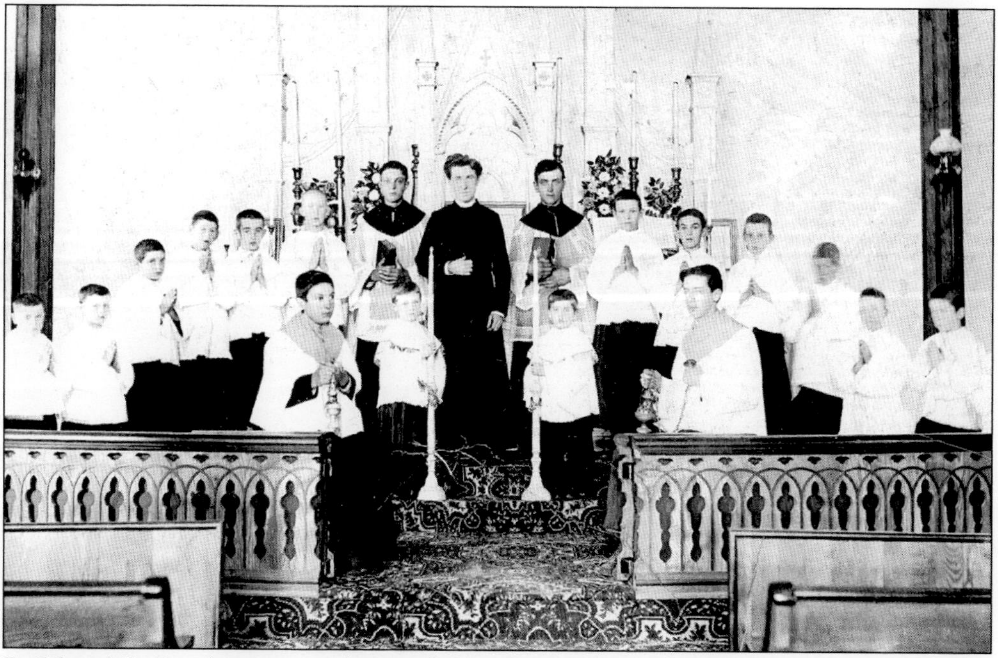

Fr. Edward R. Prendergast poses here with altar boys. Pastor of St. Joseph's from 1888 to 1908, Prendergast built a sacristy at the rear of the church and expanded the sanctuary, adding side altars and side rails. The building was heated by stoves and lit by gas. (Courtesy of Irma K. Marcy.)

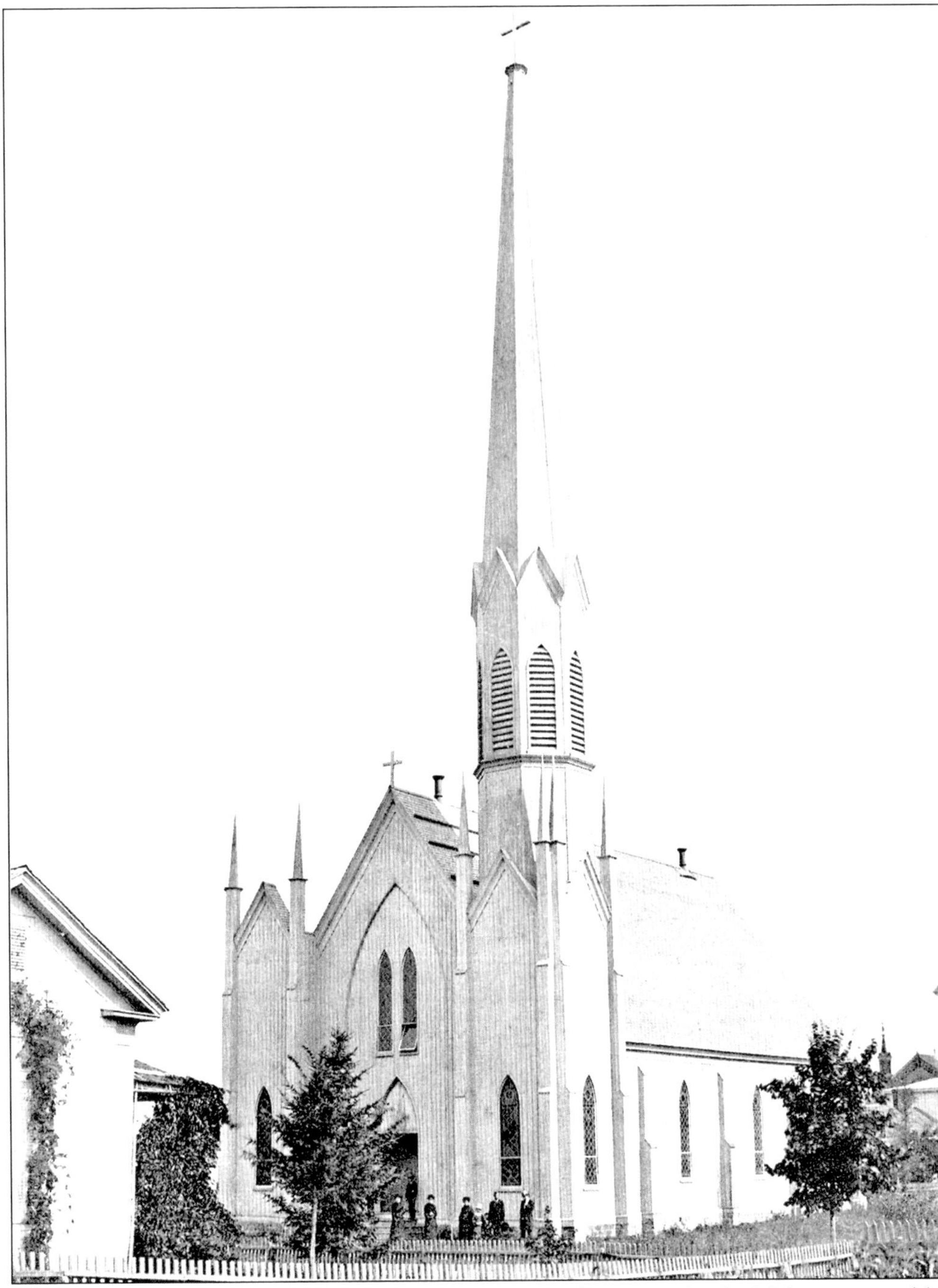

The Roman Catholic Society was founded in 1838. At that time, the faithful were served by Fr. William Beecham, an itinerant priest from Rome. Between 1841 and 1875, Boonville retained the status of a mission and was served by priests from Constableville and Port Leyden. Fr. Thomas Harty became the first resident priest in 1875. Under Harty's leadership, the congregation built St. Joseph's Catholic Church (1879) on Charles Street. The original spire (above) proved too tall for its base and was removed in 1884. (Courtesy of St. Joseph's Parish.)

Seven

FARMING, LOGGING, AND MINING

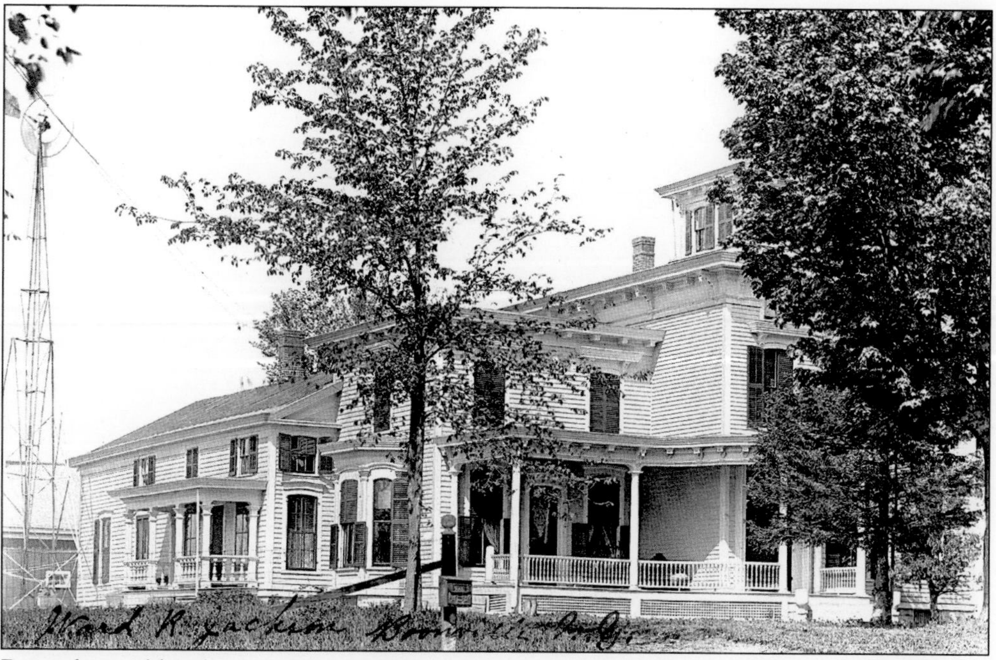

Dairy farms, like that of Ward Jackson on New York State Route 12D, ring the village of Boonville. Fluid milk became an important export in the 1880s, when the population of the urban Northeast was expanding rapidly and the demand for milk exceeded local supply. At the same time, the introduction of refrigerated transport made it possible to ship milk long distances without spoiling. (Courtesy of Larry Myers.)

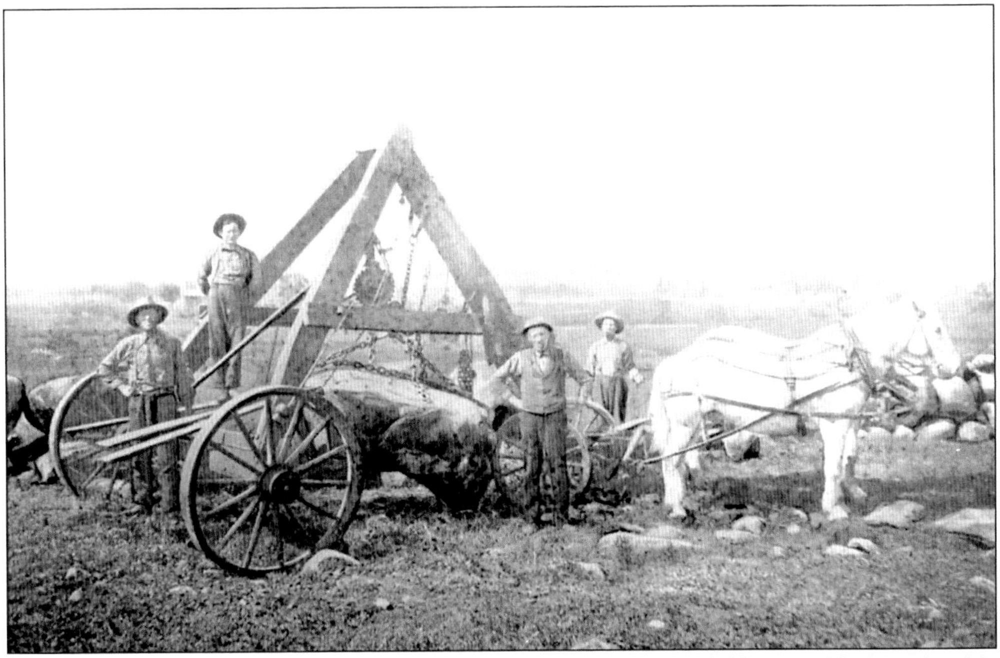

In this photograph, farmers near Collinsville remove boulders from a field using a block-and-tackle attached to a moveable tripod frame. In 1855, cheese-making farms in the Boonville area maintained about 25 percent of their improved acres in tillage and about 33 percent in pasture. (Courtesy of Ed Fynmore.)

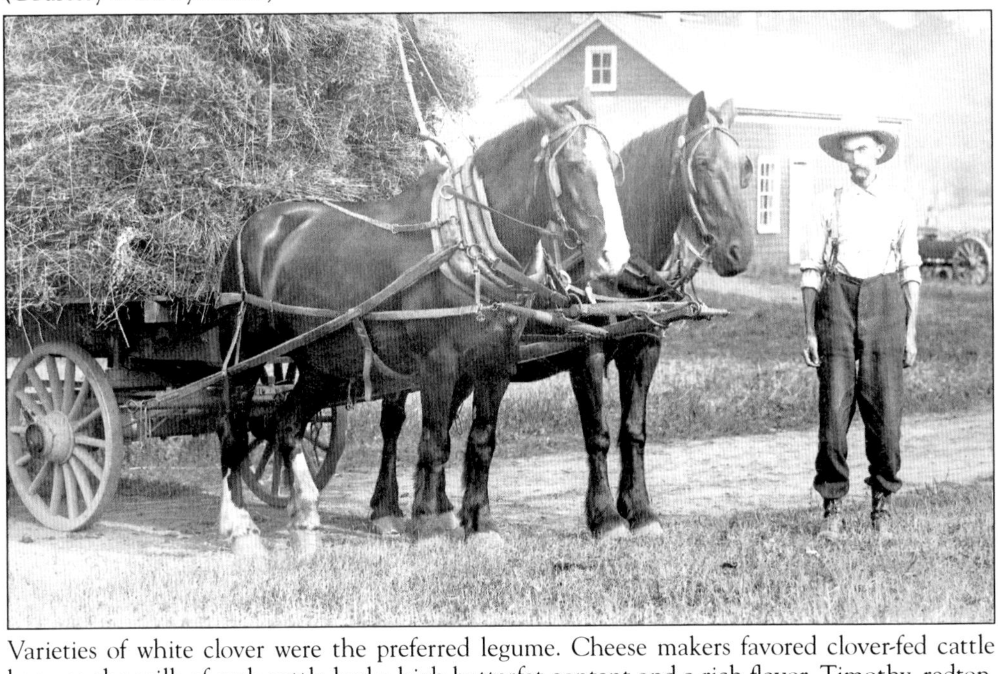

Varieties of white clover were the preferred legume. Cheese makers favored clover-fed cattle because the milk of such cattle had a high butterfat content and a rich flavor. Timothy, redtop, and orchard grasses were grown for hay. In the mid-1800s, Oneida County farmers who produced cheese harvested an estimated 1.3 to 2 tons of hay per acre. In this photograph, dairy farmer William Ransom hauls hay on Elmwood Farm. (Courtesy of Larry Myers.)

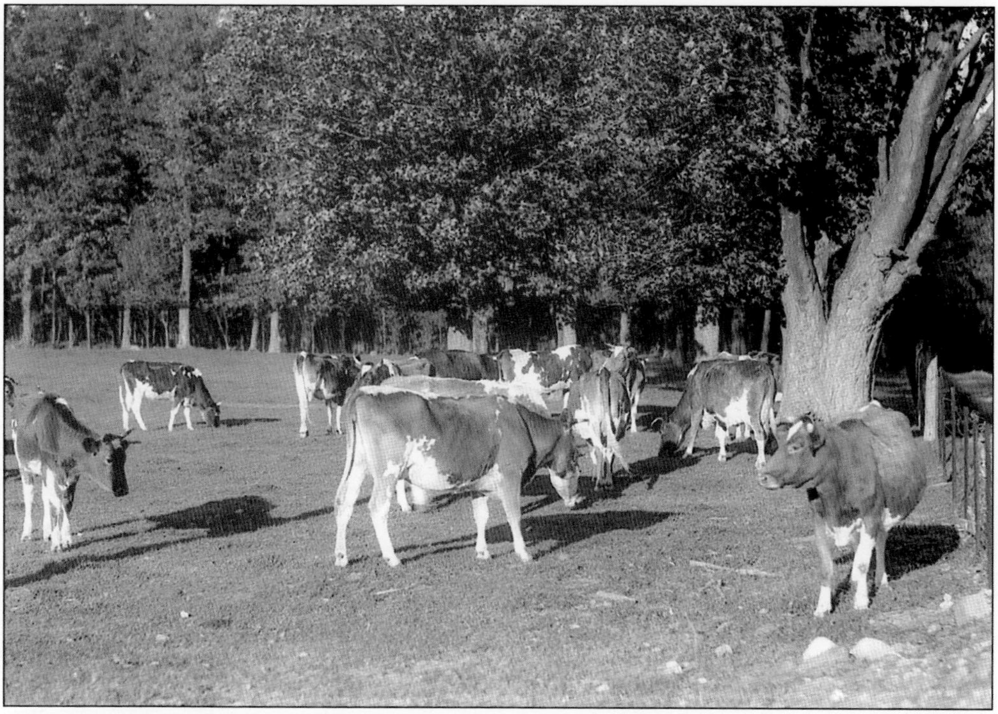

Tons of locally made cheese was transported on the Black River Canal, much of which was exported to Great Britain or the American South. In the mid-1800s, local dairy herds consisted of native cattle, descendants of interbred cattle brought to America by 17th-century immigrants. After the Civil War, farmers began to take an interest in graded cows, particularly Holsteins and Brown Swiss. (Courtesy of Ed Fynmore.)

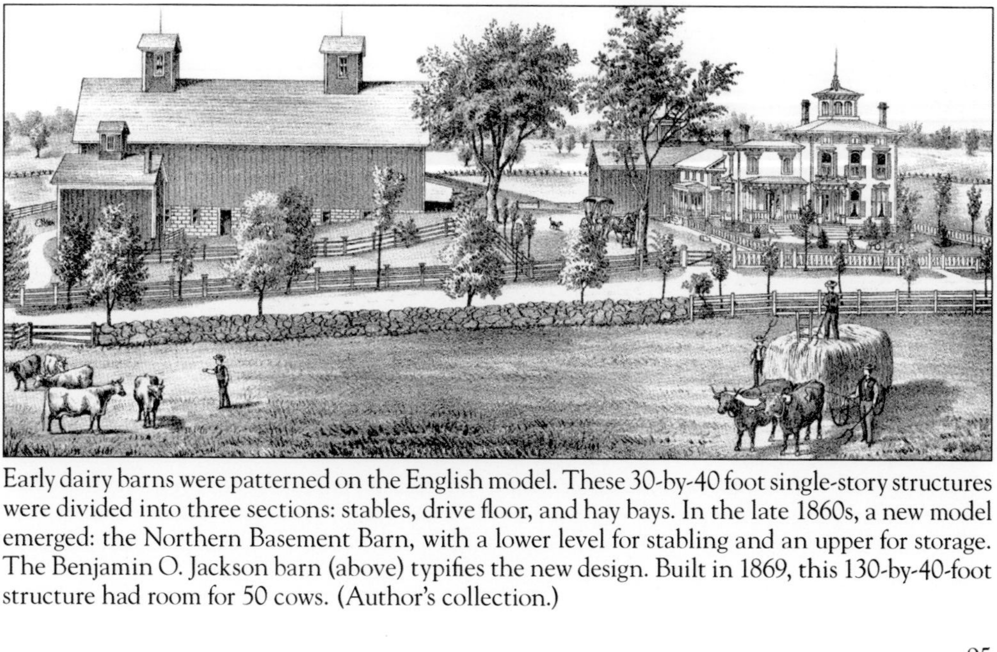

Early dairy barns were patterned on the English model. These 30-by-40 foot single-story structures were divided into three sections: stables, drive floor, and hay bays. In the late 1860s, a new model emerged: the Northern Basement Barn, with a lower level for stabling and an upper for storage. The Benjamin O. Jackson barn (above) typifies the new design. Built in 1869, this 130-by-40-foot structure had room for 50 cows. (Author's collection.)

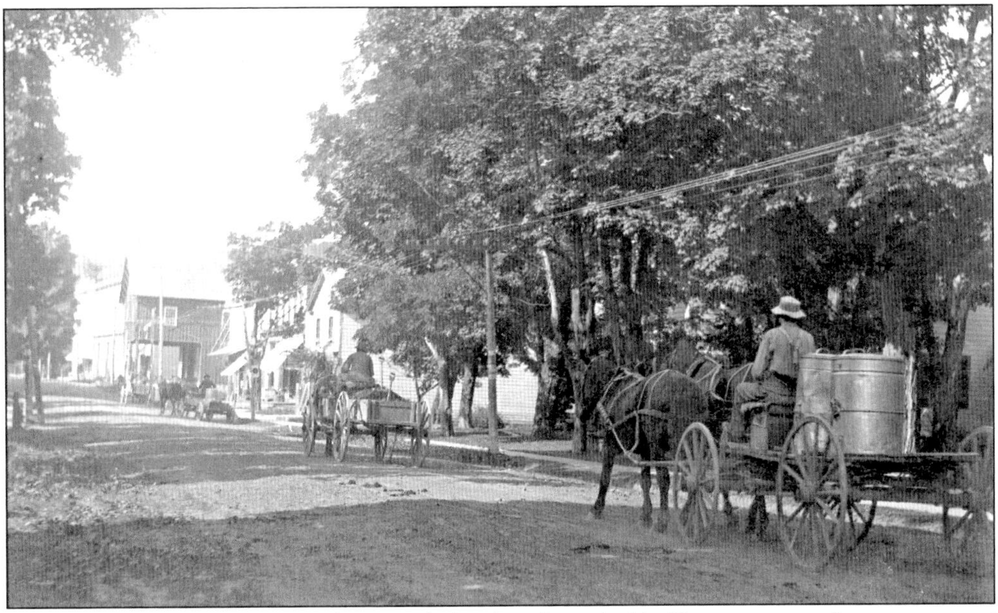

Until the late 1860s, cheese making tended to be a household affair, requiring the assistance of the entire family. For example, in 1850, John and Mary McClusky of Boonville milked 37 cows and made 6,000 pounds of cheese. To accomplish this, the couple needed the help of their five children, aged 11 to 20. The photograph above shows a farmer delivering milk in Constableville. (Courtesy of Larry Myers.)

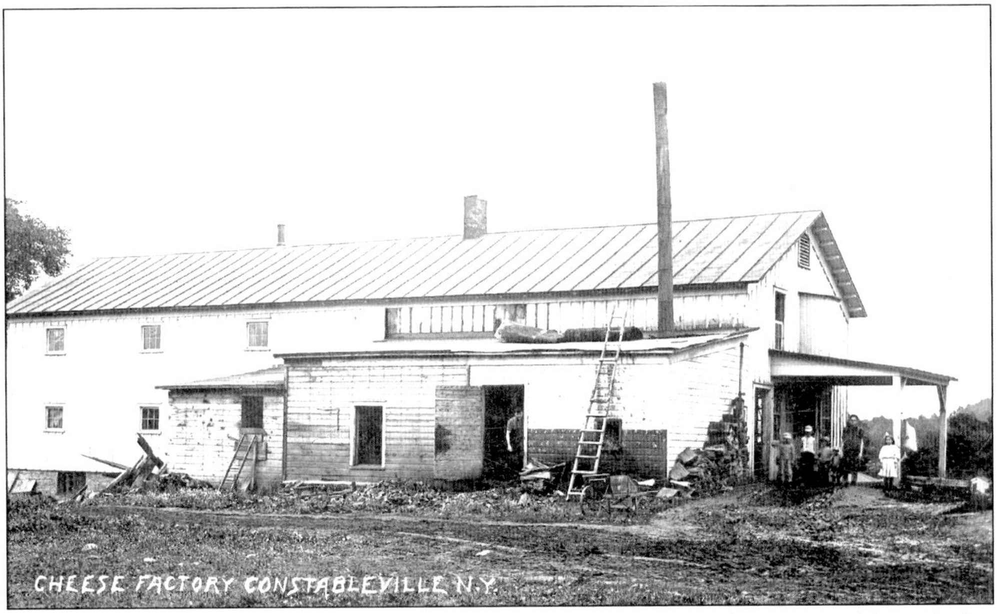

Cheese making households began to disappear as centralized cheese factories proliferated after the Civil War. Farmers frequently set up joint-stock companies with elected officers, head cheese makers, hired help, and salesmen. By pooling the milk of 300 to 600 cows, a medium-sized factory could produce 100,000 to 200,000 pounds of cheese each season. The cheese factory shown here was on the Seth Miller farm on North Street in Constableville. (Courtesy of Larry Myers.)

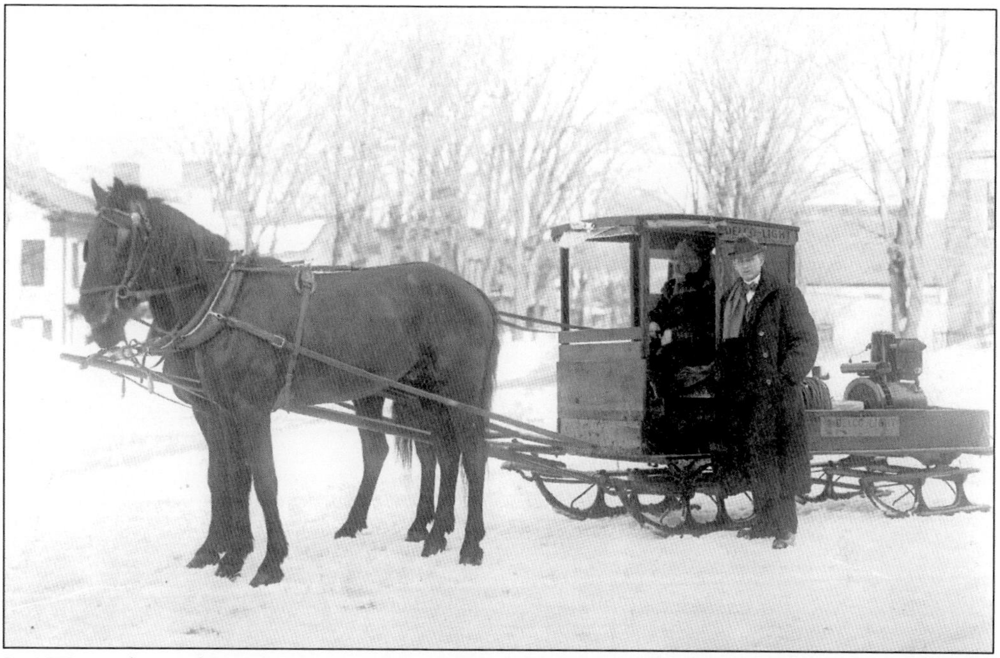

In 1919, an electric line was strung to Polaris Springs—the first outside the village limits—but rural electrification was not complete until the 1940s. Portable electric-generating units were available, however. In 1909, Delco founder Charles F. Kettering marketed a line of single-cylinder engines powered by kerosene and cooled by air. This photograph dates from 1915. (Author's collection.)

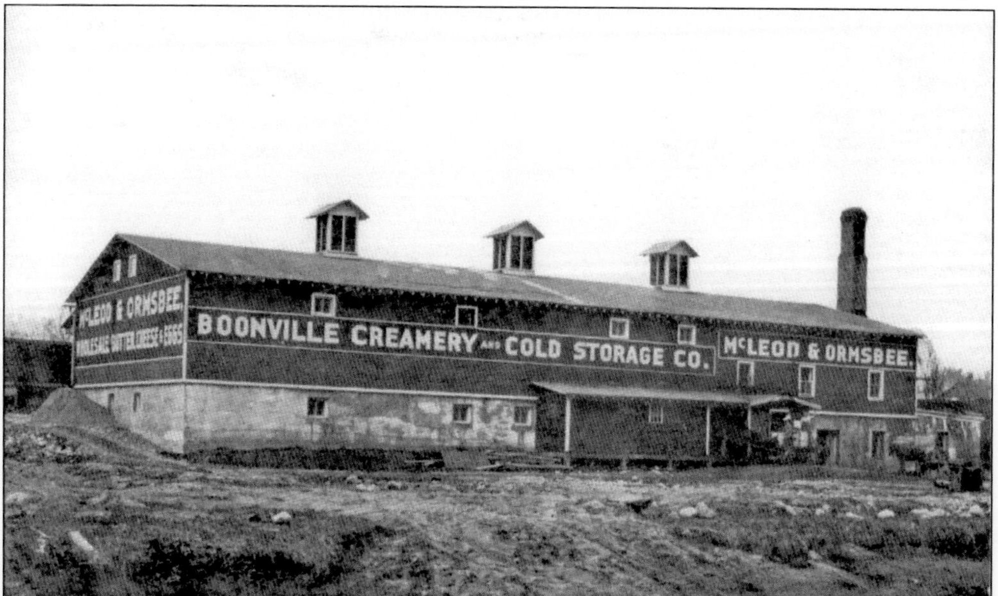

In 1911, John E. Ormsbee and Wesley McLeod founded the Boonville Creamery and Cold Storage Company. Located south of Bridge Street (Park Avenue) between the canal and the railroad, the facility was sold to the Rogers Milk Corporation in 1920 and converted into a condensery. The plant failed in 1923 and was then conveyed to the United Milk Products Company of Cleveland. (Courtesy of Larry Myers.)

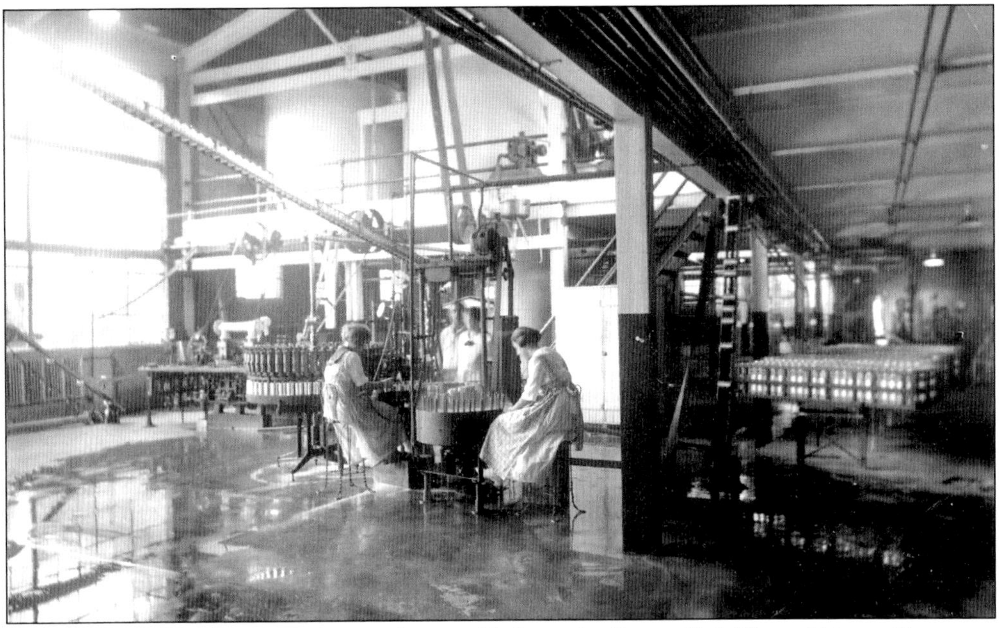

Benjamin A. Capron was instrumental in establishing the Boonville Milk and Cream Company near the junction of the Black River Canal and the Erie Canal feeder. Built in 1903, this was the first cold storage plant in town. The site was purchased by Fort Schuyler Farms in 1924 and by Sheffield Farms in 1934. The photograph above shows women processing milk at the Boonville Creamery. (Courtesy of Boonville Historical Club.)

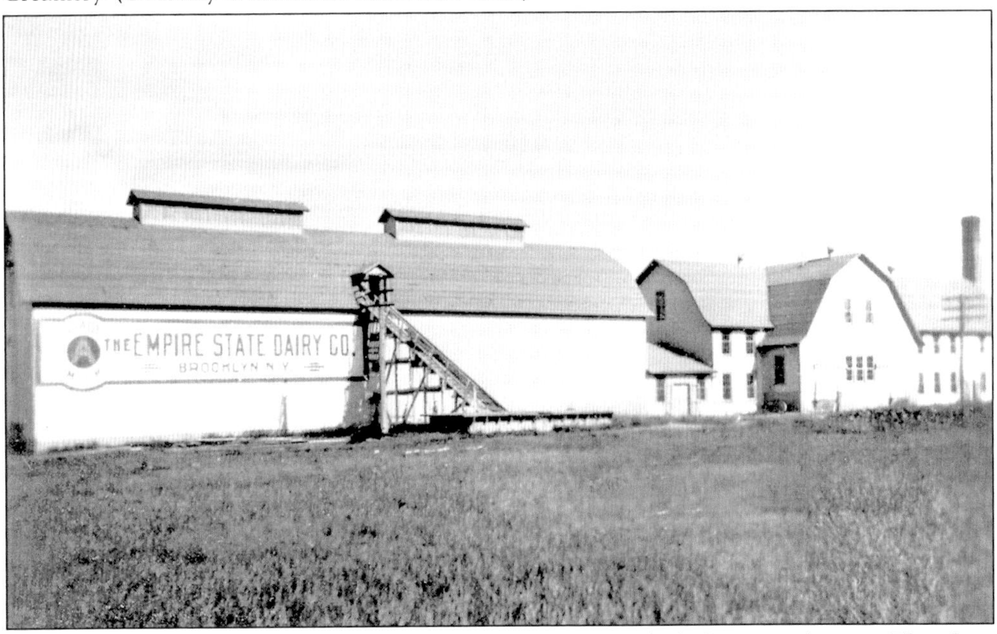

In 1922, the Boonville Dairy Company opened at the east end of Thornton Avenue. The plant was sold to Empire State Dairy Company (1922) and then to Dairymen's League Cooperative Association (1924). Following the milk strike of 1933, the plant closed for a year but reopened as Boonville Farms Co-Operative. By 1936, it had 165 patrons and processed 1,000 cases of milk daily. (Courtesy of Ed Fynmore.)

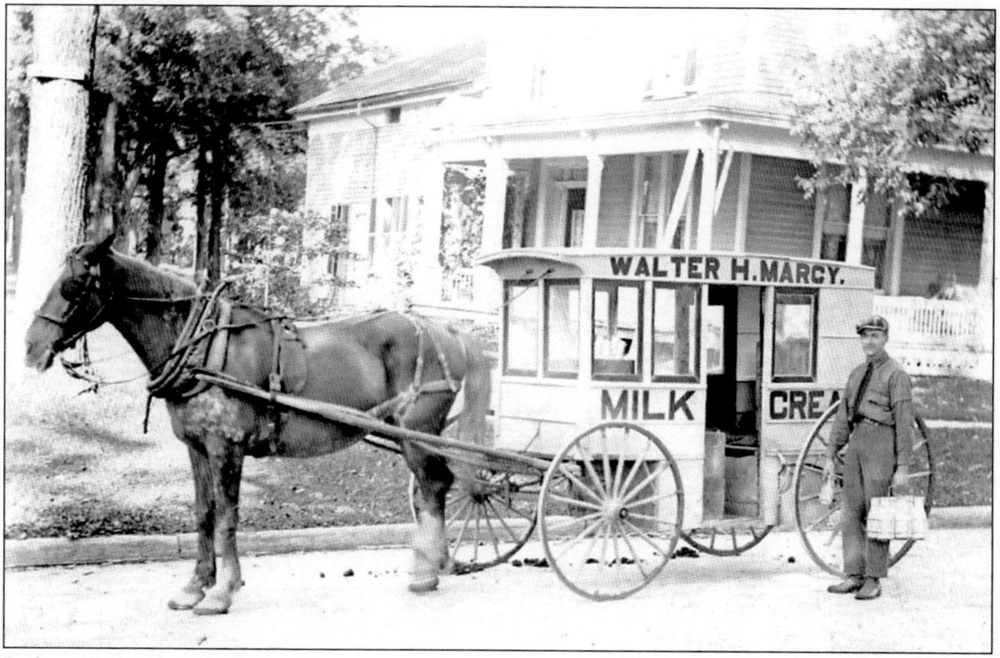

Before 1880, when milk bottles came into use, dairymen ladled milk directly from a 40-gallon can into customers' containers. Local dairies continued to use horse-drawn delivery vans into the 1930s. The 1919 photograph above shows Adolph Marcy working the family milk route. (Courtesy of Ed Fynmore.)

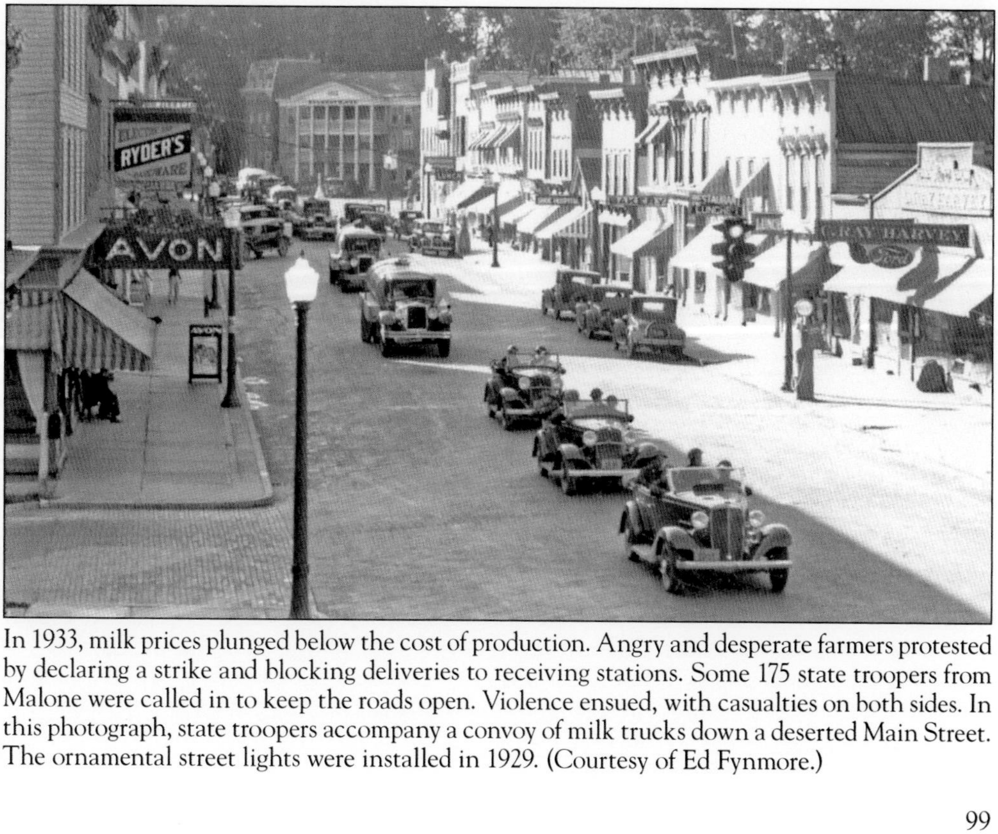

In 1933, milk prices plunged below the cost of production. Angry and desperate farmers protested by declaring a strike and blocking deliveries to receiving stations. Some 175 state troopers from Malone were called in to keep the roads open. Violence ensued, with casualties on both sides. In this photograph, state troopers accompany a convoy of milk trucks down a deserted Main Street. The ornamental street lights were installed in 1929. (Courtesy of Ed Fynmore.)

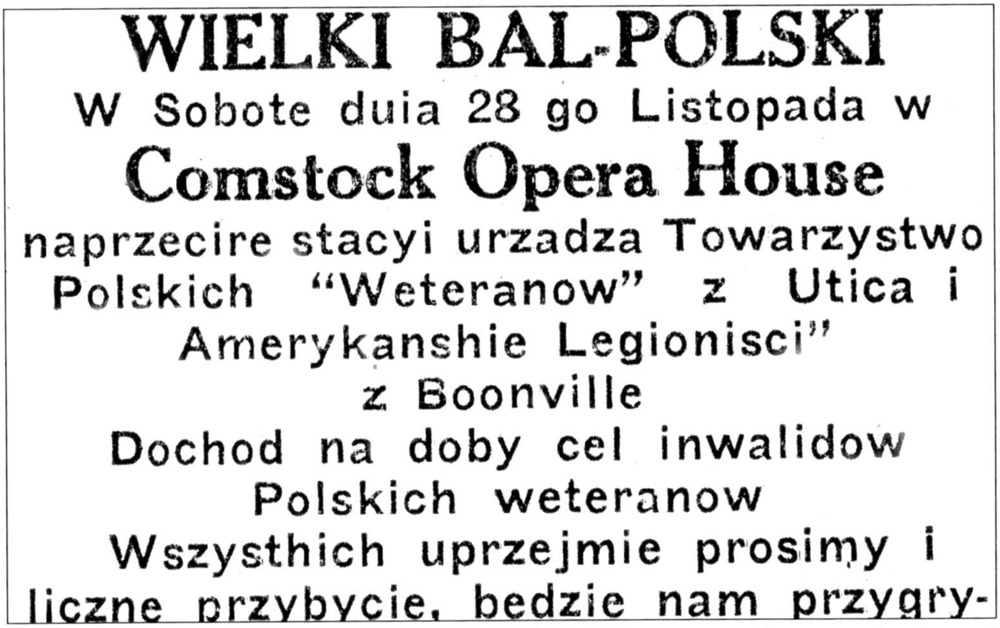

Around 1915, many Polish immigrants, preferring farming to mining or factory work, relocated in the Boonville area. This advertisement for a Saturday night dance at the Comstock Opera House is taken from the November 26, 1931, issue of the *Boonville Herald*. Today the most frequently claimed ancestries are German (23 percent), Irish (21 percent), Polish (14 percent), English (12 percent), French (9 percent), and Italian (7 percent). (Author's collection.)

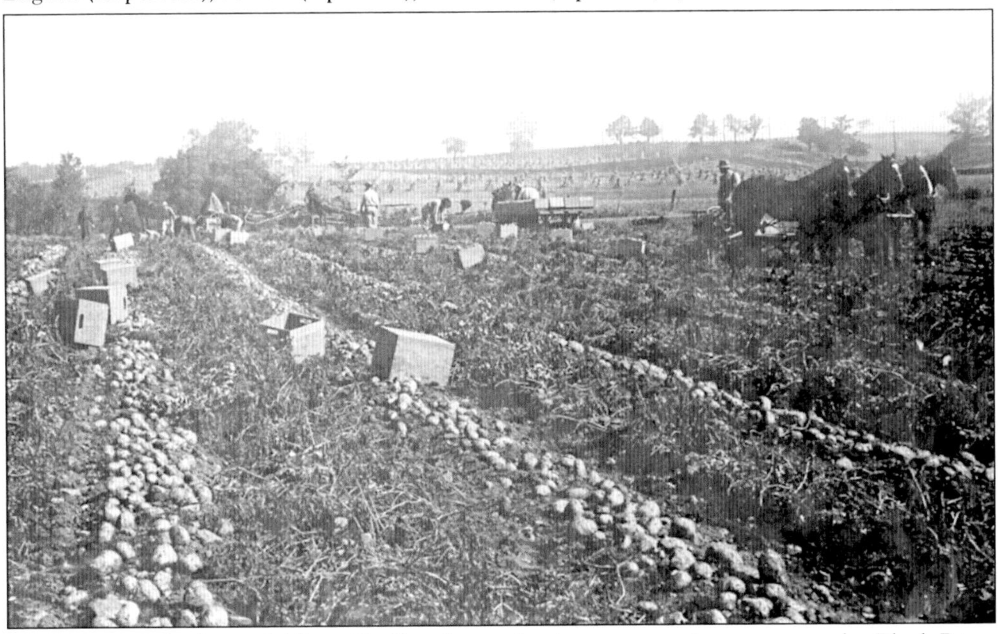

In the 1870s, Charles and Albert Traffarn began buying potatoes for export on the Black River Canal. As markets developed, potatoes became an important local crop. In 1882, for example, some 185,000 bushels of potatoes were shipped to New York City, the South, and Bermuda. At that time, growers might spend 25¢ to produce a bushel of potatoes for which they would receive 40¢ to 80¢. (Author's collection.)

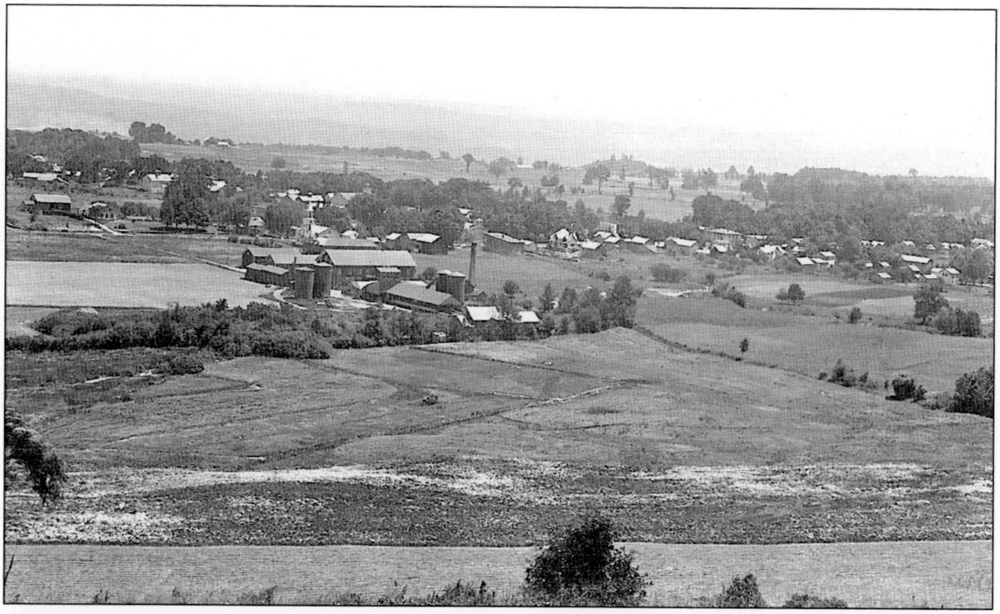

The Turin Canning and Pickling Company (1885–1911) planted corn, beans, peas, pumpkins, tomatoes, and berries on land rented from local farmers. The factory, located on Turin's Charles Street, was an important source of seasonal employment. In 1893, for example, 150 employees—mostly women—processed 1,200 wagon loads of corn, turning out 600,000 cans of finished product. (Courtesy of Larry Myers.)

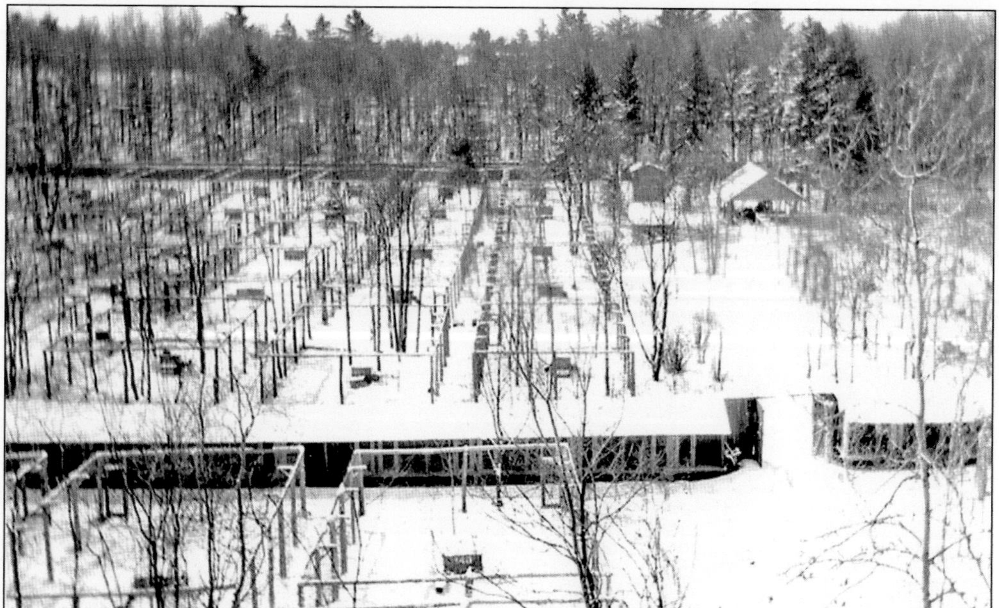

In 1920, Central New York Fur Company opened a 260-acre silver fox farm south of the village off New York State Route 12. Veterinarian W. A. Young lived on the premises and supervised the operation—reputedly, the largest in the country. At the time, a pair of registered silver fox breeding pups sold for about $1,250. In the early 1930s, the Great Depression and changing taste in fashion led to the demise of local fox farms. (Courtesy of Vincent T. Fitch.)

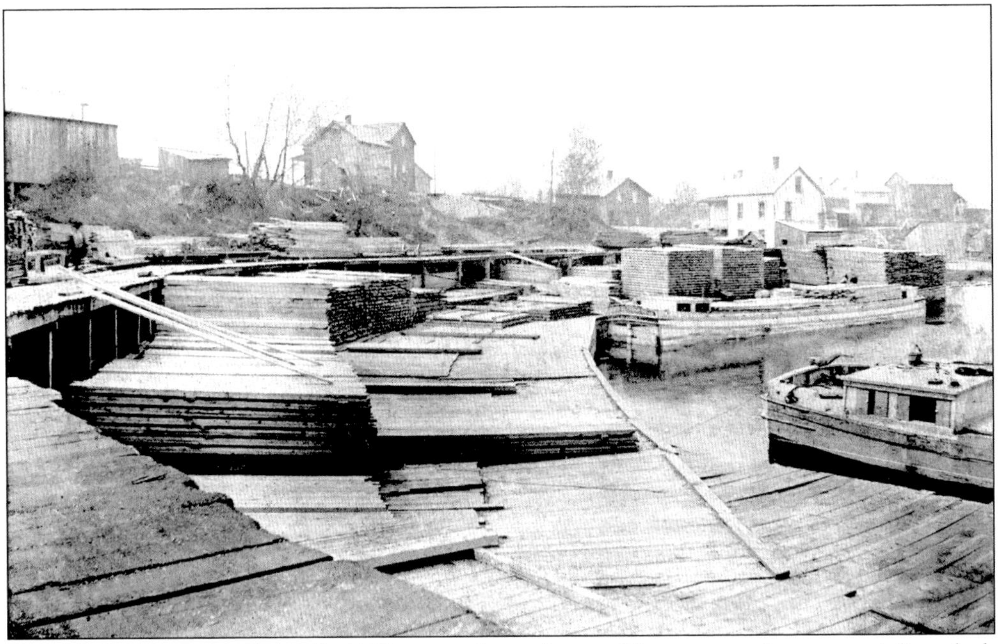

The Black River Canal (1850–1922) opened nearly a million acres of western Adirondack forestland to logging. For the first time, local sawmills were able to ship their lumber to distant markets, most notably Albany in the east and the Tonawandas in the west. In this photograph, canal boats dock at a sawmill on Forestport Pond. (Courtesy of Woodgate Free Library.)

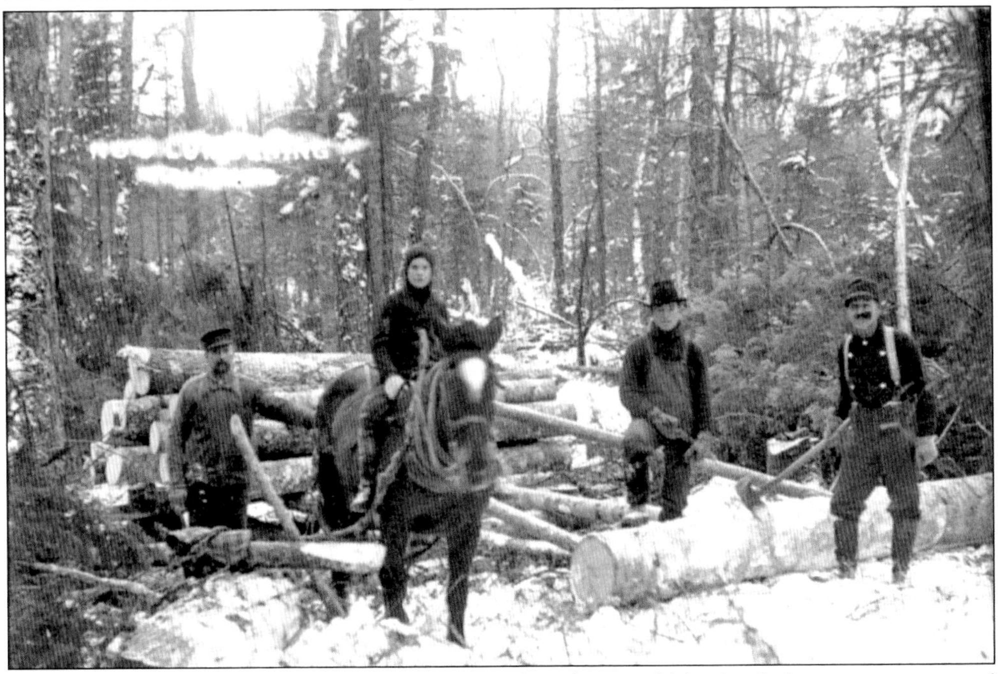

Logging was typically done during the winter when logs could be hauled over snow-covered roads to streams. There they were floated downstream with the arrival of the spring thaw. The most sought-after wood was spruce, which was cut into 13-foot-4-inch logs called "markets." (Courtesy of Larry Myers.)

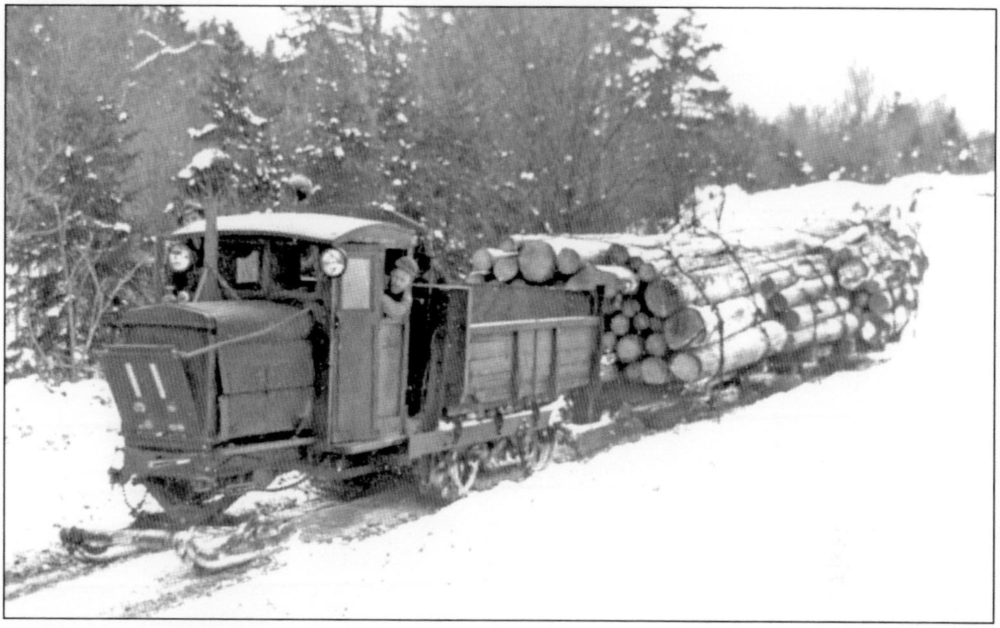

In 1918, the Gould Paper Company was the first outfit to use Linn Tractors in the Adirondacks. These gasoline-powered tractors—first manufactured in 1917 at Morris—were propelled by treads and steered with ski-like runners in front. One Linn Tractor, it was said, could do the work of 20 teams of horses. Moreover, the Linn Tractor could haul logs up steep grades, something horses could not do. (Courtesy of Ed Fynmore.)

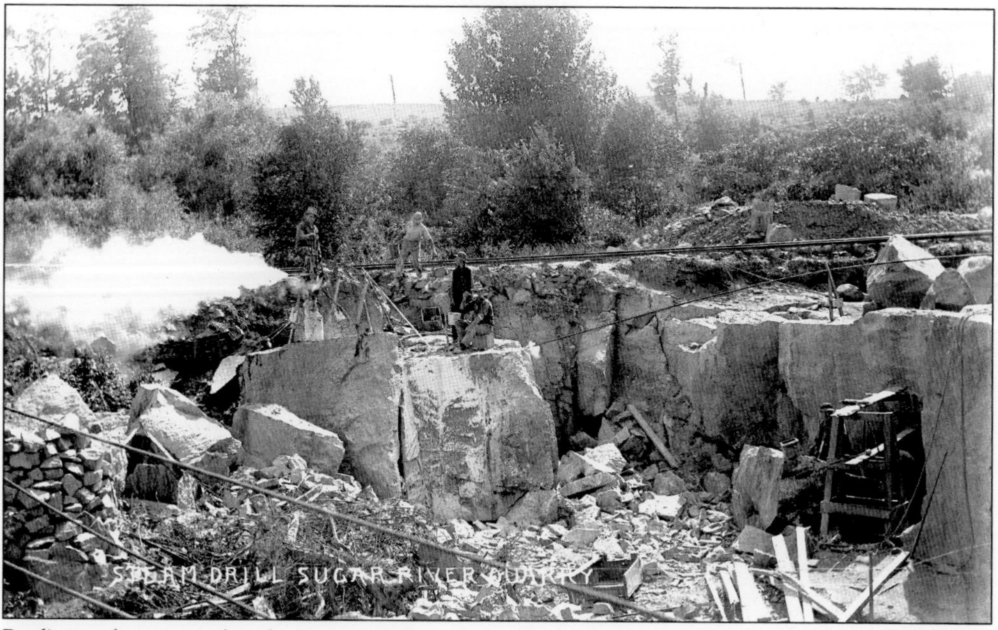

Bird's eye limestone has been quarried at Sugar River for over 200 years. Area builders used the semicrystalline limestone for residential walls and foundations. In the 1840s and 1850s, contractors used the material to build locks on the Black River Canal between Boonville and Lyons Falls. The limestone, part of the Black River formation, was deposited some 450 million years ago during the Ordovician era. (Courtesy of Ed Fynmore.)

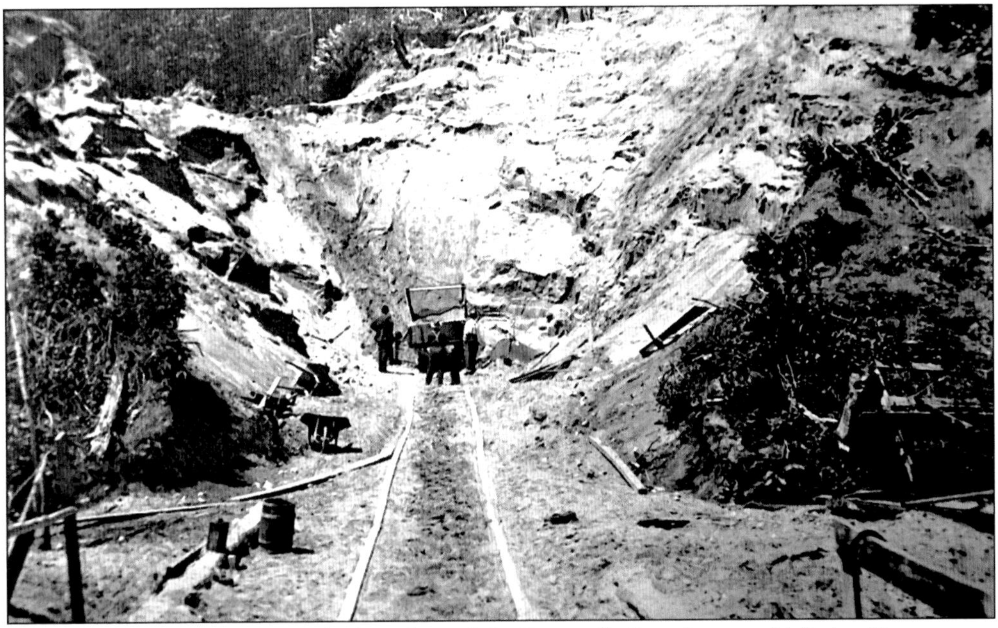

In 1865, Joseph R. Tharratt and others formed the Boonville Petroleum and Mining Company to drill for natural gas. The company discovered a gas lens on the Golden Road, but the drill broke and could not be retrieved. In the early 20th century, small quantities of silver were mined near Fall Brook. Sand, however, has traditionally been Boonville's most valuable mineral resource. (Courtesy of Ed Fynmore.)

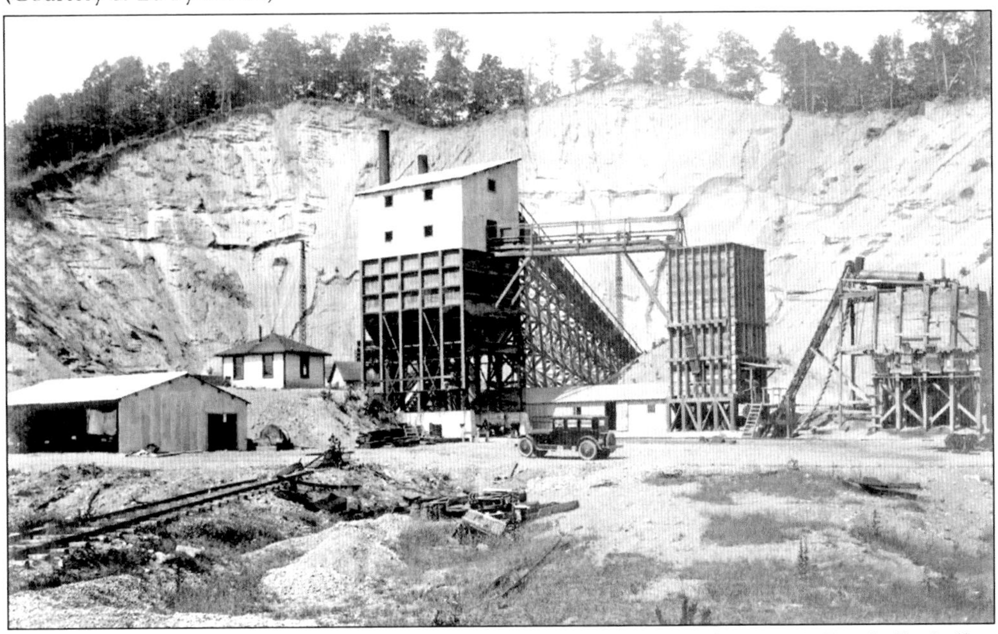

Located on the Black River Canal, the Melissa Draper pit opened in 1885. Frank E. Gallup operated the pit from 1910 until 1920 when Harold V. Owens acquired a half interest. Owens later bought Gallup out and reorganized the firm as the Boonville Sand Corporation. During the 1920s, a rail spur was built, and the plant was mechanized. Boonville Sand Corporation merged with Eastern Rock Products in 1929. (Courtesy of Ed Fynmore.)

Eight

COUNTRY ROADS

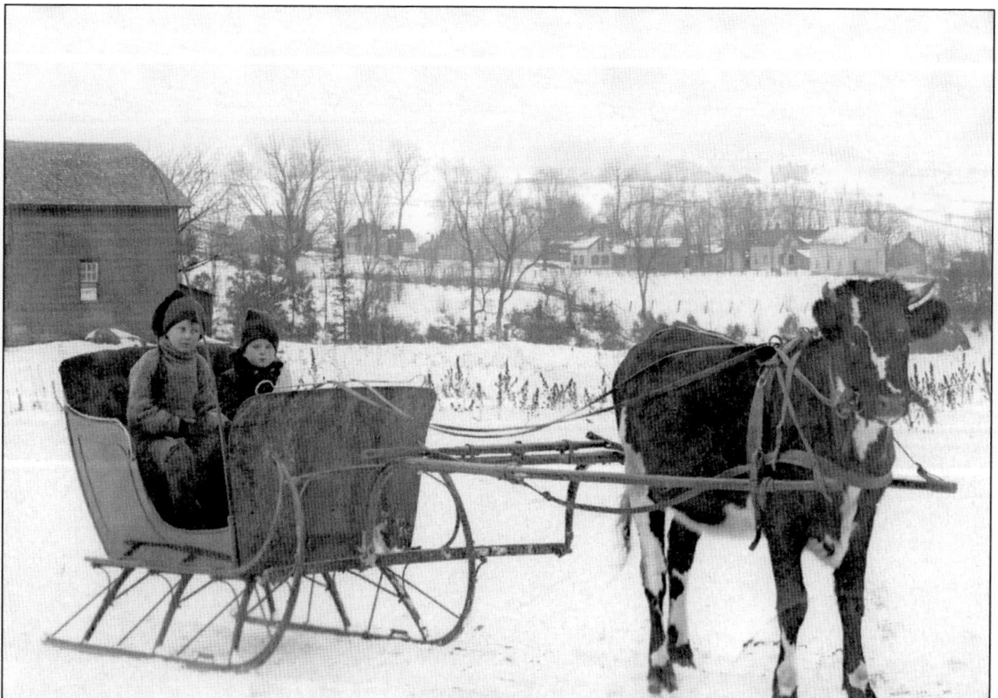

Before the late 1920s, when the use of mechanized snow plows became widespread, rural residents often banded together to keep the roads open. Ox- and horse-drawn sleighs remained an important means of winter transport well into the automobile age. When snowdrifts blocked roads, local laws permitted sleighs to cut across fields regardless of any objections landowners might have. (Courtesy of Larry Myers.)

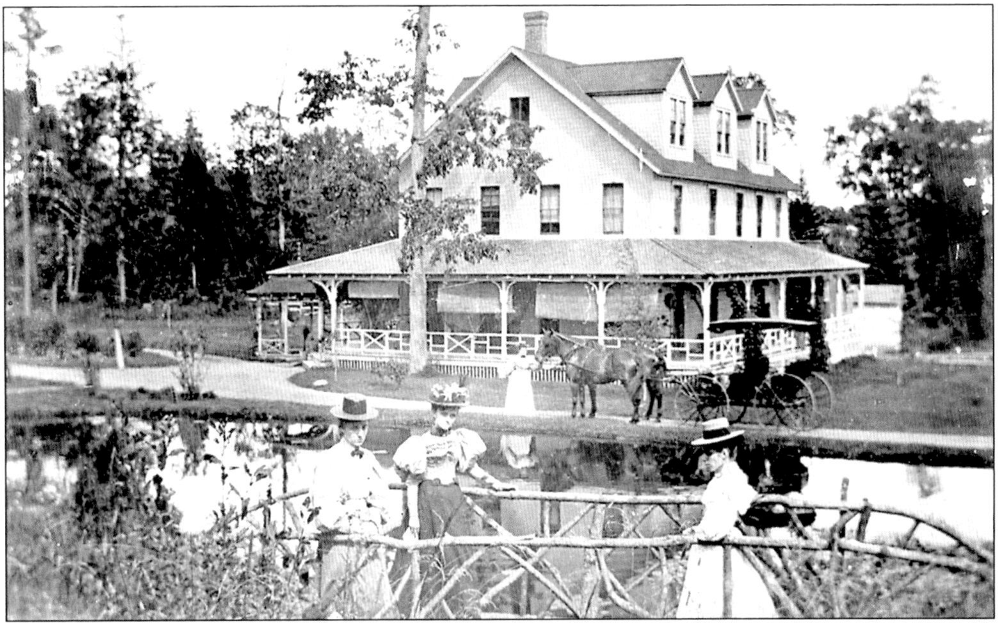

Dr. Clement T. Guillaume ran Sulphur Springs, a sanitarium located about two miles south of the village. There he organized the Boonville Mineral Springs Company in 1899 and sold bottled lithia spring water under the name Polaris. For several years, the New York Central Railroad served this water in its dining cars. After his death, Frederick Guillaume operated the plant, and in 1921, George J. Groh bought the bottling works from him. (Courtesy of Erwin Library.)

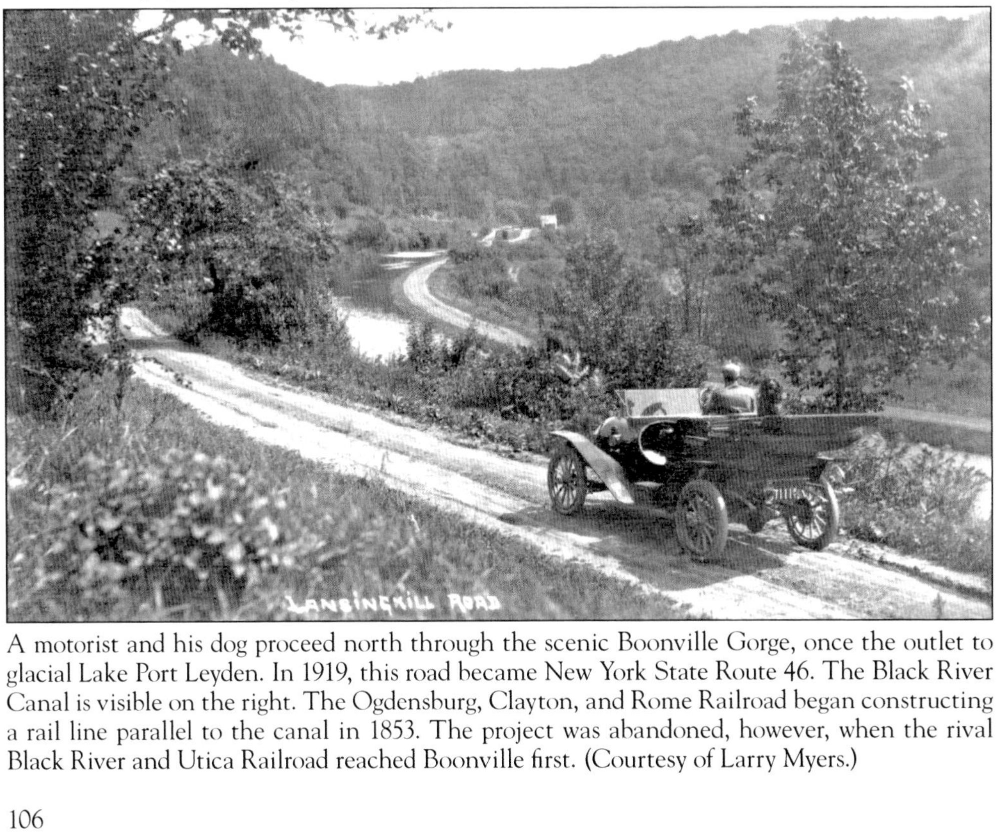

A motorist and his dog proceed north through the scenic Boonville Gorge, once the outlet to glacial Lake Port Leyden. In 1919, this road became New York State Route 46. The Black River Canal is visible on the right. The Ogdensburg, Clayton, and Rome Railroad began constructing a rail line parallel to the canal in 1853. The project was abandoned, however, when the rival Black River and Utica Railroad reached Boonville first. (Courtesy of Larry Myers.)

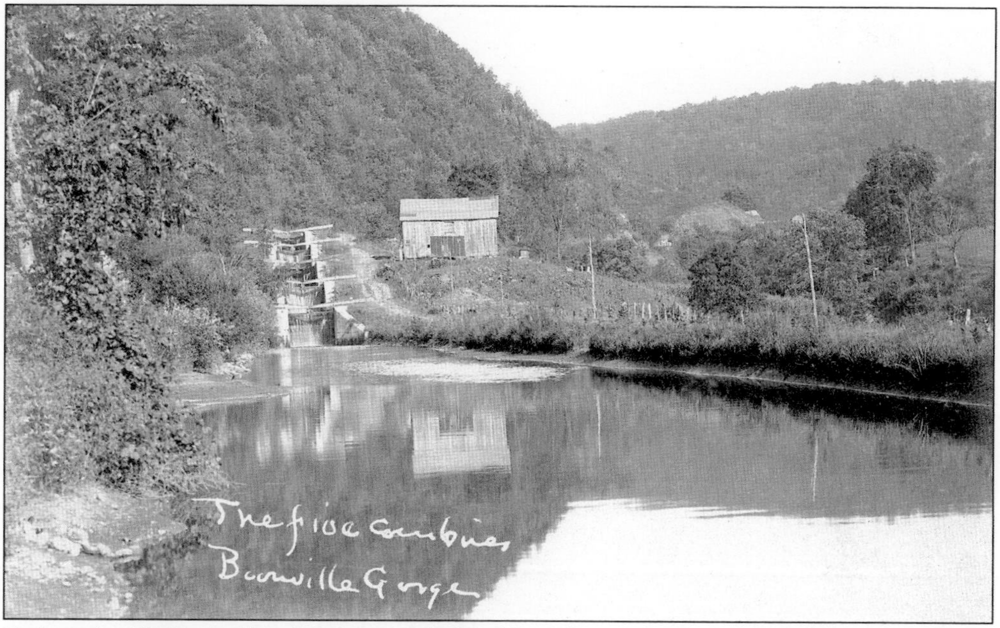

Built in the 1840s, the Five Combines, a flight of five adjacent locks, is on the Black River Canal about seven miles south of Boonville. Walter D. Edmonds immortalized the Five Combines in *Rome Haul* (1929). It is here that Dan Harrow vanquishes canal bully Jotham Klore but loses his sweetheart when he decides to abandon canalling and settle on a farm near Lyons Falls. (Courtesy of Larry Myers.)

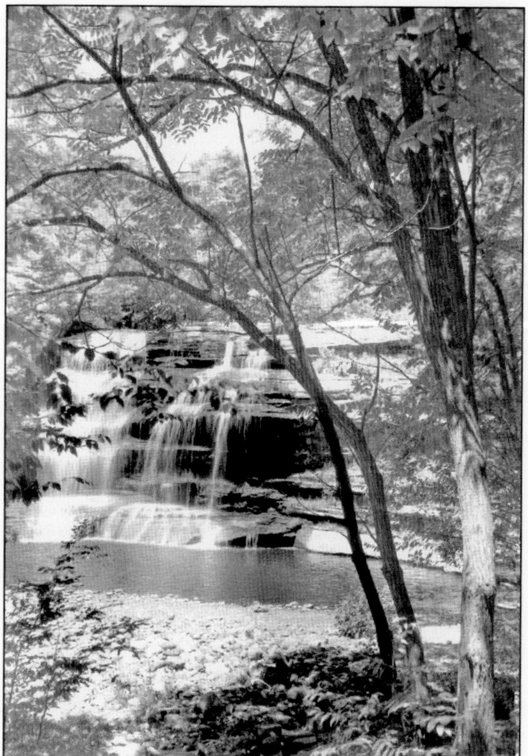

Pixley Falls State Park, located about six miles south of Boonville, was established in 1930. Built by members of the local Civilian Conservation Corps, the 372-acre park is adjacent to the Black River Canal and the former settlement of Hurlburtville. Here the Lansing Kill drops some 50 feet over Trenton limestone. (Courtesy of Oneida County Historical Society.)

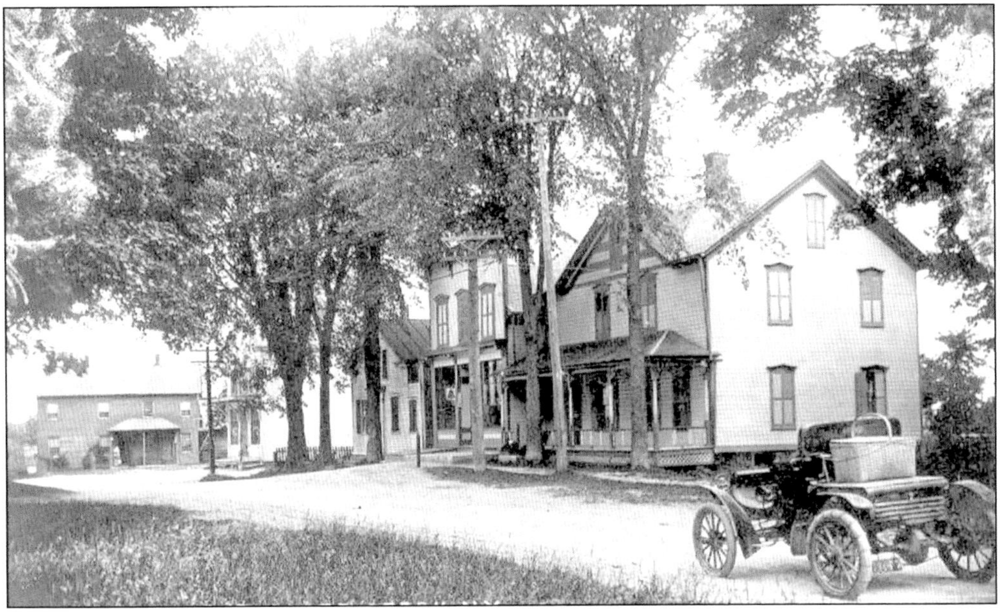

Settled about 1805 by John Platt, the village of Alder Creek lies in the southeast part of the town of Boonville. Horseback riders carried mail over this route weekly until 1819, when John Butterfield's stagecoach began running three times a week. Besides a post office, the hamlet, in 1878, had two hotels, two churches, two stores, a tannery, a carriage shop, and a shoe shop. (Courtesy of Larry Myers.)

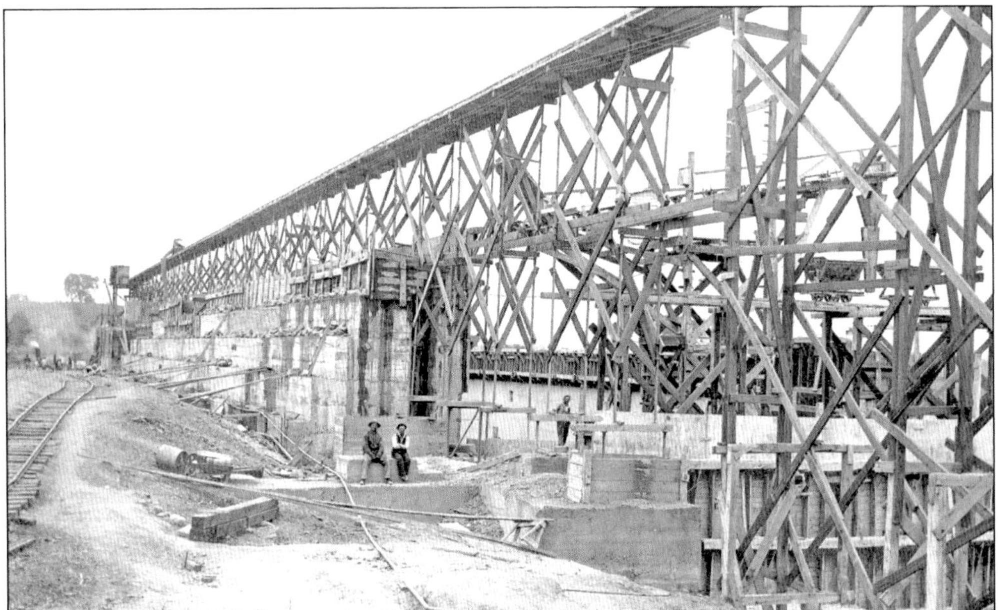

To furnish additional water for the Erie Canal, the state legislature, in 1883, ordered a new reservoir built on Black River above Forestport. Funding was inadequate, however, and the dam was not completed until December 1893. During the 1920s, the 400-acre reservoir, known as Kayuta Lake, became a popular site for summer camps. (Courtesy of Larry Myers.)

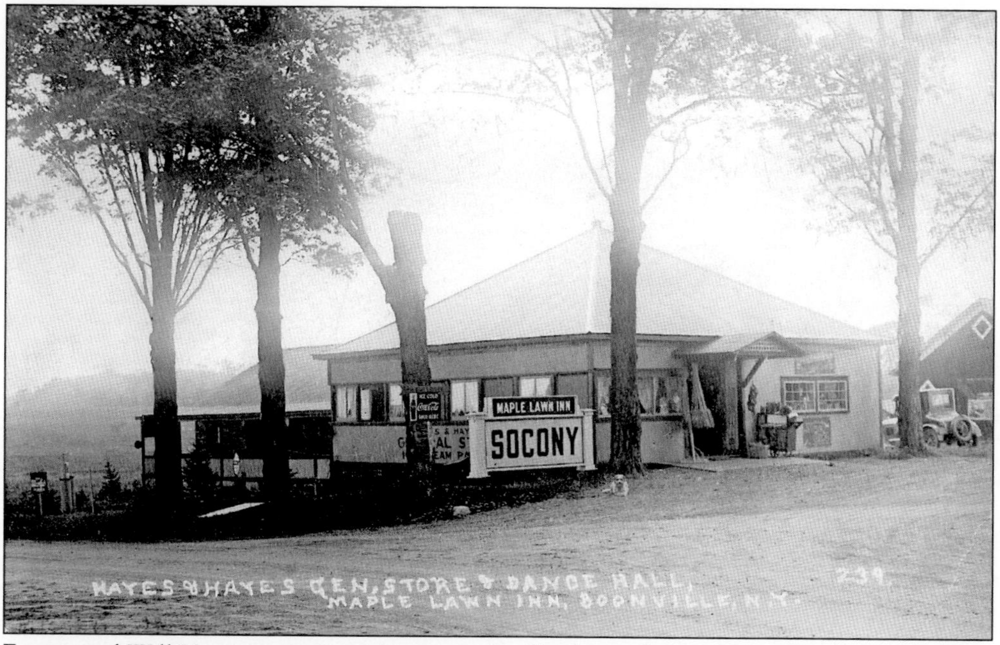

Forrest and Will Hayes ran a general store on the Hawkinsville Road. In 1926, the two cousins began holding dances in a rear annex. Three years later, they transformed their farm into Maple Lawn Golf Course. On July 27, 1931, Jack Milburn of New Hartford played 280 holes of golf in a single day—purportedly a world record. He walked an estimated 77 miles and lost six and a half pounds in body weight. (Courtesy of Larry Myers.)

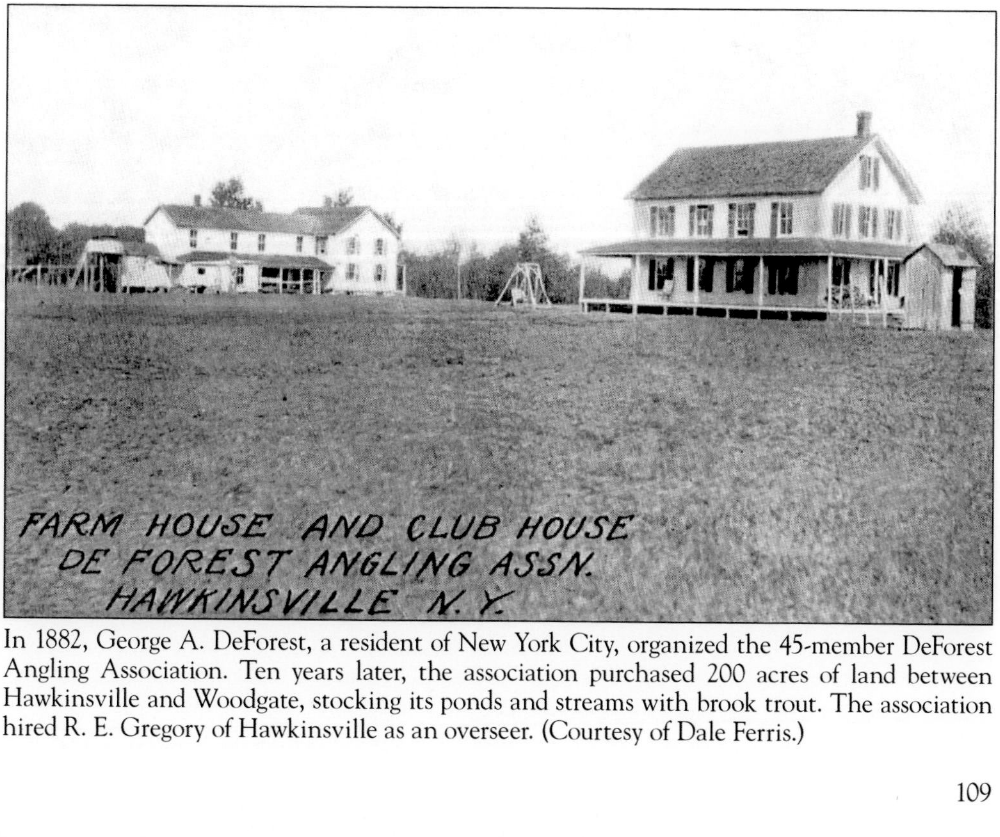

In 1882, George A. DeForest, a resident of New York City, organized the 45-member DeForest Angling Association. Ten years later, the association purchased 200 acres of land between Hawkinsville and Woodgate, stocking its ponds and streams with brook trout. The association hired R. E. Gregory of Hawkinsville as an overseer. (Courtesy of Dale Ferris.)

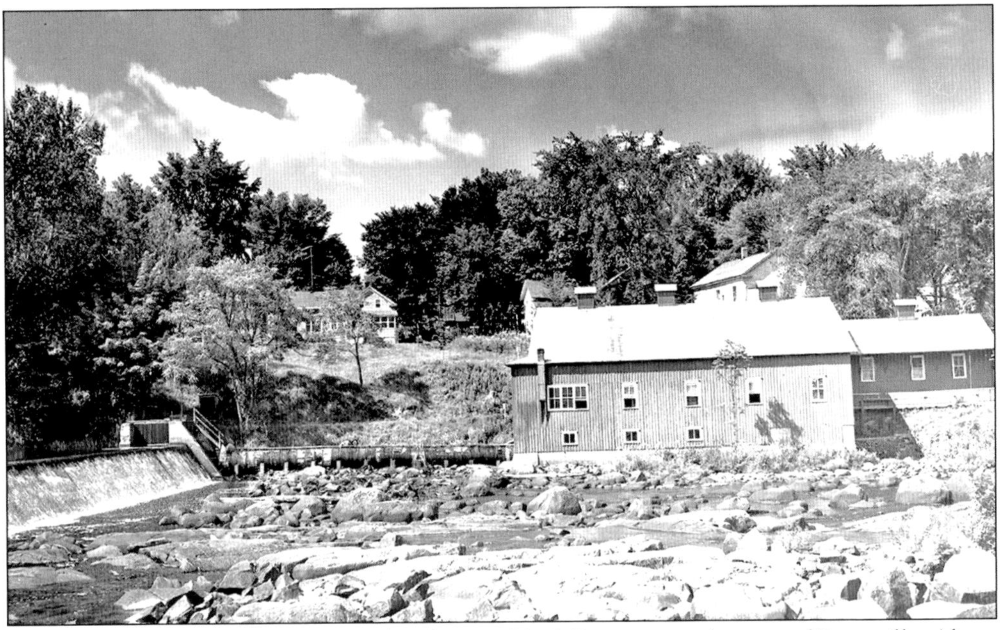

In 1824, Sterry Hawkins built a wooden dam on Black River two miles east of Boonville. About 1885, an excelsior plant began operating here. Dewitt C. West of Lowville acquired the plant in 1899 and operated it until 1910, when he sold it to Walter C. Brant, who not only enlarged and modernized the mill but replaced the wooden dam with a concrete structure in 1915. (Courtesy of Ed Fynmore.)

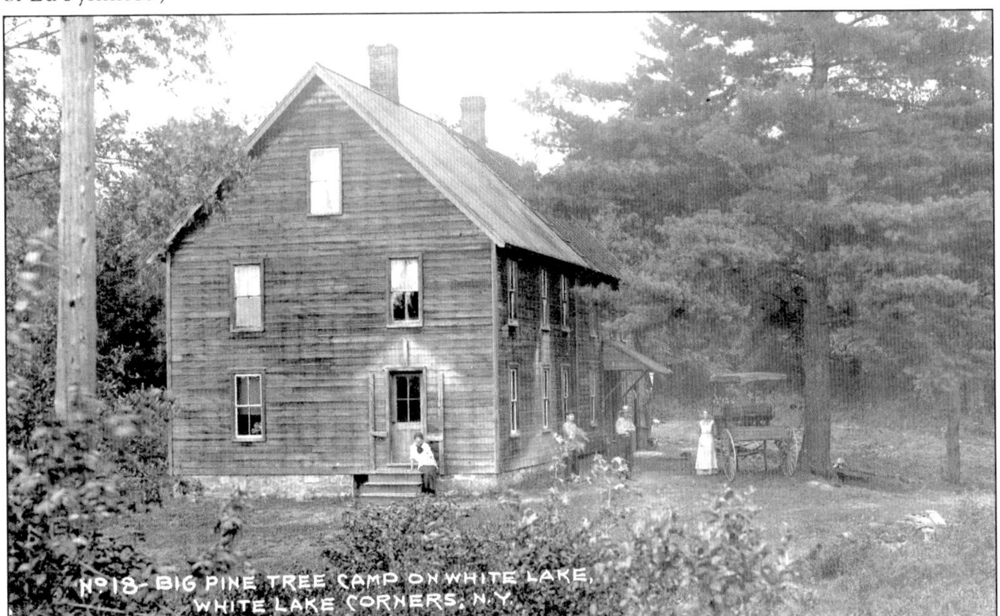

Built in 1895, Big Pine Tree Camp housed workers at the White Lake Granite Quarry. Between 1908 and 1914, Big Pine served as a seasonal home for men building New York State Route 28, the main entrance to the central Adirondacks. From 1915 to 1921, George Scheehl ran Big Pine as a summer retreat, initially charging guests $1 a day and 35¢ for meals. (Courtesy of Larry Myers.)

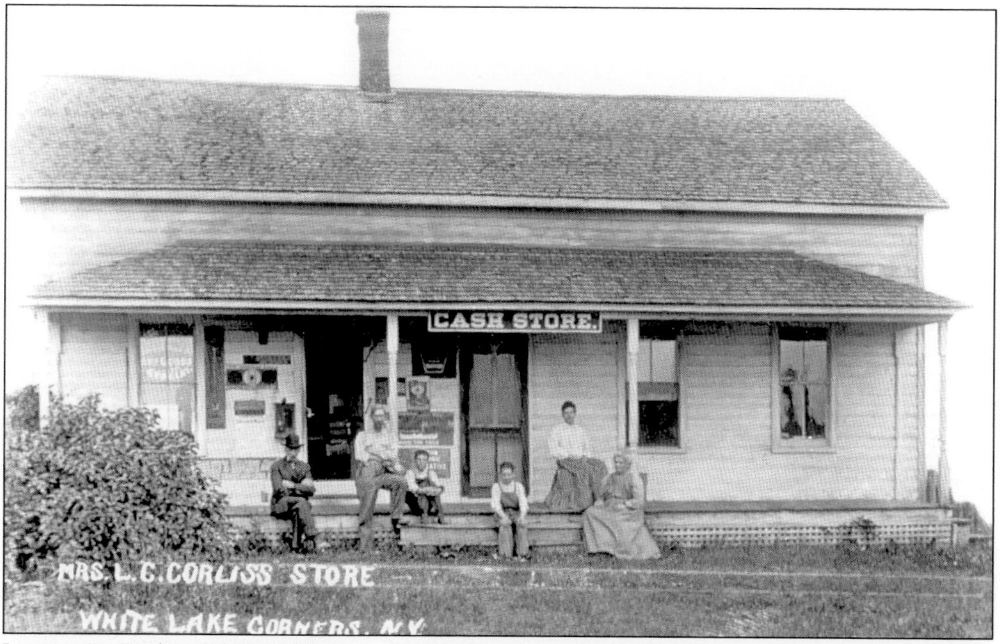

Louisa C. Corliss (1856–1938) ran a general store opposite the train station at White Lake Corners (Woodgate). The building was erected in 1878 by Charles Kronmiller. From Boonville, Woodgate could be reached by taking the 10-mile Hogsback Road, a scenic but tortuous road built atop a narrow glacial esker. Oneida County paved the road in 1934, making travel to the Fulton Chain less arduous. The photograph dates from 1912. (Courtesy of Larry Myers.)

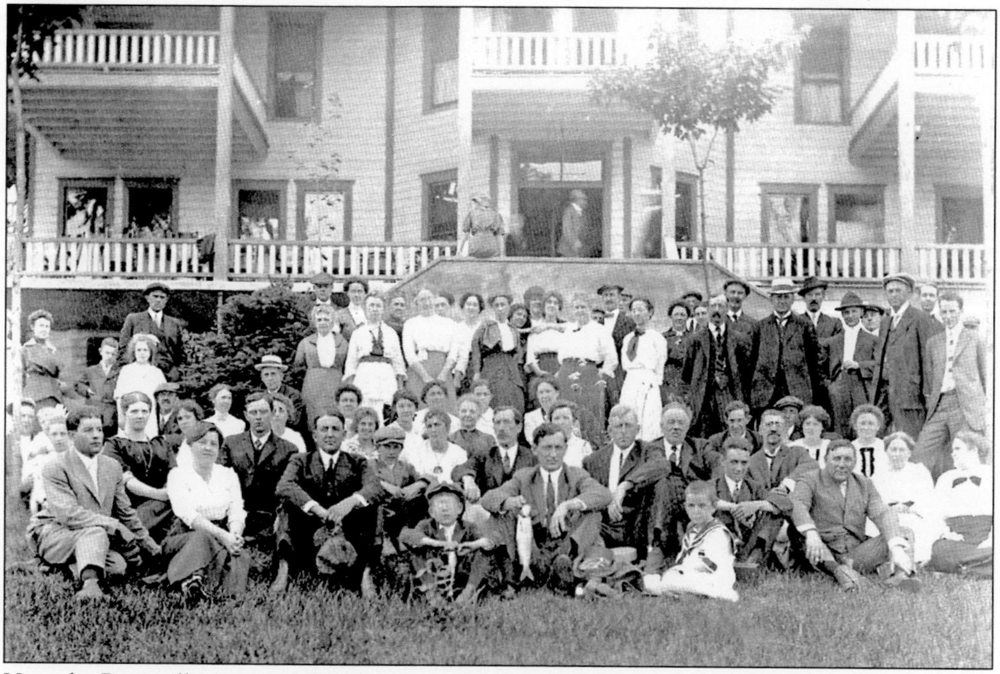

Here the Boonville Automobile Club visits the Hotel Glennmore at Big Moose Lake. Dwight B. Sperry of Watson built the hotel in 1899, naming it for his brother-in-law William Glenn. The photograph was taken by Don Ryder in 1916. (Courtesy of Ed Fynmore.)

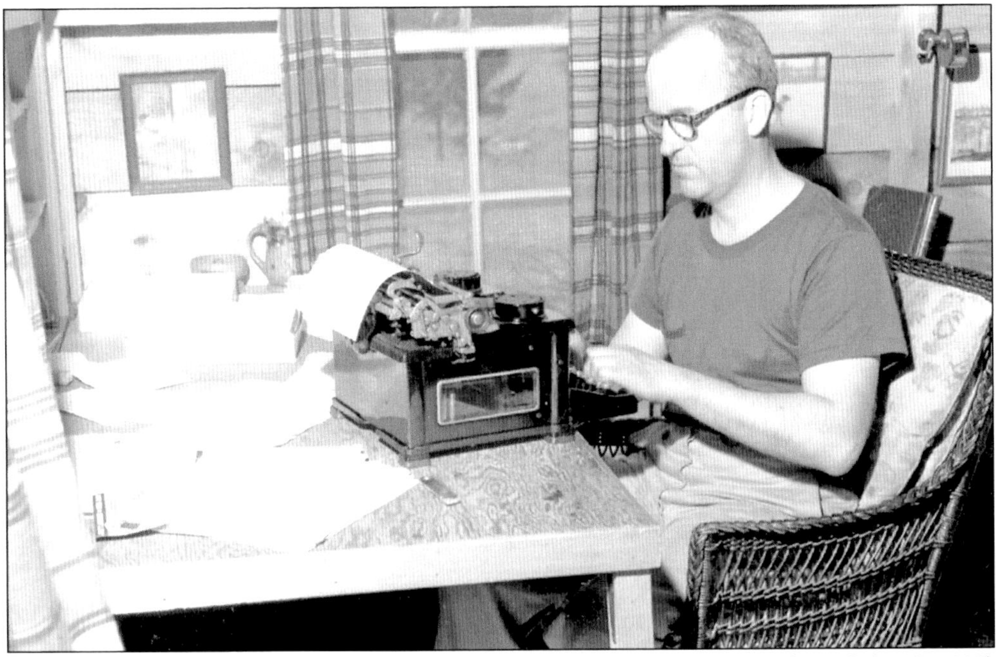

Best known for his *Drums Along the Mohawk* (1936), local author Walter D. Edmonds (1903–1999) published more than 30 books in his career, most of which are set in upstate New York. This photograph by Dante Tranquille shows Edmunds at work in his study at Northlands, located on Black River between Hawkinsville and Forestport. (Courtesy of Utica Observer-Dispatch.)

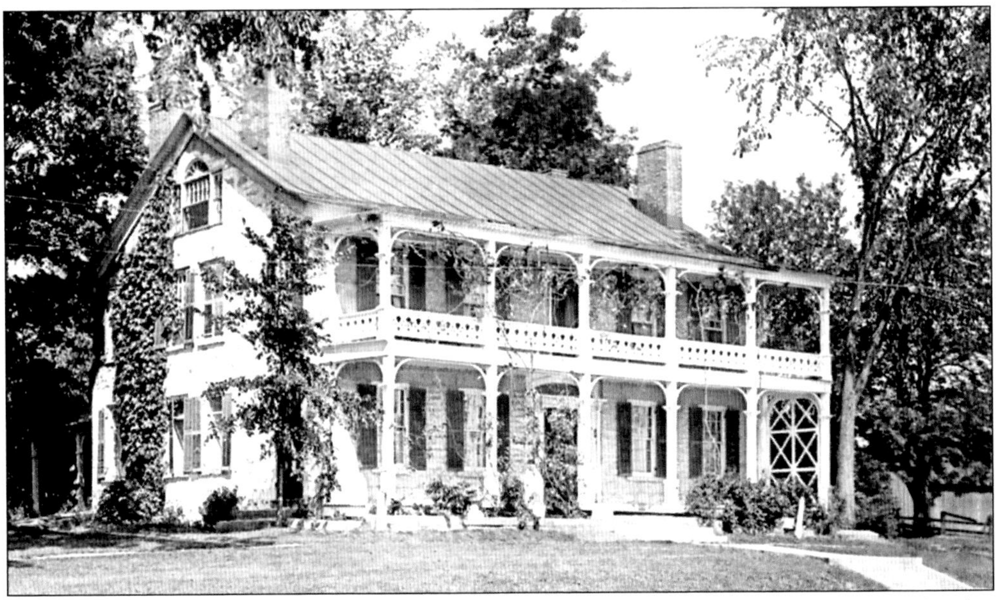

Celebrated man-of-letters Edmund Wilson (1895–1972) spent many summers in his family's Talcottville home, two miles north of Boonville. In *Upstate* (1971), Wilson claims that he discovered his literary calling there. Built from nearby Sugar River limestone around 1803, the house was acquired in 1832 by Thomas Baker, Wilson's great-grandfather. The house is situated high above Black River and enjoys a commanding view of the western Adirondacks. (Courtesy of Larry Myers.)

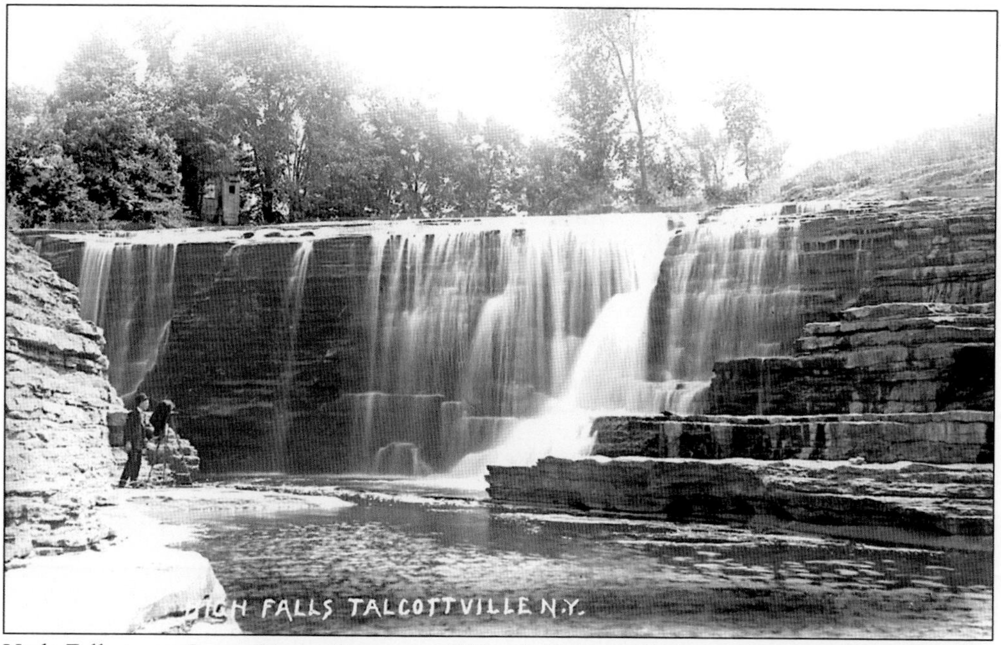

High Falls is on Sugar River adjacent to Wilson's Talcottville home. Just up the road is the settlement of Locust Grove, where C. Hart Merriam (1855–1942) grew up, practiced medicine, and wrote *Mammals of the Adirondack Region*, published in 1882 and 1884. Later, as director of the U.S. Biological Survey, Merriam became one of America's leading naturalists and is remembered today for his pioneering contributions to ecology. (Courtesy of Larry Myers.)

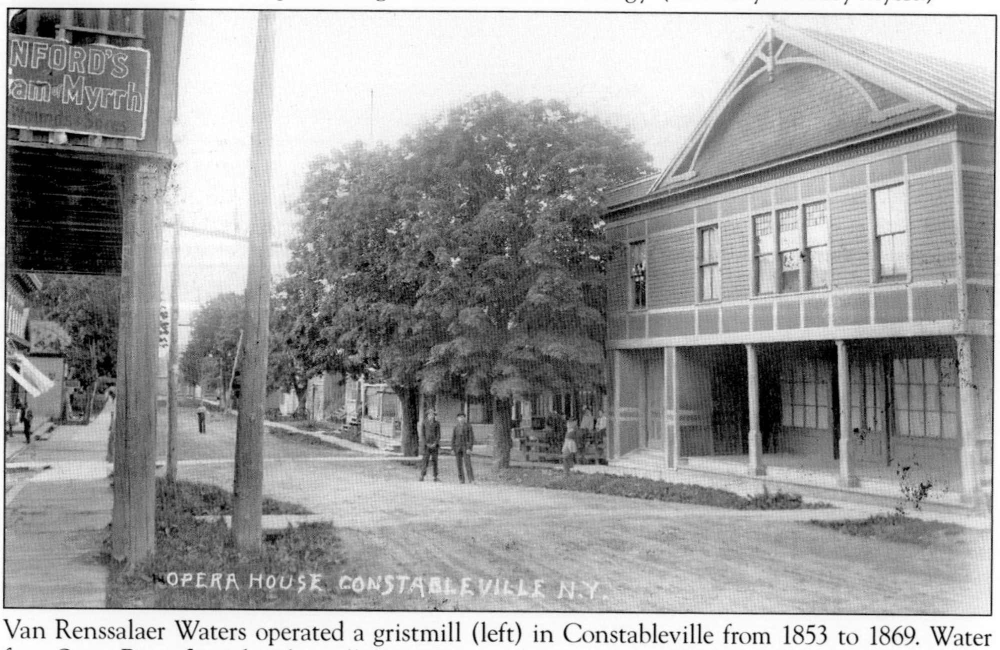

Van Renssalaer Waters operated a gristmill (left) in Constableville from 1853 to 1869. Water from Sugar River flowed to the mill through an underground conduit. Mechanics Hall, across the street, was built in the early 1860s. In 1895, the Cascade No. 1 and Deluge No. 1 fire companies purchased the building. Because the second floor often hosted dances and other community events, the building was also known as the opera house. (Courtesy of Peter Hayes.)

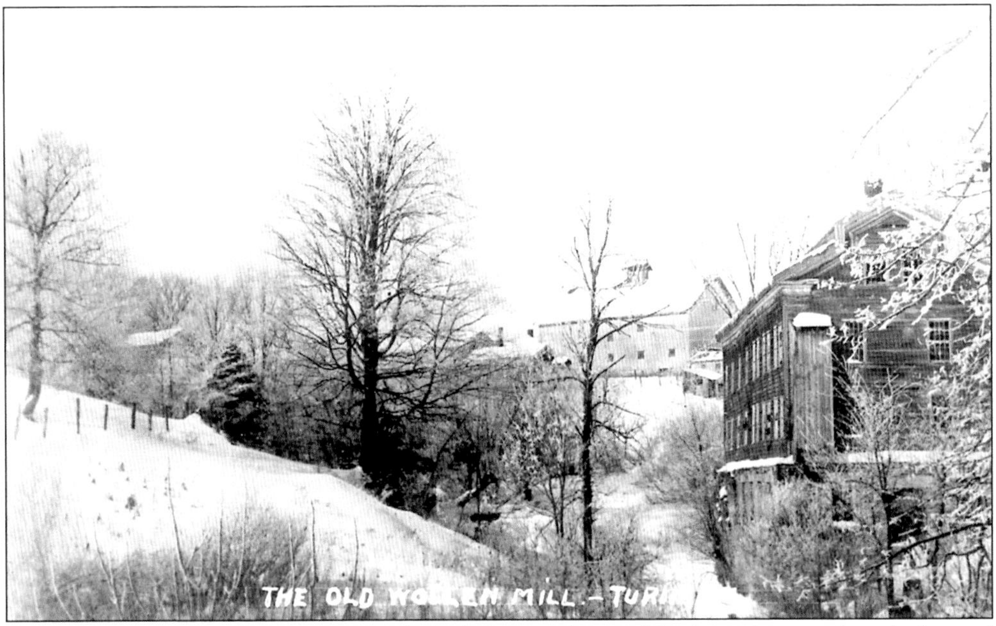

Built in 1831, the Cadwell Dewey Mill (right) manufactured high-quality woolen cloth until 1879. At its peak, the mill employed about 20 workers, most of whom lived in the settlement of Deweyville, located on Mill Creek about one and a half miles east of Turin. In 1869, a weaver might have turned out 300 to 400 yards a month and earned between 6¢ and 7¢ a yard. (Courtesy of Larry Myers.)

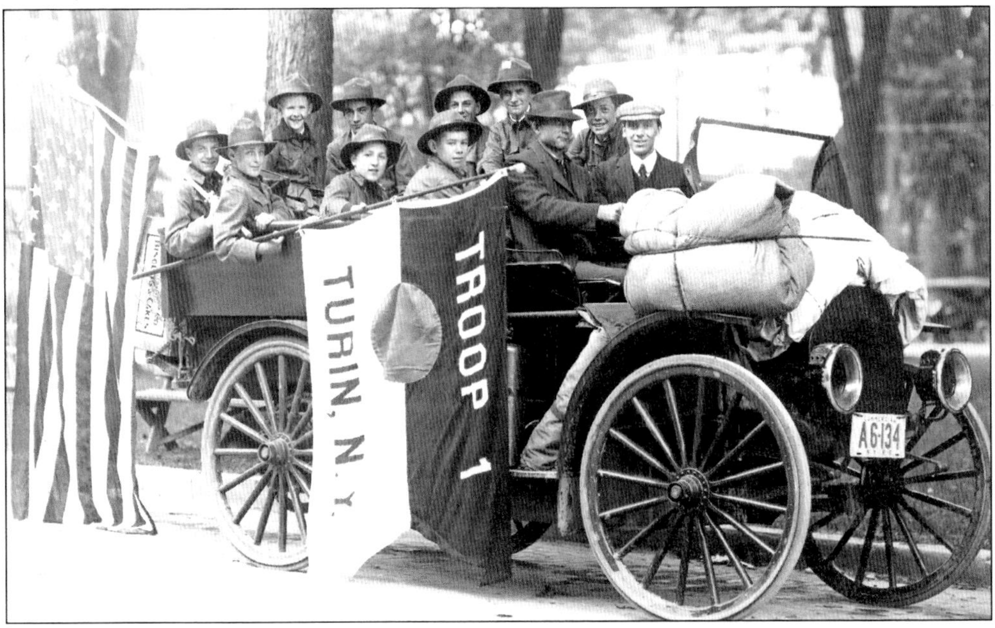

The Boonville Boy Scouts first organized in 1915 with H. G. Grubel serving as scoutmaster. In 1928, the American Legion began sponsoring the Boy Scouts, and a new 25-member troop was formed with Maurice Hammond as leader. Eleanor E. Felts organized a Girl Scout troop a few years later. In the 1916 photograph above, members of Turin Boy Scout Troop No. 1 are dressed for a parade. (Courtesy of Larry Myers.)

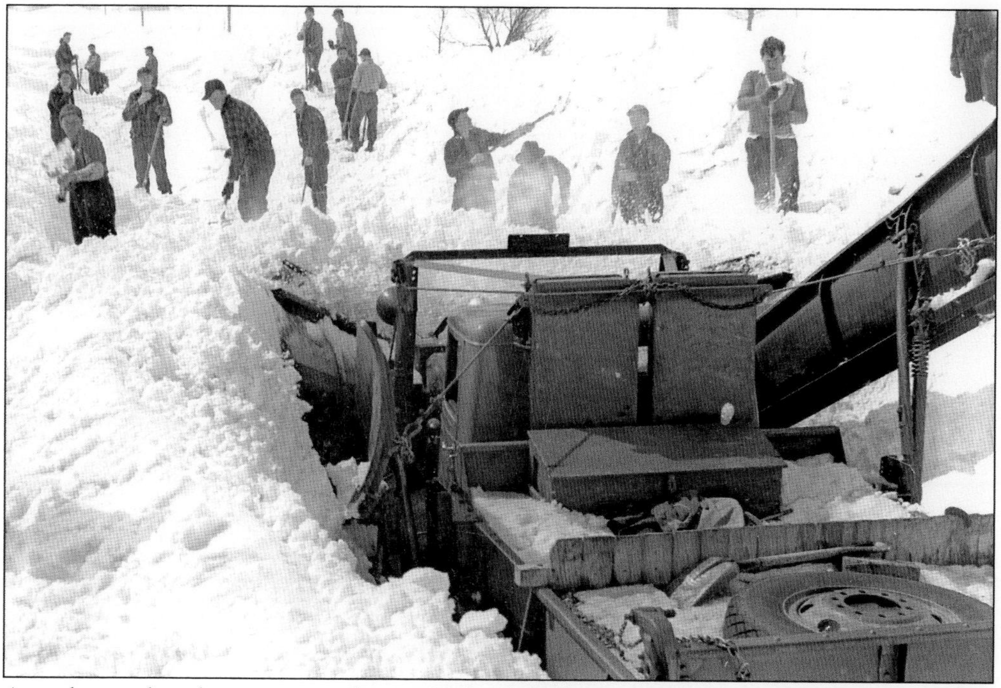

A road crew shovels out a snow plow on Mohawk Hill. In a 1914 letter to the *Boonville Herald*, George Booth of Chicago wrote, "I have lived in the Rocky mountains . . . wallowing in snow to my neck. . . . [But] I never saw as much snow as in Boonville and wonder why people stay in such a 40 degree below zero town as Boonville." (Courtesy of Chris and John Markham.)

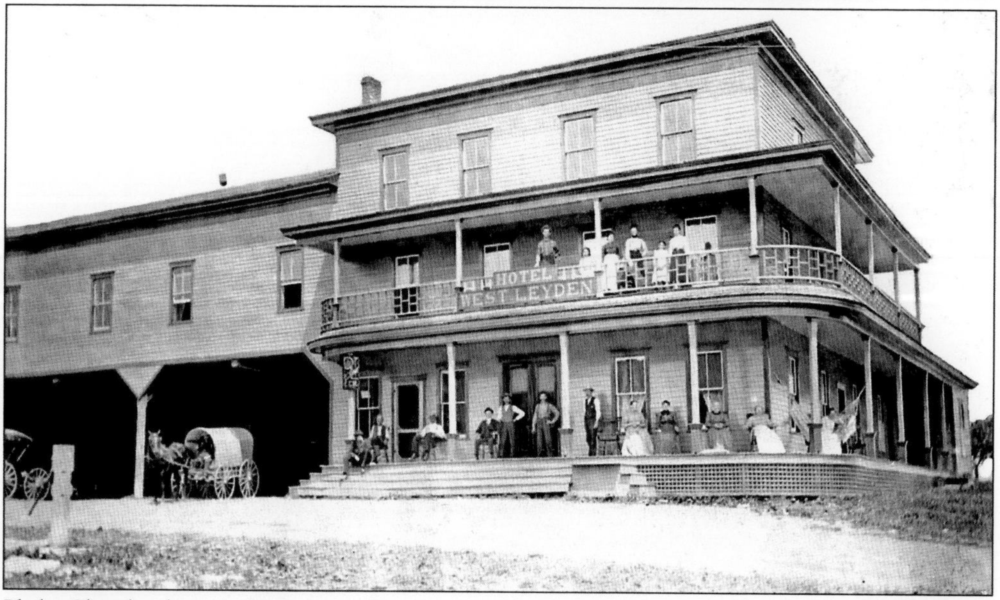

Philip Shankenberry's three-story West Leyden Hotel (1877) was an important gathering place. In 1885, Shankenberry added a two-story extension on the west. The top floor of the annex was a dance hall and the lower level housed a livery, barbershop, meat market, and blacksmith shop. The hotel burned down in 1898, and a new building, pictured here, was erected with spacious wrap-around porches on the first two floors. (Author's collection.)

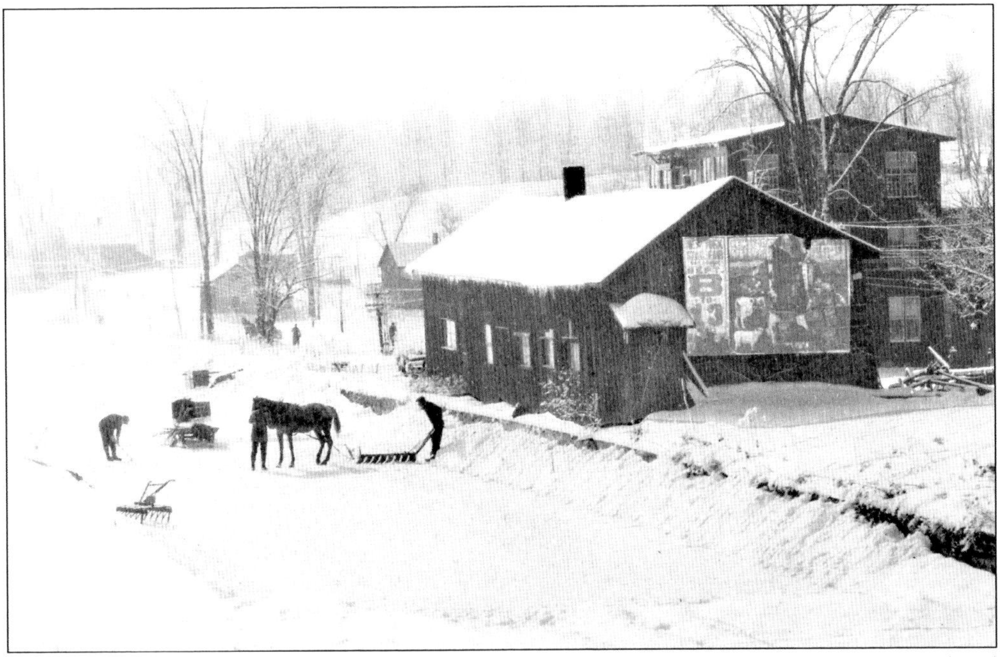

Workers cut ice on the Black River Canal in Port Leyden. Blocks of ice were stored in insulated buildings and used during the summer months. The Port Leyden Knitting Mill is visible in the center distance. (Courtesy of Larry Myers and Port Leyden Library.)

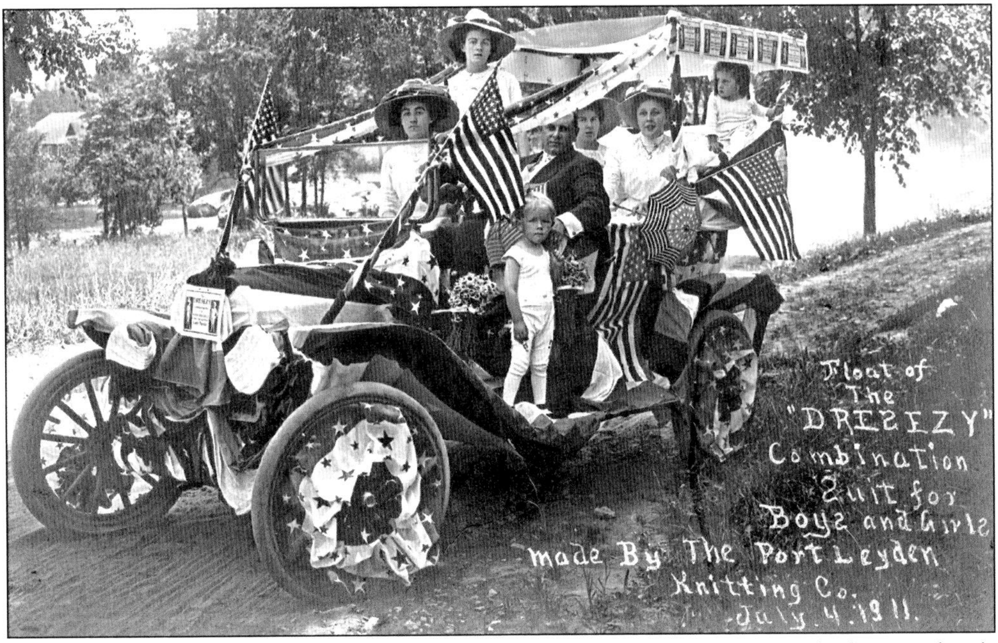

This parade float is a rolling advertisement for the Dress-Easy, a union suit for boys and girls manufactured by the Port Leyden Knitting Mill. Founded in 1907, the knitting mill was located on West Canal Street, and in the second decade of the 20th century, it employed some 60 persons, mostly women and girls. Depending on their skill, workers earned between $3 and $11 for a 54-hour week. (Courtesy of Larry Myers.)

Nine

GREAT OUTDOORS

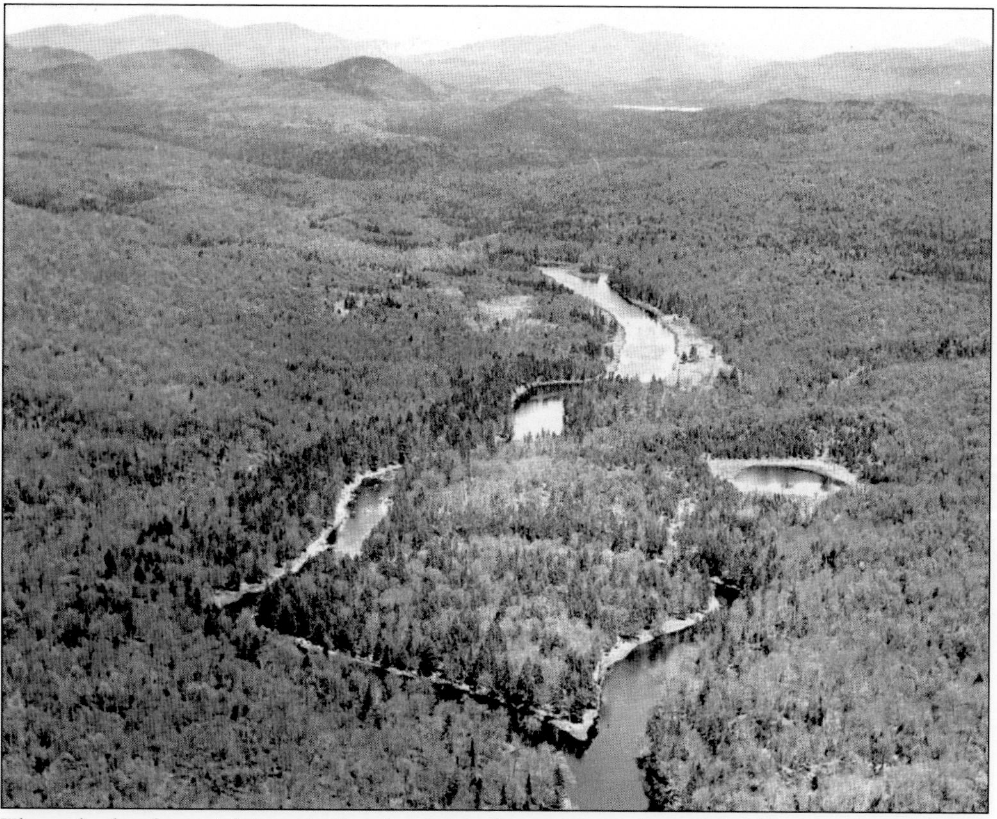

Through the financial ineptitude of a son-in-law, sea merchant John Brown of Providence, Rhode Island, was forced to accept 210,000 acres of central Adirondack land in exchange for a shipment of tea. In 1799, Brown tried to encourage settlement in the wilderness by having a road blazed from Remsen to Fulton Chain (Thendara). The aerial photograph by Dante Tranquille shows the South Branch of the Moose River. (Courtesy of Utica Observer-Dispatch.)

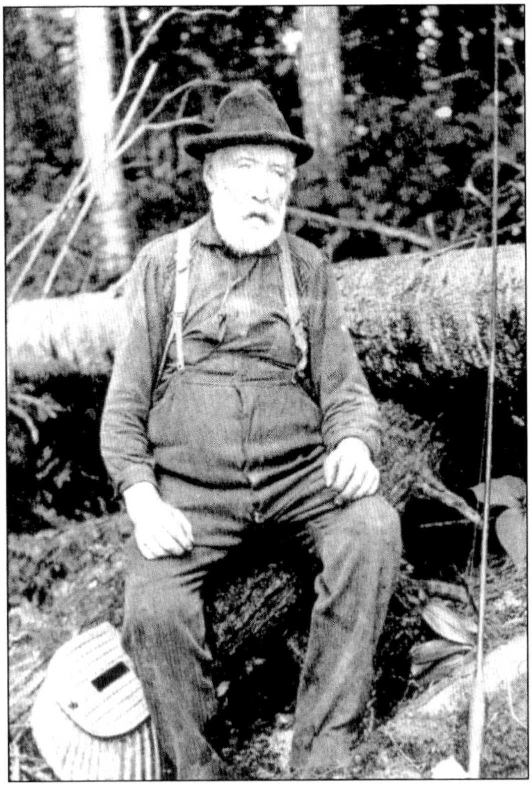

Around 1812, Charles F. Herreshoff opened Brown's Tract Road between Fulton Chain and Boonville. After sinking his fortune in an unproductive iron mine, Herreshoff took his life in 1819. Otis Arnold of Boonville began farming Herreshoff's abandoned property in 1837 and was soon taking in travelers. By 1846, Arnold found himself running one of the first Adirondack hotels. His son Edwin (pictured here) also became a well-known Adirondack guide. (Courtesy of Ed Fynmore.)

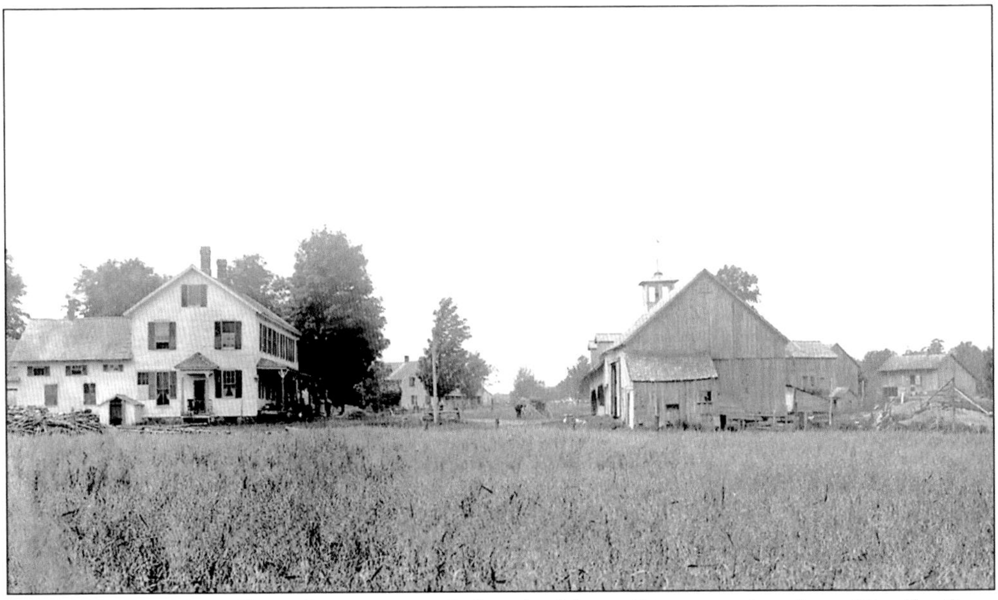

In 1859, Ava resident Abner Lawrence settled at the Moose River crossing about 10 miles from Boonville. There he set himself up as a guide and trapper. Before long, however, he found himself feeding and housing parties of travelers, and like Otis Arnold 15 miles to the north, he was soon operating a hotel: the Moose River Inn. F. A. Moore of Boonville took this photograph around 1906. (Courtesy of Ed Fynmore.)

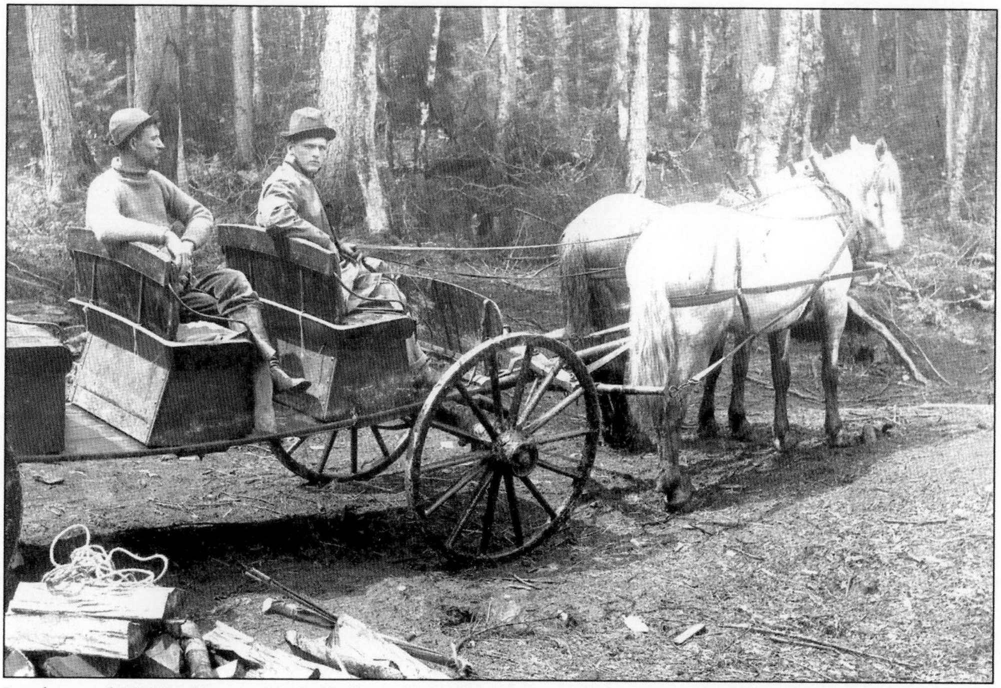

In the mid-1860s, Boonville billed itself as the "Gateway to the North Woods." Sportsmen and tourists took a train to Boonville, secured provisions there, and then proceeded over Brown's Tract Road by buckboard. The road was so rough and rutted that passengers had to be strapped into their seats. Between 1865 and 1892, George Goodsell and Charles Phelps operated one stage line, and Frank Barrett operated another. (Courtesy of Erwin Library.)

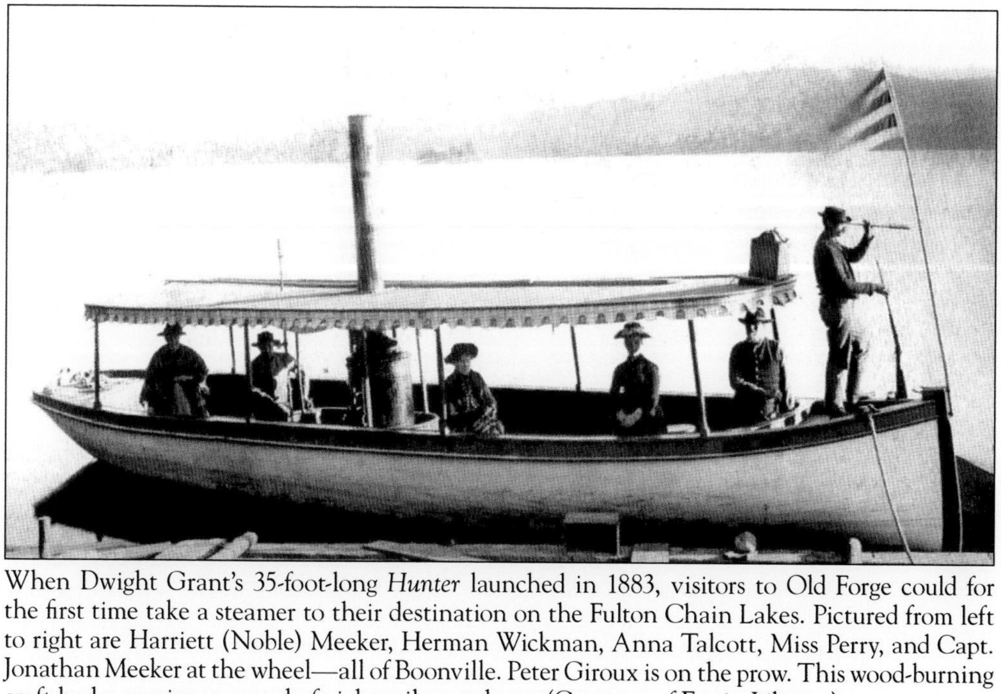

When Dwight Grant's 35-foot-long *Hunter* launched in 1883, visitors to Old Forge could for the first time take a steamer to their destination on the Fulton Chain Lakes. Pictured from left to right are Harriett (Noble) Meeker, Herman Wickman, Anna Talcott, Miss Perry, and Capt. Jonathan Meeker at the wheel—all of Boonville. Peter Giroux is on the prow. This wood-burning craft had a maximum speed of eight miles per hour. (Courtesy of Erwin Library.)

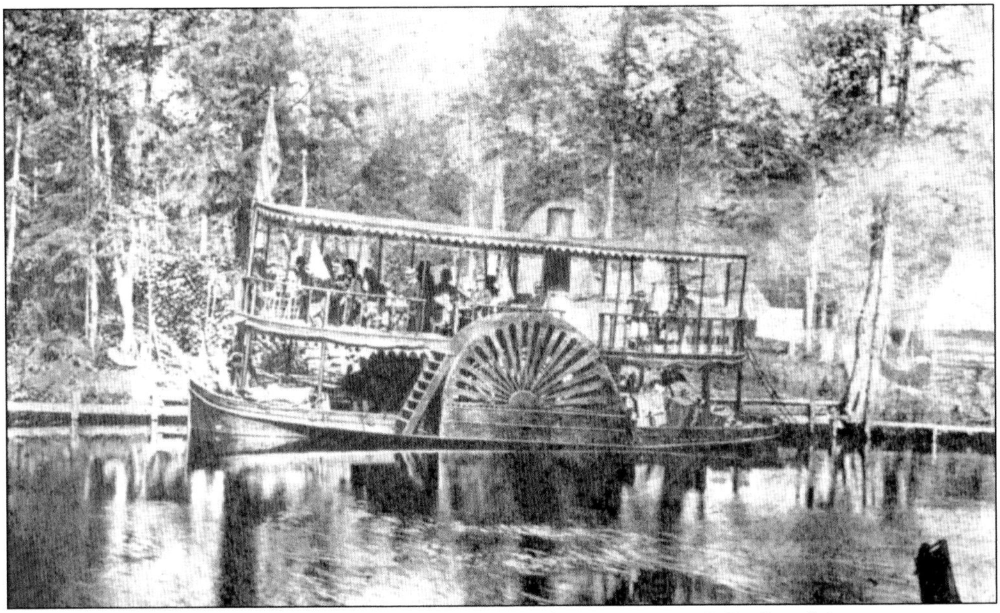

In 1889, G. H. P. Gould's narrow-gauge Fulton Chain "Peg Leg" Railroad began receiving stagecoach passengers at Moose River Settlement. With its homemade cars and wooden rails, this remarkable eight-mile line terminated at Minnehaha. After a two-hour rail journey through the woods, with passengers sometimes getting out to push, vacationers transferred to William De Camp's *Fawn* paddle wheel steamer and traveled the last five miles to Fulton Chain in relative comfort. (Courtesy of Ed Fynmore.)

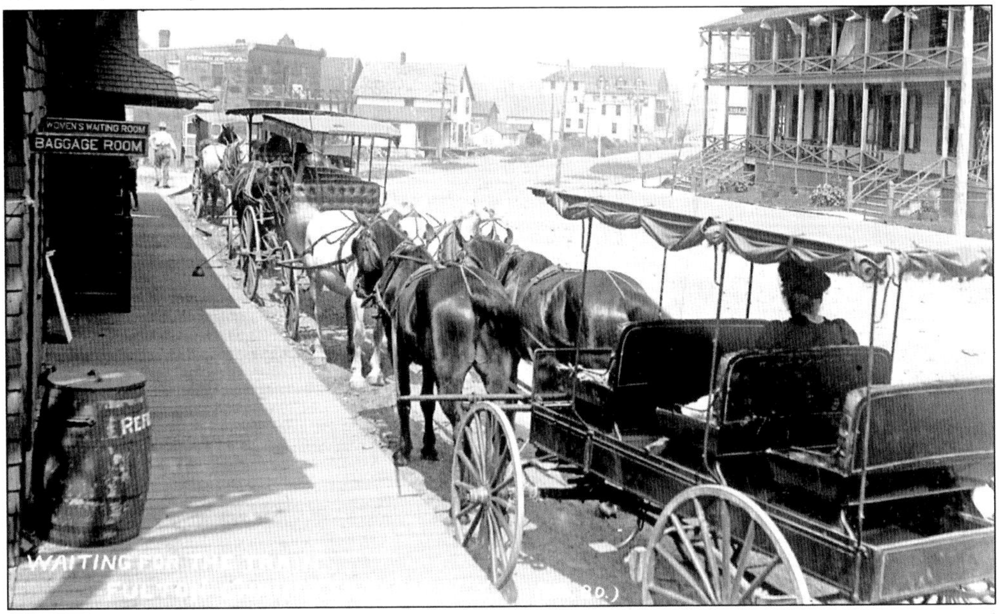

On July 1, 1892, the first train departed Remsen for Fulton Chain station. Dr. William Seward Webb built the 200-mile Adirondack and St. Lawrence Railroad in less than two years and made the central Adirondacks easily accessible to visitors. Theodore Seeber estimated that in the days of the buckboard, fewer than 1,200 tourists visited Fulton Chain annually, but that by 1896, some 25,000 vacationers were pouring in. (Courtesy of Larry Myers.)

Henry Dwight Grant (1833–1911) of Boonville was one of the great Adirondack guides. Elected to the New York State Assembly in 1874, he worked to strengthen game laws and was a moving force behind the creation of the Brown's Tract Guides' Association, in existence from 1898 to 1913. Grant is best remembered for the guide boats that he designed and built at his Post Street shop. (Author's collection.)

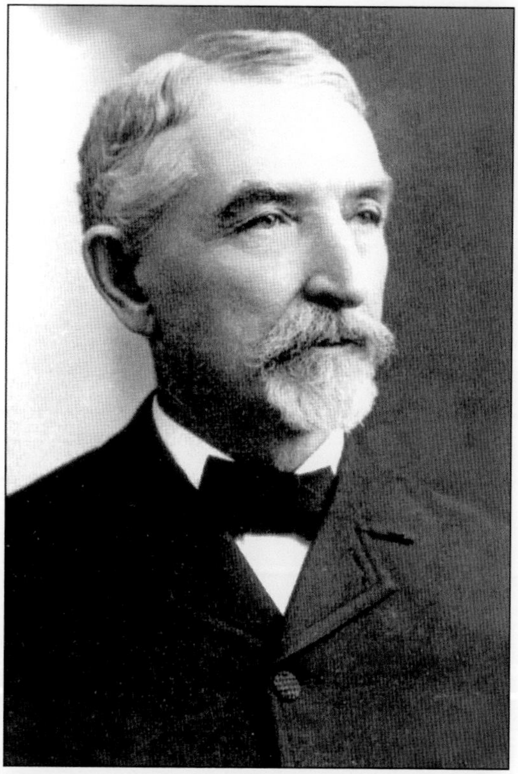

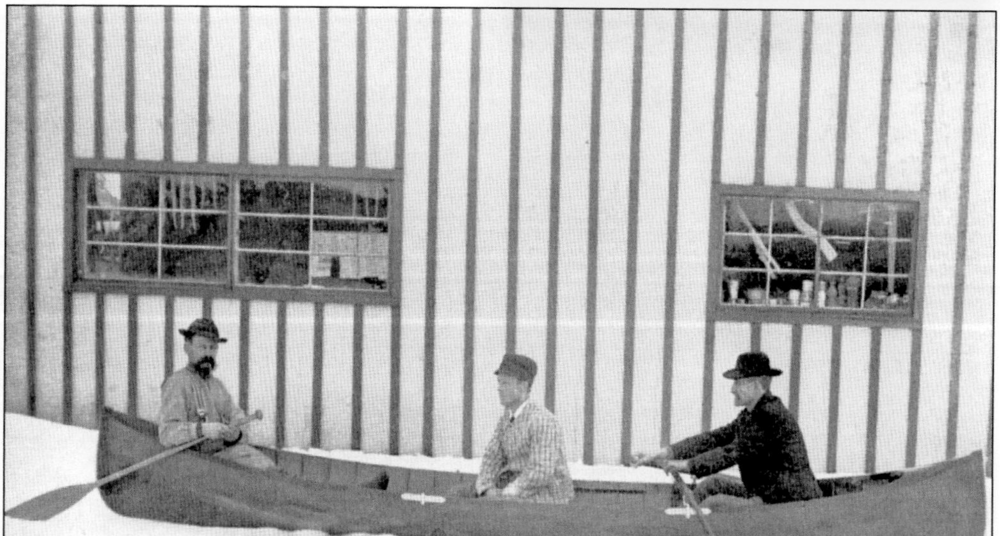

During the winter, guides often built the boats in which they would transport clients. Like a canoe, the Adirondack guide boat was tapered at both ends, but it was lighter and faster, and it was rowed rather than paddled. Here, from left to right, Theodore Seeber, Lester Fox, and Dwight Grant pose in a recently finished boat outside the Post Street workshop. The photograph dates from the 1880s. (Courtesy of Erwin Library.)

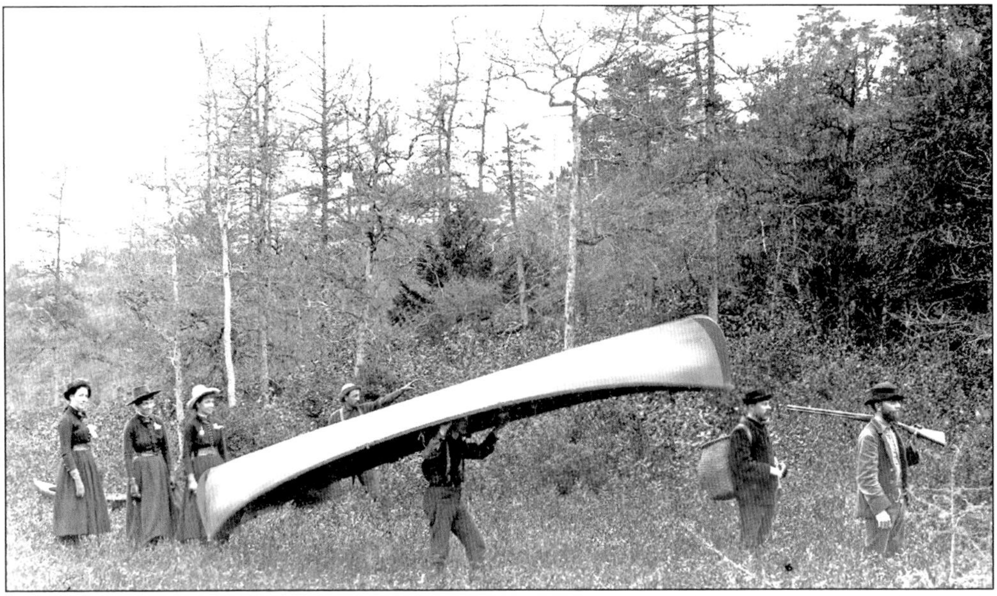

Like his father, Lewis Grant (1878–1960) built guide boats. According to Grant, a 16-foot guide boat took about 210 hours to construct and in the 1880s sold for about $70. The Grants' boat shop has been recreated and is on permanent display in the Adirondack Museum. (Courtesy of Ed Fynmore.)

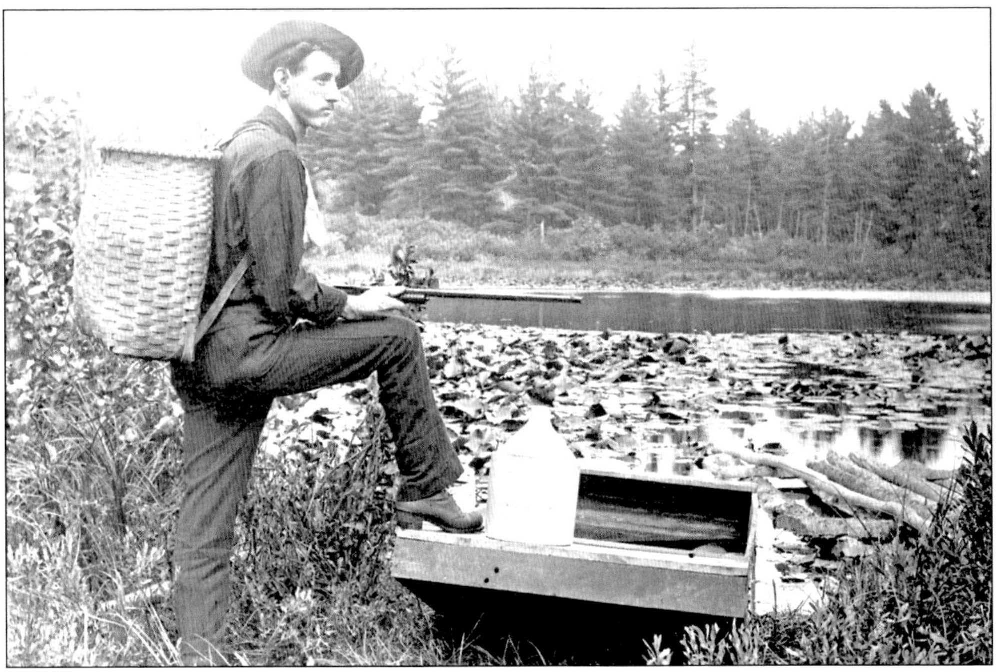

Many members of the Brown's Tract Guides' Association hailed from Boonville, including Richard Crego (first president), Gary Riggs (first vice president), and Artemus Church (perennial secretary and treasurer). The Brown's Tract Guides' Association lobbied for the strict enforcement of state game laws. It also stocked lakes with trout and attempted to reintroduce wapiti, moose, and beaver in the Adirondacks. (Author's collection.)

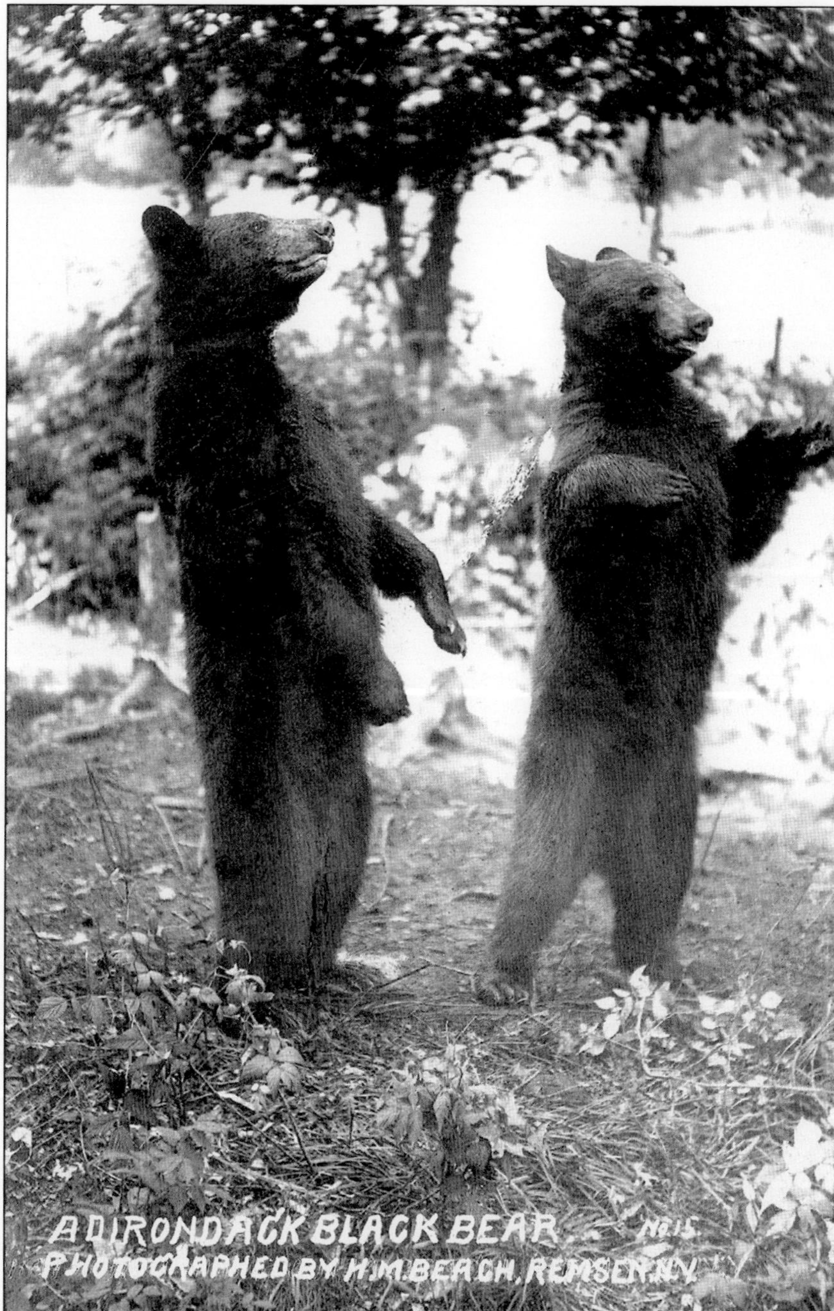

In 1884, Ava residents William Cronk and Aleck Flick set out for their Moose River camp. On the way, they picked up two apparently abandoned bear cubs. About a mile from camp, the enraged mother suddenly appeared. Instructing Flick to flee, Cronk turned to face the mother. "Cronk," according to the Rome *Daily Sentinel*, "watched his opportunity, and, seizing the bear by the tongue, which hung out of her mouth, he drew his knife with his disengaged hand and stabbed her until she fell." Flick returned to find Cronk badly mauled but alive, lying next to the dead bear. (Courtesy of George R. Davis.)

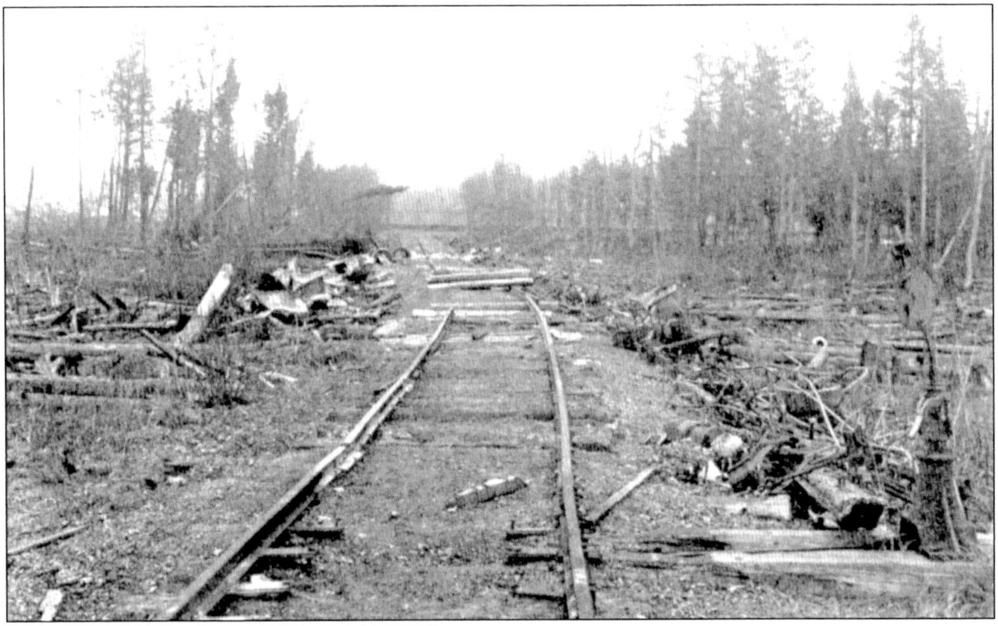

Wildfires were a serious threat in dry years, especially in recently cut areas where loggers left the ground littered with the tops of felled trees. The worst destruction occurred in 1903 when some 500,000 acres burned, including vast tracts between Boonville and Old Forge. Another bad year was 1908. Among the casualties was the hamlet of Long Lake West (above), which disappeared when a fire ignited 1,300 pounds of dynamite. (Author's collection.)

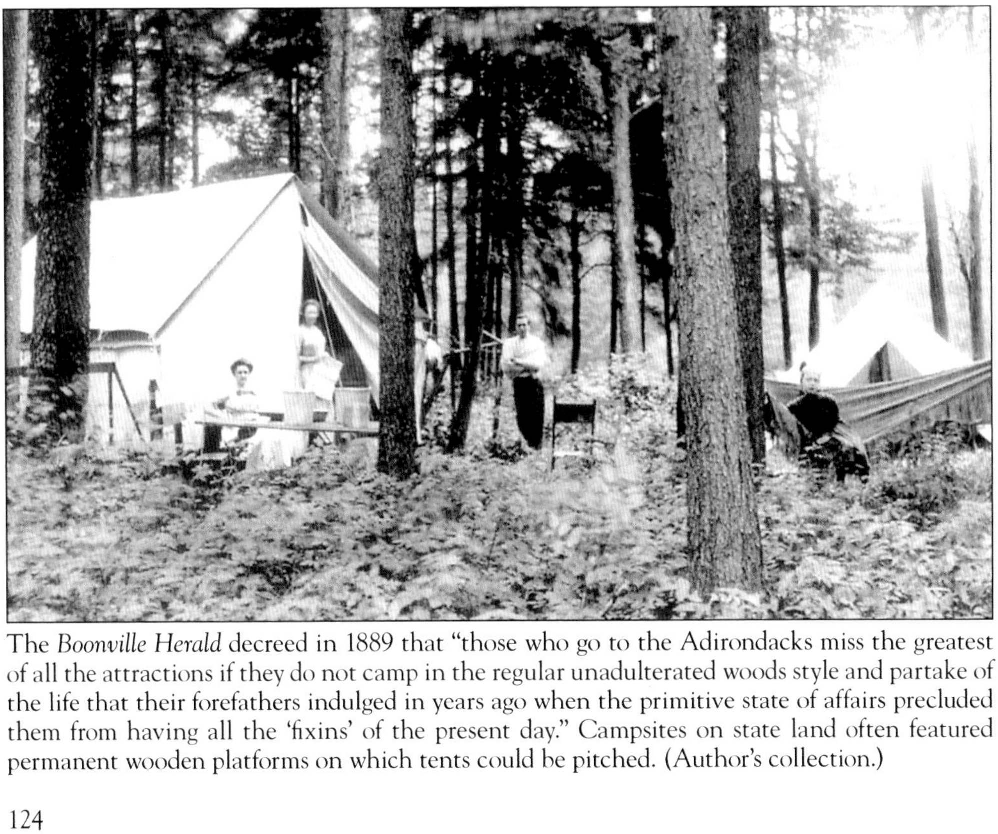

The *Boonville Herald* decreed in 1889 that "those who go to the Adirondacks miss the greatest of all the attractions if they do not camp in the regular unadulterated woods style and partake of the life that their forefathers indulged in years ago when the primitive state of affairs precluded them from having all the 'fixins' of the present day." Campsites on state land often featured permanent wooden platforms on which tents could be pitched. (Author's collection.)

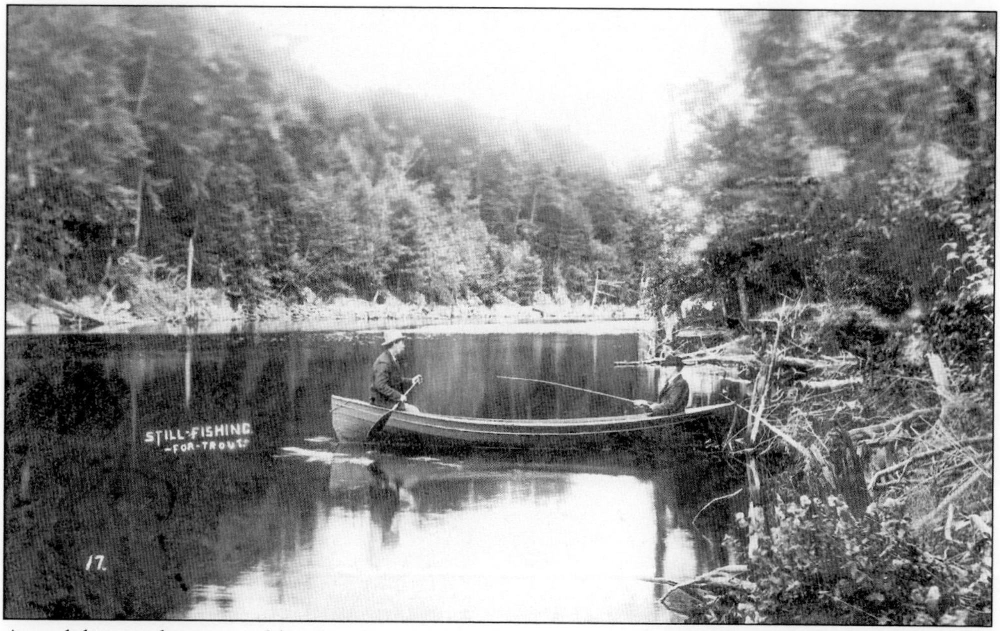

Area lakes and streams like Big Otter (above) were renowned for their abundance of brook trout, but by the late 1870s, heavy fishing pressure prompted private clubs to begin stocking their waters. In 1876, the Boonville Sportsmen's Club financed a small hatchery near the Old Forge dam, and in 1885, the club opened the Fulton Chain Hatchling House on Fourth Lake. (Courtesy of Larry Myers.)

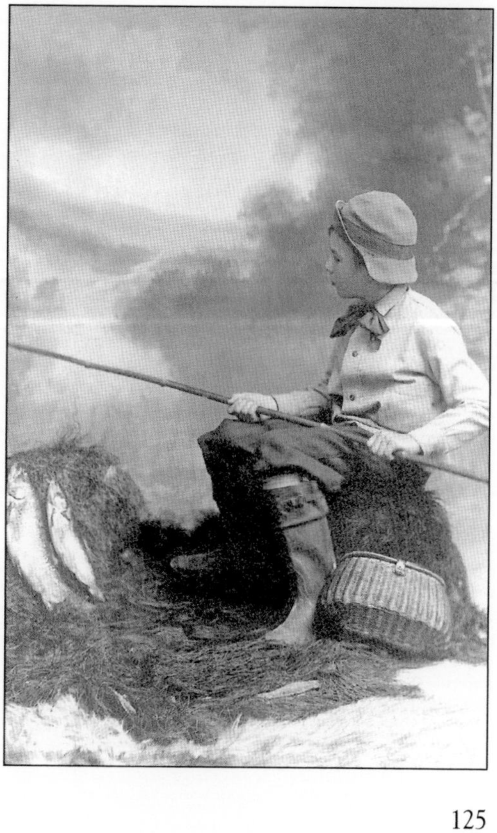

Fishermen frequently documented their catch with a studio photograph. At one time, large trout could be found close to home. In July 1909, Dr. Webster S. Seavey caught a four-and-three-quarter-pound brown trout in Mill Creek and displayed it in Henry Belknap's store. That same year, Seavey took a 12.5-pound lake trout from nearby North Pond (Echo Lake). The photograph is by George H. Pollard. (Courtesy of Jerry Putnam.)

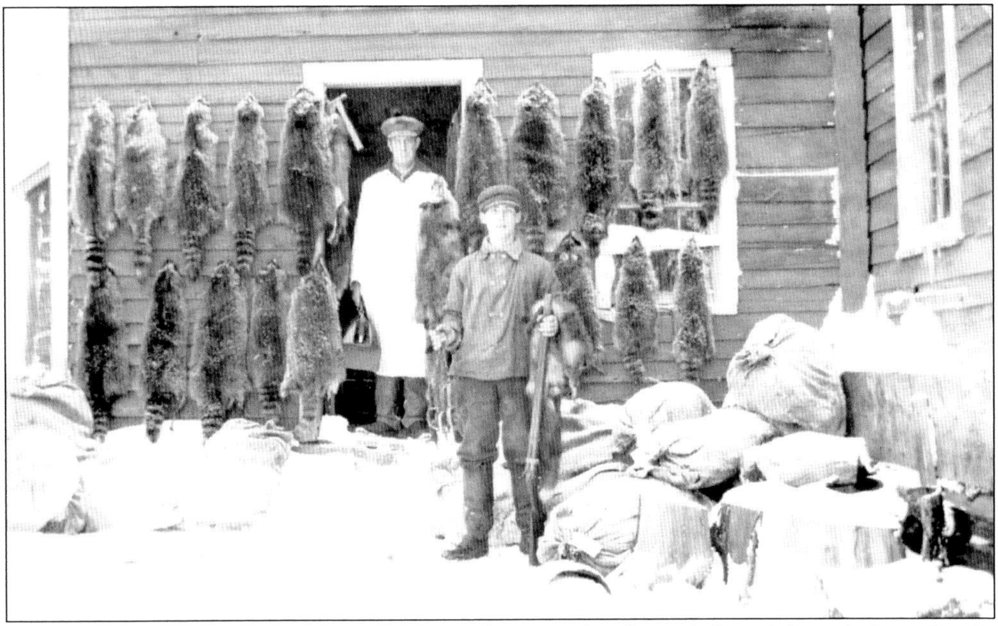

Trapping was an important source of income for many locals, including Adirondack guides. In this photograph taken about 1905, fur dealer Ed Marcy (left) and his assistant Benny Compo stand in front of a wall of raccoon pelts. In the first decade of the 20th century, Boonville had seven dealers in fur coats. The average cost of a coat at that time was about $25. (Courtesy of Irma K. Marcy.)

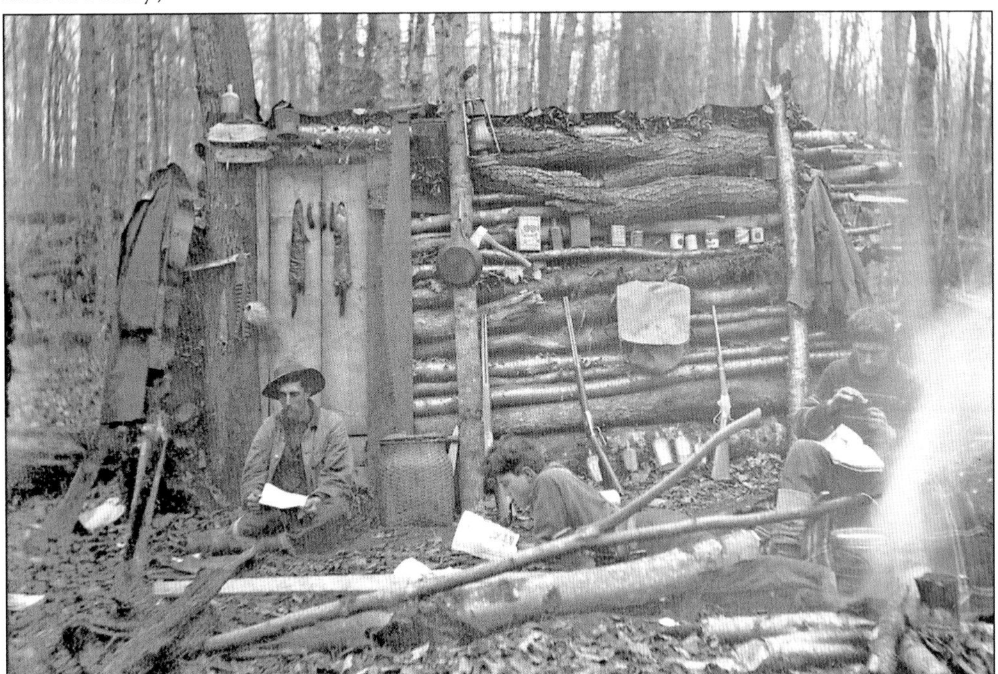

Local hunters and trappers often constructed small camps from materials left over from logging operations. Two mink pelts hang on the entrance to this camp on Big Woodhull Creek near Forestport. (Author's collection.)

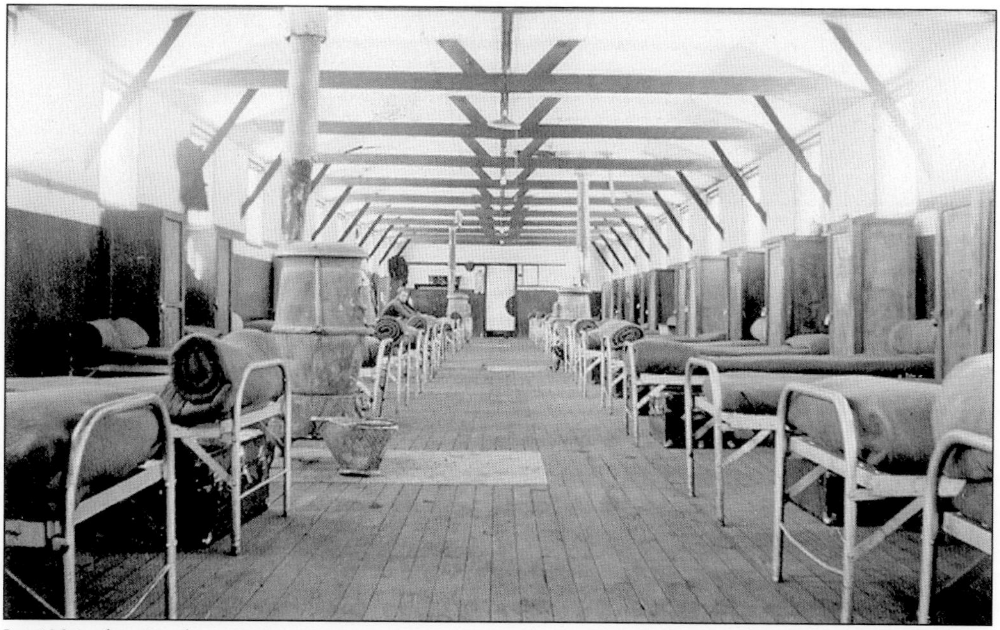

In 1934, the Civilian Conservation Corps established Camp S-122 on the Hawkinsville Road about six miles east of Boonville. The camp, with its 12 buildings, housed 200 unemployed, single men between the ages of 17 and 28 and was commanded by Lt. James Prime. Enlistees built fire breaks, fought blister rust, and by mid-1937, had planted three and a half million conifers. (Courtesy of Joe Gaetano and Marty Podskoch.)

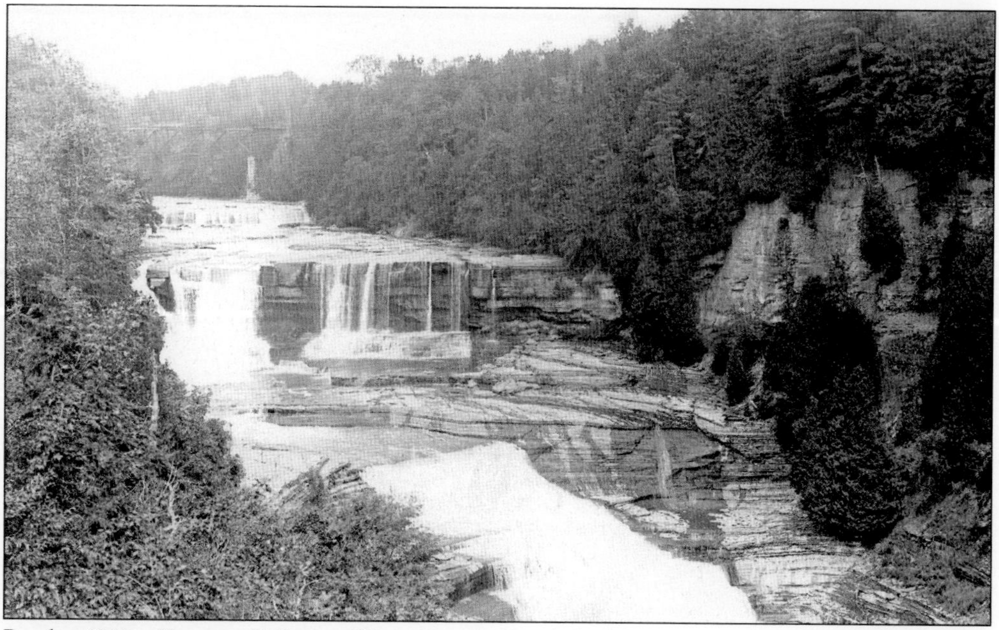

By the 1840s, Trenton Falls on West Canada Creek had become one of the premier tourist destinations in North America. With the completion of the Black River and Utica Railroad in 1855, the falls became easily accessible. One-way train fare between Boonville and Trenton was 75¢. In deference to local clergy, however, trains did not initially run on Sundays. (Courtesy of Larry Myers.)

Consistent with our mission to preserve history on a local level, this book was printed in South Carolina on American-made paper and manufactured entirely in the United States. Products carrying the accredited Forest Stewardship Council (FSC) label are printed on 100 percent FSC-certified paper.

MADE IN THE USA